Designing Multi-Device Experiences

An Ecosystem Approach to User Experiences Across Devices

Michal Levin

 Beijing · Cambridge · Farnham · Köln · Sebastopol · Tokyo

Designing Multi-Device Experiences
by Michal Levin

Published by O'Reilly Media, Inc., 1005 Gravenstein Highway North, Sebastopol, CA 95472.

O'Reilly books may be purchased for educational, business, or sales promotional use. Online editions are also available for most titles (*safari.oreilly.com*). For more information, contact our corporate/institutional sales department: (800) 998-9938 or *corporate@oreilly.com*.

Editors: Mary Treseler

Developmental Editors: Patricia Bosewell and Amy Jollymore

Production Editor: Melanie Yarbrough

Copyeditor: Rachel Monaghan

Proofreader: Rachel Head

Indexer: Ron Strauss

Cover Designer: Randy Comer

Interior Designers: Ron Bilodeau and Monica Kamsvaag

Illustrators: Justine Tiu and Rebecca Demarest

Compositor: Melanie Yarbrough

January 2014: First Edition.

Revision History for the First Edition:

2014-01-24   First release

See *http://oreilly.com/catalog/errata.csp?isbn=0636920027089* for release details.

978-1-449-34038-4

[TI]

[*contents*]

Preface

Multi-Device Design Today

We have entered a multi-device world.

Until recently, design models for online products considered only the computer or mobile phone as a standalone platform. Now, in our increasingly connected world, people own multiple devices—PCs, smartphones, tablets, TVs, and more—and are already using them *together*, switching between them, in order to accomplish a single goal. These devices relate to one another in a variety of ways, and together can form powerful ensembles that can better assist people in achieving their goals.

Still, most products today offer the same experience across all devices, often using their existing desktop experience as the model and making minor adjustments for device-specific size and form factor. That is an acceptable stopgap measure, but it's not necessarily best suited to user needs and goals. This kind of design approach, which I call *consistent design*, provides users with access to all the content from any device at any time, but unfortunately it ignores a key factor in users' behaviors, needs, and experiences: *context*.

People don't necessarily need *everything, all the time, on all devices*. Different devices are often used in different ways, in different contexts, as part of different activities. Thus, the greater benefit would come from people getting *the right thing, at the right time, on the best (available) device*.

Adopting such a context-driven perspective means we need to start looking at multiple devices as part of a bigger ecosystem, rather than treating them as silos. In this ecosystem, devices can relate to one another in a variety of ways (for example, complementing or continuing one another's roles), and together—as a holistic structure—better equip people to complete their tasks.

Why I Wrote This Book

This book is intended to help you make decisions about your design projects—not just how to create a product for the smartphone or a product version for the tablet, but rather how to deliver a product *ecosystem* that serves the end-to-end user journey across devices that are already available in our connected world. This book will hopefully be a first step in paving the way toward better multi-device experiences that go beyond duplicating existing models to embrace instead the full potential of an ecosystem.

In *The Medium Is the Message*, Marshall McLuhan asserted:

> When faced with a totally new situation, we tend always to attach ourselves to the objects, to the flavor of the most recent past. We look at the present through a rear-view mirror. We march backwards into the future.[1]

I see a similar pathway in the way we approach multi-device experiences today.

It is very difficult, impossible even, for any of us to fully understand the extent to which this new multi-device world will reshape the way we experience, work with, and interact with the environment and with one another. However, we can start working toward that by detaching ourselves from the familiar comfort zone, and adopting new perspectives that take full advantage of the new opportunities presented by the growing set of connected devices in front of us.

In this book, I'd like to introduce a new ecosystem framework for designing multi-device experiences—one that focuses on context. At the root of this framework is the realization that along with different devices, people's needs, behaviors, usage patterns, and settings also change en route to their goals.

This framework is based on three key approaches for addressing the emerging relationships between different devices: *consistent*, *continuous*, and *complementary*.

These approaches provide the building blocks for designing multi-device experiences, establishing a broader product narrative that puts people—rather than technology—in the center.

Who Should Read This Book

This book provides a roadmap for how to think about multi-device experience design. If you're involved—or planning to get involved—in product design and development, this book is for you. Whether you are an engineer, a product manager, a user experience (UX) practitioner, a grad student, or an entrepreneur, this book is for you. Truly, collaboration among these roles is instrumental to creating the best product experiences.

Before we think about delivering a product to a specific device, we need to consider the broader multi-device strategy. If you are a product manager, you are responsible for the product strategy, roadmap, and feature prioritization. I hope this book helps you consider how to prioritize building a multi-device experience—from stationary to mobile—for your product vision.

One of the biggest challenges we face today in creating ecosystem experiences is the many technological hurdles that prevent us from adopting a big-picture view. If you are an engineer, I hope this book inspires you to explore solutions that can overcome these hurdles. The multi-device world needs technological muscle power to create these ecosystem experiences.

At the end of the day, it's all about the people, and we need to find a way to help devices better serve the needs of our users. If you are a UX designer, your role is to create the magic that combines the product technology and features into a seamless, fluid experience that delights people. This emerging environment is an opportunity for you to set the path for the future. You are the person who will teach and encourage people to find meaning within all these devices and technologies.

How This Book Is Organized

This book is divided into eight chapters. Chapter 1 introduces the concept of an ecosystem and progresses into design approaches that can be used to create a rich, successful product ecosystem. Chapters 2 through 4 provide a walkthrough of the 3Cs framework—consistent, continuous, and complementary—and explore those approaches across multiple products, physical environments, and platforms. The book ends with a discussion of how to measure ecosystem success and overcome the challenges we currently face in this space (Chapters 5 through 8). Here's a closer look at what you'll find in this book:

Chapter 1, An Ecosystem of Connected Devices
> This chapter presents the main set of events and conditions leading to the emergence of the multi-device world. It defines the concept of ecosystem—borrowed from our natural world—and applies it to our digital lives today, where we are surrounded by numerous connected devices. Following this, I introduce the three key design approaches for addressing multi-device design: consistent, continuous, and complementary.

Chapter 2, The Consistent Design Approach
> This chapter introduces and explains the consistent design approach, in which the basic experience is replicated across the different devices, porting the same content and core features in a like manner. We then explore this approach with three products— Google Search, Trulia, and Hulu Plus—and cover ways you can handle the plethora of devices and platforms out there.

Chapter 3, The Continuous Design Approach
> This chapter focuses on the continuous approach, where the user experience shifts between devices; one device picks up where the other leaves off. Products like Apple AirPlay, the Amazon Kindle, Allrecipes, Eventbrite, POP, and Pocket show how multiple devices can be used to support continuation of both a single activity and a sequence of activities composing a broader user goal.

Chapter 4, The Complementary Design Approach
> This chapter dives into the third design approach—complementary—analyzing how it can offer a richer experience when multiple devices interact as an ensemble. We'll explore different types of relationships between devices through a variety of products, from collaborative game play to media to entertainment, accompanied by a case study on building a second-screen experience.

Chapter 5, Integrated Design Approaches
> Following the basic exploration of each separate approach in the 3Cs framework, this chapter discusses how and why many designs integrate several approaches across devices. It presents the key questions to ask when you are approaching ecosystem design and demonstrates the benefits and important takeaways of some of the product examples used in previous chapters, as well as new products.

Chapter 6, Beyond the Core Devices

This chapter takes ecosystem experiences into a broader world of devices and appliances that go beyond the four core devices of smartphones, tablets, PCs, and TVs. Concepts like the Internet of Things and ubiquitous computing are discussed, demonstrating how—even in more complex ecosystems—the 3Cs still serve as an instrumental framework to multi-device design. Discussions of the Quantified Self movement, QR codes, and a case study on building an Internet of Things platform provide additional design insights about the connected world we're headed toward.

Chapter 7, Multi-Device Analytics

This chapter focuses on product analysis as a means to learn user behaviors and engagement patterns, as well as an important way to measure ecosystem success. It introduces a multi-device analytics approach and discusses some new concepts designed to address multi-device measurement challenges. Case studies on multi-device measurement using Google Analytics and paving the ecosystem way with A/B testing complement the discussion with hands-on guidance.

Chapter 8, Transforming Challenges

This chapter discusses the ecosystem challenges we're facing today both as consumers and as product developers. On the consumer side, there are hurdles around setting up the ecosystem, getting it going, and dealing with app overload. From the product development perspective, the ecosystem approach presents challenges in terms of organizational structure, walled gardens, and time (and resources) to market. This chapter explores possible solutions to address these challenges and prepare ourselves for a world where everything—people, information, and things—will be more connected than ever before.

Online Resources

Over time, I have found a few websites particularly useful when contemplating multi-device design and the ecosystem of devices. Some of the ones I like most include:

- Scott Jenson, Exploring the World Beyond Mobile (*http://jenson.org/*)

- LukeW, Ideation + Design (*http://www.lukew.com/*)

- Punchcut Perspectives (*http://punchcut.com/perspectives*)

- Cisco.com, Internet of Everything—Connecting the Unconnected (*http://www.cisco.com/web/tomorrow-starts-here/index.html*)

- Our Mobile Planet (*http://bit.ly/18WlzXJ*)

Conventions Used in This Book

This book contains a set of perspectives, aiming to equip you with a thought framework that can guide you as you approach multi-device experience design, along with various practical, hands-on design principles that can already be applied in your day-to-day work.

As you progress through the book, you will find case studies, first-person stories, spotlight discussions, and analysis questions woven through the chapters. All these components work together to provide a comprehensive picture of the multi-device space.

[TIP] OR [NOTE]

Indicates a tip, suggestion, or general note relating to the nearby text.

Question to the Reader

Contains a question relevant to the discussion at hand.

Comments and Questions

Please address comments and questions concerning this book to the publisher:

O'Reilly Media, Inc.
1005 Gravenstein Highway North
Sebastopol, CA 95472
(800) 998-9938 (in the United States or Canada)
(707) 829-0515 (international or local)
(707) 829-0104 (fax)

We have a web page for this book, where we list errata, examples, and any additional information. You can access this page at:

http://oreil.ly/design_multidevice_exp

To comment or ask technical questions about this book, send email to:

bookquestions@oreilly.com

For more information about our books, courses, conferences, and news, see our website at *http://www.oreilly.com*.

Find us on Facebook: *http://facebook.com/oreilly*

Follow us on Twitter: *http://twitter.com/oreillymedia*

Watch us on YouTube: *http://www.youtube.com/oreillymedia*

Safari® Books Online

Safari Books Online (*www.safaribooksonline.com*) is an on-demand digital library that delivers expert content in both book and video form from the world's leading authors in technology and business.

Technology professionals, software developers, web designers, and business and creative professionals use Safari Books Online as their primary resource for research, problem solving, learning, and certification training.

Safari Books Online offers a range of product mixes and pricing programs for organizations, government agencies, and individuals. Subscribers have access to thousands of books, training videos, and prepublication manuscripts in one fully searchable database from publishers like O'Reilly Media, Prentice Hall Professional, Addison-Wesley Professional, Microsoft Press, Sams, Que, Peachpit Press, Focal Press, Cisco Press, John Wiley & Sons, Syngress, Morgan Kaufmann, IBM Redbooks, Packt, Adobe Press, FT Press, Apress, Manning, New Riders, McGraw-Hill, Jones & Bartlett, Course Technology, and dozens more. For more information about Safari Books Online, please visit us online.

Acknowledgments

Many good people helped make this book a reality. I'm deeply thankful for each and every one of you, and would like to especially acknowledge the following people.

Mary Treseler, my editor at O'Reilly, gave me the opportunity to engage in this remarkable journey, and accompanied me along the way. Thank you so much for your ongoing mentorship, support, guidance, and encouragement. It made a world of difference.

Patricia Bosewell and Amy Jollymore, my developmental editors, helped me craft the literary art of this book. Being a first-time author, I learned so much from you about what great writing means. Thank you for that, and for making all the pieces work together synergistically.

Justine Tiu, my graphic designer, worked with me relentlessly on the visual art of this book. Thank you for making this book beautiful.

All my esteemed reviewers provided so much useful feedback that truly turned this book around. Samantha Starmer, Scott Jenson, Dan Saffer, Karl Fast, Ran Makavy, Adam Ungstad, Austin Govella, Tom Boates, Lane Halley, and Chris Risdon: thank you for your great advice and thoughts, and for challenging me to stretch my limits even further.

All the book contributors took the time to share their knowledge and experience through discussions and case studies. Scott Jenson, Nir Eyal, Ori Shaashua, Eyal Baumel, Daniel Waisberg, Rochelle King, and Michael Spiegelman: thank you for complementing the book with your invaluable contributions.

At Google, I would like to particularly thank Rob Peterson, Jon Wiley, Mike Gordon, Brian Fitzpatrick, and Emily Wood for their help and support. Also, I would like to thank Shuly Galili, Gil Ben Artzy, Liron Petrushka, and Yael Winer from UpWest Labs for their ongoing encouragement, as well as the opportunity to mentor dozens of the best startup companies out there. A special thanks to the entire staff at O'Reilly for making this book happen, in the smoothest way possible.

Last but definitely not least, I would like to thank my loved ones, my dear friends and family, who stood by me all along the way. Writing a book while maintaining a fulltime job at Google meant working consistently late nights and weekends for over a year. I'm indebted to you for your unbounded support, encouragement, and love during all this time. I couldn't have done it without you.

#Grateful #Humbled

NOTES

1. Marshall McLuhan and Quentin Fiore, *The Medium Is the Message* (New York: Bantam Books, 1967).

[1]

An Ecosystem of Connected Devices

What does it mean to design a product in a world where people own multiple devices and use them interchangeably? This chapter describes how we got to this multi-device era, and introduces a new ecosystem design framework to help us both navigate and influence this new reality.

We have entered a world of multi-device experiences. Our lives have become a series of interactions with multiple digital devices, enabling each of us to learn, buy, compare, search, navigate, connect, and manage every aspect of modern life.

Consider the hours we spend with devices every day—interacting with our smartphones, working on our laptops, engaging with our tablets, watching shows on television, playing with our video game consoles, and tracking steps on our fitness wristbands. For many of us, the following are true:

- We spend more time interacting with devices than with people.

- We often interact with more than one device at a time.

The number of connected devices has officially exceeded the 7 billion mark, outnumbering people (and toothbrushes) on the planet.[1] By 2020, this number is expected to pass 24(!) billion.[2] This inconceivable quantity not only attests to the growing role of these devices in our digital lives, but also signals *an increasing number of devices per person*. Many individuals now own multiple connected devices—PCs, smartphones, tablets, TVs, and more—and they are already using them together, switching between them, in order to accomplish their goals. Ninety percent of consumers use multiple devices to complete a task over time—for example, shopping for an item might entail (1) searching and exploring options at home on the PC, (2) checking product information and comparing prices in-store using your smartphone, and (3) writing product reviews on a tablet.[3] Eighty-six percent of consumers use their smartphones while engaging with other devices and during other media consumption activities, as shown in Figure 1-1.

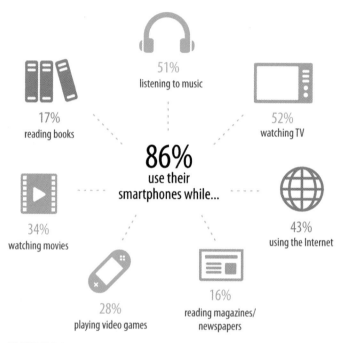

51%
listening to music

17%
reading books

52%
watching TV

86%
use their
smartphones while...

34%
watching movies

43%
using the Internet

28%
playing video games

16%
reading magazines/
newspapers

FIGURE 1-1
Multitasking view—activities take place and other devices are used simultaneously with the smartphone.[4]

While each device plays an important role in many of our daily activities, *their real power exists in how they are used together with other devices.* This multi-device usage sets the foundation of a product *ecosystem*.

The Concept of an Ecosystem

Biologists use the term *ecosystem* to describe interconnections within our natural world—a community of living organisms (plants, animals, and microbes) in conjunction with the nonliving components of their environment (elements like air, water, and mineral soil), interacting as a system. An ecosystem essentially describes a network of interactions—among organisms, and between those organisms and their environment—which together create an ecology that is greater than the sum of its parts.

In looking at the world of online apps and electronics today, we can see a type of ecosystem emerging. In this system—this climate of multiple devices—we see smartphones, tablets, laptops, TVs, and other connected devices all interacting with one another and wirelessly sharing data. These interactions are shaped by the different ways in which individuals use the content and services that flow between devices, in different contexts, en route to their goals (Figure 1-2).

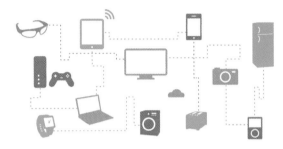

FIGURE 1-2

An ecosystem of connected devices, including those that are already available today and a few that will join soon.

The growing number of connected devices, especially mobile ones, is progressively changing the way people perceive, experience, and interact with products and each other. Our mission as designers and product creators is to understand the different relationships between connected devices, as well as how individuals relate to them, in order to create natural, fluid multi-device experiences that allow these dynamic changes. These experiences should focus on how the (increasing) set of connected devices can best serve users' needs as they move between activities and contexts throughout the day.

You can choose to build your product as an isolated cell on each device, replicating the same basic experience, and thus offering independent access to *everything, everywhere, anytime.* Or you can foster an ecosystem approach that captures the dynamically changing needs and contexts that accompany shifting devices, putting the emphasis on delivering the *right thing* at the *right place* at the *right time.*

The latter—the context-driven approach—is where I believe we'll find our biggest opportunities.

The 3Cs Framework: Consistent, Continuous, and Complementary

In this era of proliferating connected devices, one goal is becoming clear: clients want to see their products on as many screens as possible. At the very least, we'll need to get a product up and running across the basic, core set of screens already deeply embedded in our daily lives: the smartphone, tablet, PC, and TV.

How do we handle this design complexity, given the myriad devices on the market already (and those that are on the way)? How should we approach a multi-device experience design without overwhelming our users, and being overwhelmed ourselves?

When I was struggling with these questions a while back, I was inspired by the multi-screen patterns work done by Precious in 2011.[5] The company's pioneering work established a conceptual model for approaching the emerging multi-device world. However, as I deepened my work in this space, I noticed several challenges that arise when we try to make clear distinctions between the different patterns; this is due in part to particular pattern overlaps and semantic blurs across them. To cut through the confusion, I adopted a framework, or set of building blocks, that has proven to be durable and immensely relevant for approaching ecosystem design. I call the framework *3Cs: consistent, continuous,* and *complementary.*

In *consistent design*, the same basic experience is replicated between devices, keeping the content, flow, structure, and core feature set consistent across the ecosystem. Some adjustments are made to accommodate device-specific attributes (mainly screen size and interaction model), but overall the experience can be fully consumed, in an independent manner, on any device.

Spotify is a good example of consistent design. It enables users to discover and listen to their favorite music from everywhere—their computers, their mobile phones, their tablets, and their home entertainment systems.

While consistent design provides access to everything, anywhere, anytime—a first important step in bringing value to users through multi-device use—it often doesn't capture the full potential of an ecosystem. Consistency overlooks several significant factors involved in the user's experience: context (delivering the *right thing* at the *right time*), multi-device relationships (ways devices can supplement and support one another), determining the best device for the task, and scaling the experience to a fully connected world (that goes beyond smartphones, tablets, PCs, and TVs).

To accommodate these needs, we need two additional design building blocks—continuous and complementary design.

The hallmark of *continuous design* is that the experience is passed on from one device to another, either continuing the same activity (watching a movie, reading a book) or progressing through a sequence of different activities, taking place in different contexts but all channeled toward achieving the same end goal (like getting ready to go to work in the morning).

The hallmark of *complementary design* is that devices complement one another (with relevant info/functionality), creating a new experience as a connected group. This experience can encompass two forms of device relationship: collaboration and control.

Google Chromecast, which turns a smartphone or tablet into a remote control for the TV, is one example of such experience design. These devices can then be used to browse the content on TV, control playback, and adjust volume.

The 3Cs provide a framework for thinking about how users accomplish a single goal using multiple devices. Rather than providing a technology-focused framework—stemming from device form factor, size, and resolution—the 3Cs focus on *people*, looking at the relationships between individuals and their devices, and how the latter can support them along their task flow en route to their goal.

Using an analogy from the music world, let's imagine that devices can be used in any of the following ways to elevate a user's experience:

- As a solo instrument, where each performs the entire piece from start to end (consistent)

- As a step in a sequence, by splitting the music into pieces and playing them with other instruments, one after the other (continuous)

- As part of an ensemble, where instruments play together in a coordinated manner to create a harmonized music piece (complementary)

In this musical group, *you* are the conductor...and sometimes even the composer. You decide which devices take part in the multi-device composition, what role each one plays, and how they all orchestrate the complete ecosystem experience. How?

In the following chapters, we will review many different multi-device experience examples through the lens of the 3Cs, demonstrating different relationships between devices, and how they can serve individuals in their tasks. As you will see, the 3Cs help you decide what flows and functionality should be featured when, and how the experience elements should be distributed across devices.

Bear in mind that each design approach is useful for addressing certain user contexts and use cases. For that reason, no single approach is useful in all situations, and quite often the best design employs several approaches (more on that in Chapter 5).

By mapping the variety of contexts across an experience, and then framing the roles each device plays in the overall ecosystem, we can create a clear narrative and mental model for that multi-device experience. Once *we* have this clear understanding in mind, we can translate it to design decisions for each device and for interaction points between devices. In doing so, we can help users navigate (and make sense of) the increasing complexity involved in having more and more devices, guiding them toward a more effective, productive, and delightful multi-device usage.

A Glance at the Past: Portable Computer Ads from the 1980s

Figures 1-3 and 1-4 are two portable computer newspaper ads that illustrate well how far technology has come in less than 30 years.

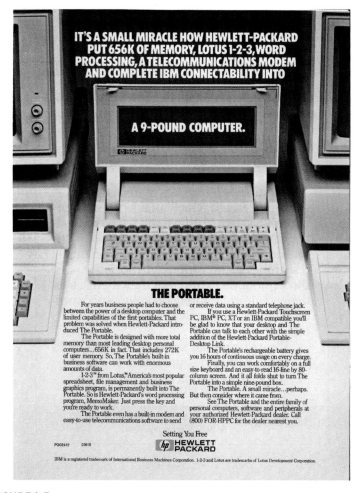

FIGURE 1-3

Hewlett-Packard, 1984 ad for The Portable computer—a nine-pound computer, with 656 KB memory; by comparison, smartphones today weigh on average 130 grams (0.286 pounds) and offer 1–2 GB RAM and 16–32 GB internal memory.

FIGURE 1-4

IBM 1984 portable personal computer ad ("The first IBM PC you can pick up and take with you"). This computer weighed 30 pounds, and was the approximate size of stationary computers today.

But how did we arrive at this multi-device era? Why are its opportunities so unique?

Single-Device Design Is History (Don't I Know It!)

As a UX designer, I can remember how not that long ago we all labored over the personal computer (PC) when designing a mass-market product. Our parameters were bounded: a single device, stationary, in landscape format, with relatively high resolution, and based on mouse and keyboard interaction.

Life was definitely simpler in many ways, but even back then, we had our share of design challenges for these shifting environments: ever-changing screen resolutions; multiple browsers with no common standard; and various technical limitations in terms of interaction design, latency, and implementation.

While those challenges represented the growing pains of a technology evolution, our current era is a technology *revolution*.

By *multi-device revolution*, I'm referring to the fast-growing number and diversity of connected devices—from smartphones, tablets, PCs, and TVs, through smartwatches, smartglasses, wristband activity trackers, smartfridges, and connected toothbrushes, to (soon enough) any physical object that can be connected to the Internet via sensors (what is known as the *Internet of Things*, which we'll discuss in Chapter 6). However, this revolution is not characterized just by new screen sizes, input methods, form factors, or increasing processing power. It also introduces new ways these multiple devices enable us to connect, operate, interact, work, and affect our surroundings—ways we didn't have before.

If we look back, we can see that three processes in particular were supremely influential in changing the multi-device landscape from a UX perspective: smartphones as a commodity, burgeoning application stores, and the emergence of tablets on the market. These processes signify the critical transformation from a single-device–focused design to the need to adopt an ecosystem approach to multi-device design.

HELLO SMARTPHONES

In June 2007, Apple launched its first iPhone device, a game-changing move in the mobile industry. A brand new, shiny device replaced the old tactile phone. It came with a slick, touch-based interaction, a rich feature set, a better graphical display, and processing power exceeding that of *Apollo 11* when it first went to the moon.[6] A year later, the App Store launch truly brought this device to life, with thousands of apps for entertainment, content, media, and other services (as discussed in the next section). As a side effect, iPhone owners consumed significantly more data than traditional cell phone users, which in turn encouraged mobile providers to offer subsidies on the device, given their compensating revenue from the increased data rates from these customers. All these factors contributed to accelerated adoption of the device.

The Android platform, introduced officially in October 2008, significantly reinforced smartphone adoption, with new kinds of devices from various manufacturers being offered at a lower cost. Soon enough, the face of mobile devices changed completely.

This change sparked (among other transformations) a sharp UX paradigm shift from the dominant design practices of the time, due to the move from tactile-based devices with a full physical keypad to touch-based displays where the entire interaction takes place on the screen itself.

Table 1-1 outlines the main differences in key user experience design aspects, in terms of both industrial design and interaction design.

TABLE 1-1. Comparison between the prevalent mobile device design before the iPhone was launched (left) and after (right)

	BEFORE	AFTER
Industrial design and form factor (sample of devices)		
Interaction model	Tactile	Touch
Interface manipulation	Indirect manipulation Users interact with physical keys below (and next to) the screen, through which they control the elements on the screen.	Directly on screen Users interact right with the elements on-screen.
Physical keys	Full physical keypad (usually 21-key–based, including navigation and action keys) and additional side buttons (like power on/off, volume up/down).	One home button on iPhone, three keys in Android, and additional side buttons (like power on/off, volume up/down).
Touchpoints	Supports a single keypress at a time	Supports touching multiple points on the screen simultaneously
Gestures	Supports only keypresses (no gestures)	Supports both button taps on-screen and gesture-based interactions (like swipe, pinch, rotate, and spread)
Orientation	Portrait only	Portrait and landscape
Focus and selection states	Two separate states (can have different visual treatments, and trigger different events)	Both merged into selection state (have a single visual effect, and can trigger only one event for selection)
Short and long press	Supports both	Supports both

These changes required everyone involved in product development and/or consumption to alter the way they approached mobile devices, and to establish new mental models, use habits, and best practices around the new mobile experience.

But the changes didn't stop there.

HELLO APP STORES

In July 2008, Apple launched its App Store for iPhone, and the mobile space was open for business. This move gave third-party developers the long-awaited freedom to build powerful mobile applications for everyone: no longer was the device strictly governed by mobile operators or handset manufacturers, but rather applications were developed by the people, for the people. Everyone could potentially build a mobile application, or develop a mobile version for an existing desktop product. The smartphone was finally recast from being a fancy, high-priced enterprise device (mostly used for calling, texting, and some browsing) into a multi-functional device offering a rich, dynamic world of content, features, and services.

In the first weekend after the App Store was launched, 10 *million* applications were downloaded. In less than a year, 1.4 billion apps had been downloaded, and more than 200,000 apps were available in the App Store.

Soon after Apple's App Store opened, many competitors followed suit, further enhancing smartphone adoption. In October 2008, Google introduced its Android Market. By August 2010, 1 billion apps had been downloaded from the Android market; in 2009 BlackBerry App World, Nokia Ovi Store, and Palm App Catalog opened; in 2010 Microsoft joined the party with Windows 7 Phone marketplace, and so did Samsung with its apps marketplace. Today, even the Nintendo DSi and Sony PlayStation Portable have application stores.

"There's an app for that" has quickly become the new catchphrase, serving as yet another signal of the profound effect (depicted in Figure 1-5) application stores have had on mobile development and design.

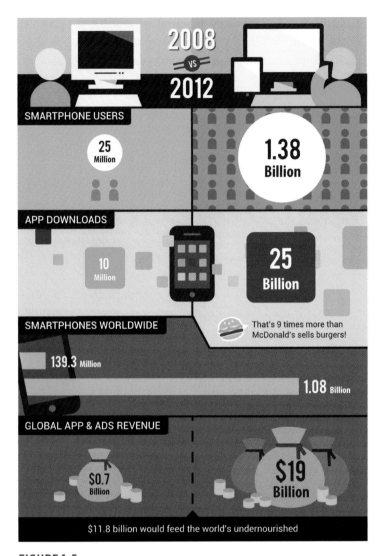

FIGURE 1-5.

Infographic comparing key mobile stats between 2008 and 2012. Can you believe this all happened in less than five years?[7]

In less than five years, mobile phones have practically become an extension of ourselves. Users *love* their smartphones, and use them everywhere—at home, work, the family dinner table, a restaurant, a store, a coffee shop, the doctor's office, the airport, the movie theater, the bathroom, on public transport, on a date, and even at church. If that's not enough, a recent study showed that 15% of iPhone owners said they would rather give up sex than go for a weekend without their iPhones.[8]

Four percent actually reported using their phones *during* sex (probably a topic for yet another book), and 65% reported they couldn't *live* without their devices. (If that's not love, I wonder what is.)

With the rapid success of the smartphone, its wide adoption, and its deep assimilation into our daily activities, it was just a matter of time until new devices joined the party. And they did.

Discussion: On Native Apps, Web Apps, and Everything in Between

For a few years now, whenever someone has considered building a mobile app, one of the debates that has immediately come up is which development path to choose. Native app? Web app? Or maybe a hybrid app?

Before going into the pros and cons of each approach, let's first understand what each of these app types means:

Native apps

> These apps live on the device itself. Accordingly, they are specific to the device platform on which they reside (e.g., iOS or Android), and require separate development per platform. These apps need to be downloaded and installed through an application store, and can then be accessed via a dedicated icon on the home screen. Native apps can access and use all the device's sensor data (GPS, accelerometer, camera, etc.), as well as benefiting from native platform components like UI elements (buttons, sliders, tabs, and other controls), interaction patterns (gestures, transitions), and core features (contact list, call log). These apps can also run in the background, work offline, and integrate into the central notification system. Most of the mobile apps today are native.

Web apps

> Also commonly referred to as HTML5 apps, these apps run in the web browser. These "apps" are effectively websites (typically written in HTML5) that users access just like any other website—through a URL entered in the device's browser. Upon first connecting to the website, users can install the app—an action that puts the app icon on the home screen (providing similar access to native apps). The difference is that in this case, the icon is a shortcut to the designated URL.
>
> As web apps are run by the browser, they do not require a separate code base per platform; a single instance can be used across platforms.

Visually, web apps can look very much like native apps, and they can incorporate gestures and transitions (as supported by HTML5). At the same time, HTML5 apps do not (yet) match native apps' quality of experience (in terms of performance, smoothness, gesture slickness, etc.), and certain native OS features are (still) unavailable from the browser, such as the central notification system, some sensor data, and advanced gestures.

Hybrid apps

As the name implies, hybrid apps are a combination of native apps and web apps (see Figure 1-6). They are essentially HTML5 apps wrapped inside a native container. They live on the device itself and run inside a native wrapper, which uses the device's browser engine to render the HTML5 code. Just like native apps, they are installed through the application store.

This hybrid structure aims to take advantage of the best of both worlds: keeping a single code base for all platforms (like web apps), and having access to extended device capabilities such as the accelerometer, GPS, camera, and device storage (like native apps).

Development frameworks such as Sencha, PhoneGap, Titanium, and others provide tools to build hybrid apps that can work on iOS and Android, as well as BlackBerry, Windows Phone, and more.

FIGURE 1-6

Untappd (created by PhoneGap) is an example of a hybrid mobile app. It is shown here (left to right) on Android, iOS, and Windows Phone, respectively. Untappd has a native app look and feel, and it even follows each platform's specific UI principles (e.g., the tabs location), strengthening platform affinity.

Deciding which development path you should take depends on multiple factors related to your company, your product, your users, and your product timeline. To help you with the task, Table 1-2 lists nine questions that will guide you through selecting the approach that best fits your needs.

TABLE 1-2. Comparison of native, web, and hybrid apps—the green bar indicates an advantage for that development path, while red highlights a disadvantage

	NATIVE APP	WEB APP	HYBRID APP
Need for speed	Faster graphics and performance	Slower	Slower
Need for device sensors (GPS, camera, etc.)?	Native apps provide access to all the device's features	Access to device is limited from the browser	A web-to-native abstraction layer allows extended access to the device's sensors
Limited development resources?	Requires separate, specialized development per platform	Single HTML5 code base across platforms	Single HTML5 code base across platforms
Crunched for time?	Slower implementation due to the need to develop multiple app variants and get them approved in the app stores	Fastest implementation and deployment	Faster implementation and deployment
Prioritizes premium design? Complex UX design?	Provides slicker, higher-quality, and more personalized UX. Allows use of device-specific gestures.	HTML5 is still more limited in UX capabilities. Might have a very similar look and feel, but inferior interaction.	HTML5 is still more limited in UX capabilities. Might have a very similar look and feel, but inferior interaction.
Large amounts of data transfer?	Faster data transfer	(Still) slower due to reliance on network speed	(Still) slower due to reliance on network speed
Expecting frequent updates?	Requires maintaining multiple specialized mobile variants and distributing the updates through the app stores	App can be changed and pushed out instantly to the entire user base	Requires changing only a single code base, but the distribution is still through the app stores

	NATIVE APP	WEB APP	HYBRID APP
Need the app to work offline?	Supports offline use	Cannot work without connectivity	Supports offline use
Plan to mone-tize content?	Much better in-app purchasing system also tied to other users' purchases on the platform	No structured support. Can offer a shop-ping cart on the website, but still doesn't compare to the native app.	No structured support. Can offer a shop-ping cart on the website, but still doesn't compare to the native app.

Note that the assessments in Table 1-2 are based on the current state of technology and may change with time, narrowing down some of the gaps that exist today and possibly expanding others.

In any case, remember that users don't really care if the app is native, web, or hybrid. What they *do* care about is being able to find the app they need, and that app offering a fast, slick, effective, and delightful user experience that helps them in their activities.

HELLO TABLETS

In April 2010, Apple expanded its family and introduced the iPad to the world. On the first day alone, 300,000 iPads were sold, and sales reached 14.8 million during the first year. As with its ancestor, the iPhone, it was really the App Store that made the iPad truly magical, and sales continued to skyrocket, with cumulative totals reaching 67 million units in just two years.[9]

In parallel, Google stirred up the tablet market even more, releasing Android OS for tablets in 2011 and gaining 39% market share within less than a year.[10] In less than three years, tablets reached 10% market penetration, becoming the fastest-growing device in the history of con-sumer electronics.[11]

The tablet, similarly to the smartphone, not only created new use modes and behavior patterns around it, but also changed the ways we use existing devices in what I call the *interaction effect*: the usage pat-terns of one device change depending on the availability of another device. This change can manifest in using the devices more, using the devices less, or using them differently—in conjunction with one another, for example.

In the case of tablets, their increasing use led to a decline in other media and device usage; for instance, 20% of tablet owners are using print magazines less, 25% are using fewer print books, and 27% are using print newspapers less often. Furthermore, desktop computers, laptop computers, ereaders, and portable media players are also used less.[12]

But there was another interaction effect created by tablets, one that demonstrates the strength of (and need for) multi-device experiences. According to a 2011 Neilsen Company survey, 70% of tablet owners used their tablets *while watching TV*—a use scenario that constituted the largest share of their total time with the tablet (30%), as Figure 1-7 illustrates.

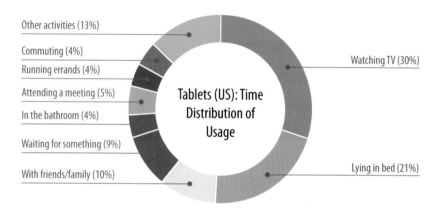

FIGURE 1-7.
Time distribution of tablet usage in the US market.[13]

This made the TV the device most used in conjunction with the tablet, pulling it into the ecosystem as one of its core devices (as well as granting tablets the title of "TV buddies"). Not only that, but this joint usage involved users engaging with the tablet for TV-specific activities during a show: looking up information related to the TV program they're watching (29%), searching product information for an ad (19%), and looking up coupons or deals related to a commercial (16%).[14] These behaviors emerged organically, through users searching for information using a web browser, before there were any specialized apps for that purpose. Can you imagine the UX opportunities embodied in building multi-device experiences that *are* specifically tailored to this use case? Apps that offer users relevant, real-time information and activities while they're watching TV? Today, we already have an abundance of such apps (also referred to as *second-screen experiences*), and we will further analyze some of them in the next chapters.

At a higher level, this strong tie between the TV and the tablet, as well as other interaction effects taking place between the ecosystem devices, is a highly important data point when we're considering multi-device experiences.[15] These interaction effects provide insights into users' evolving habits, use patterns, and mental models. As a result, they can (and should) help drive product and design decisions regarding key questions like which devices should take part in the experience, how the experience should be distributed across devices, what the integration points between devices should be, and where (if at all) offering a collaborative device interaction is beneficial to users.

It's an Ecosystem!

The three processes just described—smartphones becoming a commodity, application stores gaining speed, and tablets joining the party—all contributed to the emergence of an ecosystem, with four devices at its core: the smartphone, tablet, PC, and TV.

In this ecosystem, a few important principles emerge that will accompany us throughout the book:

- We are in the midst of an important behavioral shift to a multi-device model; product design is no longer just about the desktop platform because there's a prosperous ecosystem of connected devices that complements it, and that continues to grow.

- These connected devices can form a multi-device experience as a connected group (rather than just a set of silo devices). In other words, the ecosystem experience can employ any of the three design approaches—consistent, continuous, and complementary—or a combination of them.

- The ecosystem is not bound to the four core devices. These devices are currently the most commonly used, and thus serve as the basis; however, as more connected devices are introduced, they can join the ecosystem, further expanding the contexts of use and device relationships it accommodates.

- The more we embrace the potential of an ecosystem by adapting the experience per device and building the required bridges between them (acknowledging the different use cases in varying contexts), the more we can simplify the experience on each device, and provide an overall holistic experience that is greater than its parts.

Bear in mind that the multi-device era is still in its early stages. Thus, use patterns across devices are just starting to take shape, and even the ones that seem to stabilize will probably change soon enough, as more devices join the ecosystem and introduce new, disruptive ways to connect and interact with the environment and one another.

At this point in time, the most important goal we should focus on is *learning*. We should explore and experiment with building multi-device experiences that can continuously drive us to create better products, that are more intimately tailored to individual users' changing needs. In this process, we need to encourage the open mind, inquisitive spirit, and broad thinking that are instrumental in taking the leap from a single-device approach to an ecosystem one. As you will see throughout the book, this new multi-device world opens up many new opportunities to innovate—not only by looking into future needs and use cases that will naturally arise, but also through rethinking some of our existing design approaches to current challenges. The latter is where much of the power lies: disrupting widespread perceptions and assumptions regarding what is possible in light of the new ecosystem possibilities we have.

Summary

- Particular conditions brought about the multi-device era and the unique factors that differentiate it from anything we've seen before.

- The multi-device era introduces an ecosystem, similar to that of the natural world. In the multi-device ecosystem, a variety of devices interact with one another as an ecology, and their interactions are shaped by how individuals use the devices in a variety of contexts en route to completing their information and entertainment goals.

- The three key processes that signify the critical transformation from a single-device model to an ecosystem approach were the entry of smartphones as a commodity, the burgeoning application market, and the success of tablets.

- The 3Cs framework consists of three principal approaches—consistent, continuous, and complementary—for handling the design complexity introduced by the numerous devices on the market (and those yet to be invented).

NOTES

1. Cisco.com, "Cisco Visual Networking Index: Global Media Data Traffic Forecast Update: 2012–2017," February 6, 2013, *http://bit.ly/1c0HYnW*.

2. "GSMA Announces That the Proliferation of Connected Devices Will Create a US$1.2 Trillion Revenue Opportunity for Mobile Operators by 2020," PR Newswire, October 10, 2011, *http://prn.to/19cuKWx*.

3. Google, "The New Multi-Screen World: Understanding Cross-Platform Consumer Behavior," August 2012, *http://bit.ly/1gVzizF*.

4. Google/Ipsos OTX MediaCT, US, "Our Mobile Planet: United States," May 2012, *http://bit.ly/1bQ26bo*.

5. Christophe Stoll, "Multiscreen Patterns," May 26, 2011, *http://bit.ly/1fmA87Y*.

6. Richard Stengel, "Making Sense of Our Wireless World," *Time Magazine*, August 27, 2012, *http://www.time.com/time/magazine/article/0,9171,2122243,00.html*.

7. "Number of Smartphones Sold to End Users Worldwide from 2007 to 2012 (in Million Units)," Statista, February 2013, *http://bit.ly/Jx8aM9*; "Strategy Analytics: Worldwide Smartphone Population Tops 1 Billion in Q3 2012," Business Wire, October 17, 2012, *http://bit.ly/1kSjiPn*; Rob Thurner, "The Latest App Download Statistics," *Smart Insights*, March 29, 2012, *http://bit.ly/1hZhib8*; Jeff Sonderman, "Mobile App Revenue Exceeds Ad Revenue," December 4, 2012, *http://bit.ly/1jf2w1o*; Chris Quick, "With Smartphone Adoption on the Rise, Opportunity for Marketers Is Calling," Nielsen, September 15, 2009, *http://bit.ly/1jf2AhI*; "A History of App Stores: Apple, Google, and Everyone Else" (infographic), WebpageFX, August 15, 2011, *http://bit.ly/1bNWZIC*.

8. Sam Liard, "Are You Addicted to Your Smartphone?" Mashable, September 5, 2012, *http://mashable.com/2012/09/05/addicted-smartphone/*.

9. Sam Costello, "What Are iPad Sales All Time?" About.com (based on Apple Quarterly Finance Report), October 23, 2013, *http://abt.cm/1dmA32t*.

10. Robin Wauters, "Android Reaches 39% Tablet OS Market Share 2012," TechCrunch (based on research by Strategy Analytics), January 26, 2012, *http://tcrn.ch/19Swgrc*.

11. Michael DeGusta, "Are Smart Phones Spreading Faster Than Any Technology in Human History?" *MIT Technology Review*, May 9, 2012, *http://bit.ly/1fEBvj0*.

12. "In the U.S., Tablets Are TV Buddies While e-Readers Make Great Bedfellows," Nielsen, May 19, 2011, *http://bit.ly/1khyS9G*.

13. "Double Vision—Global Trends in Tablet and Smartphone Use While Watching TV," Nielsen, April 5, 2012, *http://bit.ly/1cAsIuu*.

14. "State of the Media: U.S. Digital Consumer Report, Q3–Q4 2011," Nielsen, 2012, *http://bit.ly/J5amtF*.

15. Chapter 7 focuses on multi-device data analytics.

[2]

The Consistent Design Approach

This chapter introduces the first of the 3Cs framework—the consistent approach to multi-device design. We'll see how this approach, by which the same core experience is ported across devices (with some adjustments per device), sets the stage for multi-device design. It is, however, only Act One.

To lay the groundwork for the upcoming discussion of the three design approaches in operation, I'll first focus on each one in isolation, provide examples of how it is employed in existing products, and extract important design takeaways. In later chapters, I'll discuss how the different approaches coexist and intertwine to construct a richer ecosystem experience, composed of a broader set of contexts and meeting broader user needs. With this foundation, we'll be able to spread our wings even wider into the world of the Internet of Things (IoT). We will analyze the new opportunities a fully connected world introduces, the challenges that go along with them, and how we can overcome those hurdles and create even more innovative, creative, and successful experiences.

By learning to identify and incorporate these multi-device approaches into your design process and design thinking, you will be able to build better experiences for your users—experiences that span across space and time, devices and things, and the digital and physical, but that still remain true to the core essence of UX: people. If you focus on people, put their needs and goals in the center, all else will follow. This basic notion will never be changed by technology, no matter how sophisticated it may get.

What Is Consistent Design?

Consistent design, the most common multi-device approach applied today, happens when the same essential experience, with the same content and features, is ported across devices in a like manner (see Figure 2-1). In many cases, it's the desktop experience (which most products already have) that is replicated on the mobile device, with some adjustments made to accommodate different devices' characteristics.

FIGURE 2-1

The consistent approach: the same content offering is replicated across devices, with some adjustments to accommodate each device's characteristics.

These adjustments address differences between devices in facets like form factor, screen size, interaction model (touch, keys, voice), and sensors (GPS, accelerometer, gyroscope, and others). They can be visual—adapting screen layouts, grids, and user interface (UI) element size—but they can also involve other experience layers, like information architecture (IA).

For example, a common visual adjustment is taking a standard multi-column page layout on a desktop website and organizing it as a single column on a smartphone to fit its smaller screen size. Additionally, UI elements like buttons and images often change in size between devices, to optimally fit the available screen real estate.

An example of an IA adjustment is shifting the navigation model from a flat hierarchy on the desktop (where several levels of menu items are offered on the same page) to a deep hierarchy on mobile devices (dividing the content along several screens, which require more drill-down steps). An alternative practice that has gained popularity on mobile devices is placing the entire navigation menu behind a "hamburger" icon (▤), usually located at the top-left corner of the page.

This way, the same navigation structure and organization can remain consistent across all devices, keeping the interface adjustments between devices mostly visual. In big-screen devices, the full menu is exposed on screen at all times, while in smaller-screen devices the same menu is one click away, located behind a dedicated control, helping to keep the screen design clean and clear. (See Figure 2-2.)

FIGURE 2-2

Mashable's responsive web design for desktop, tablet, and smartphone. The three-column tiled layout on the desktop changes into two columns on the tablet, and is then condensed into a single list column on the smartphone. Also, while on the bigger screens the main navigation bar is placed horizontally at the top across the entire desktop site, on the smartphone it is hidden behind a "hamburger" icon at the top-left.

The design adjustments between devices highlight an important principle of the consistent approach: *consistent doesn't mean identical.*

The design can't be 100% identical across the different devices, and it shouldn't be. Different devices vary in size, display, input method, interaction model, use mode, context, and more, as outlined in Table 2-1.

TABLE 2-1. A summary of some of the main differences between devices, which require design optimizations per device

	SMARTPHONE	TABLET	DESKTOP/ LAPTOP	TELEVISION
Display size[1]	4–5"	7–10.1"	15–27"	32–60"
Proximity	6–12"	10–18"	12–22"	5–15"
Where used	Practically everywhere	Mostly at home, but also on the go	Mostly at the office/home	Home
Use mode	Mobile	Mobile	Mostly stationary	Stationary
Viewing mode	Lean back and lean forward	Lean back	Lean forward	Lean back
Interaction model	Touch-based— direct manipulation on-screen. Also, voice interaction is becoming more prevalent.	Touch-based—direct manipulation on-screen	Dominated by keyboard and mouse (indirect manipula-tion)	Mostly reliant on standard remote controls, limited to four-way arrow and selection
Attention pattern	Series of many short interactions all day long. Highly interrupt driven. Most people look at their phones about 150 times a day (that means about once every 6.5 minutes), mainly to check incom-ing email and text messages.[2]	Longer engage-ment—more of a leisure device used to consume content	Longer engage-ment—used mostly in the work environ-ment, and for search/ explora-tion tasks at home	Longer engage-ment—mostly passive, con-suming media. Attention is often split between the TV and another mobile device (smartphone/ tablet) used in parallel.
Device sharing	Very private device. Reluctance to share with others.	Shared device— usually among fam-ily members (including toddlers).	At work— usually pri-vate. At home—can be shared. Still, relies on different logins, thus preserving privacy even when device is shared.	Shared between family members. Furthermore, the experience itself is often social (watch-ing with friends/ family).

Main features and sensors	GPS, proximity, accelerometer, gyroscope, compass, pressure, WiFi, camera, microphone, Bluetooth, ambient light sensor, back-illuminated sensor.	GPS, proximity, accelerometer, gyroscope, compass, pressure, WiFi, camera, microphone, Bluetooth, ambient light sensor, back-illuminated sensor.	Varies, but mostly WiFi, webcam, microphone, Bluetooth, ambient light sensor.	None on standard TVs. Smart TVs offer WiFi, as well sensors like presence, light, ambient light, and motion.

OPTIMIZING THE CONSISTENT EXPERIENCE

Looking through these differences, you can clearly see that you cannot merely take a certain experience design *as is* and scale it to fit different devices. You need to consider functional and visual optimizations per device. Three main optimization facets are described next.

Optimizing for layout

Optimizing for layout means changing screen layouts and adapting UI elements to fit the different devices' screen sizes, resolutions, and orientations (see Figure 2-3). As we saw earlier, these adjustments refer to properties like screen grid, image size, button size, font size, spacing, and alignment.

FIGURE 2-3

Philip House design adjustments across different screen sizes and orientations (via *http://mediaqueri.es/*).

When it comes to screen size, the smartphone presents the most constraints, due to its small screen size. While this is a limiting factor in terms of design flexibility, it also has a strong advantage: constraints force you to focus the design on the most important content and actions, crystallizing the core essence of the user experience. Not only that, but these constraints also encourage you to be more creative, as you have fewer tools available to craft a useful, usable, and engaging experience.

In his famous book *Mobile First*, Luke Wroblewski discusses how embracing mobile phone constraints (rather than trying to fight them) can ultimately lead to better, stronger, more focused designs.[3] When you simply don't have enough space to accommodate all the content and features that exist on other devices (like the PC), or listed in the product requirements doc, you and your team have to go through a tough prioritization process, which eventually leads to cleaner, simpler designs that are truly focused on the main needs and goals of your users. As Jonah Lehrer put it in his book, *Imagine: How Creativity Works* (Houghton Mifflin), "The imagination is unleashed by constraints. You break out of the box by stepping into shackles."[4]

Optimizing for touch

With touch-based interaction, UI elements need to accommodate the human finger size (which is significantly bigger than a mouse cursor target). This requires, for example, using bigger, more spaced-out buttons instead of dense links, as often used on desktop sites (see Figure 2-4).

[TIP]

The key size displayed on the mobile interface doesn't always need to reflect one-to-one the touch-sensitive area of that key. For example, iPhone and Windows phone keyboards alter the hit target area around each letter continuously as users type, based on the probability that each letter will be selected given the input typed so far. This allows them to display smaller-size keys on screen while optimizing for typing errors.

FIGURE 2-4

A Facebook post displayed at the bottom in the web interface (collection of action links) and at the top in the mobile interface (bigger, more spread out buttons).

Furthermore, a touch interface doesn't allow for the hover state (i.e., you can't "mouse over" a target for more information or options, as an intermediate/educational step before taking an action). Given that hover has become one of the most dominant interaction triggers in desktop interfaces, designing a mobile experience without it—especially when you're porting an existing desktop one—requires design changes. Finally, gestures have practically become a standard in mobile interfaces. Interactions like swipe, pinch, and spread often offer quick and easy ways to complete an action. Thus, when designing or porting an experience to the mobile device, you must account for this interaction layer.

Optimizing for form factor

When considering the use mode and features of the different devices, you can make some functional enhancements to help improve the experience for each device. A simple example is adding a Call or Get

Directions button to a place page when it is accessed on a smartphone. Another example is promoting voice input on mobile devices, where typing is slower and more error-prone.

Form factor also impacts the physical attributes of device use—for example, smartphones often rely on one-thumb operation, while tablets are gripped on both sides. These different configurations impact the relative accessibility of different areas on the screen to the user, and thus affect the UX design considerations. A good demonstration of this is the iOS split keyboard for the iPad, which accounts for the way a user holds the iPad in an effort to make typing easier (see Figure 2-5).

FIGURE 2-5

The iOS 5 split keyboard, which accounts for the way iPads are commonly held on both sides. The keyboard is split in half, offering one-thumb access to all the letters in an effort to make typing easier.

KEEPING THE CORE EXPERIENCE CONSISTENT

When it comes to consistent design, you need to constantly keep in mind the delicate balance between *consistency across the ecosystem* and *optimized experience per device*.

We've discussed the optimization part of the equation, so let's have a look now at where consistency should be applied:

Consistent core functionality across devices
   The vital components of the experience—those features that are considered its lifeblood and are part of the *minimum viable product* (MVP)—should be kept consistent across devices. When it comes

to consistent design, each device is independent, a fully functional unit that should allow users to consume the entire core experience using it.

In addition, consistent elements should work the same between devices (as much as possible) in the way they are triggered, configured, and interacted with.

Consistent IA across devices

The basic information structure, organization, and terminology should be kept consistent across devices, even if the navigation model needs to be adjusted for certain devices (as we saw at the beginning of the chapter). IA is a fundamental building block of the experience, and an essential component in establishing a clear mental model around the product structure and flow.

Consistent look and feel across devices

A common visual language should be used across devices to help people establish not only the brand personality, but also the cognitive and affective tie between devices. Research has shown that visual design plays an important role in shaping user's responses to products, as well as their perceptions about functionality, usability, and credibility.[5] Having different visual designs across devices might signal to people different functionality, flow, or offerings (when that is not the case), as well as increasing the learning curve.

When you use the consistent approach, where different devices provide access to the same content and features (even with mild adjustments), people expect to get the same core user experience and follow the same behavior patterns. Drawing from the physical world, you might think about consistent experience as a coffee chain like Starbucks. People visiting different branches expect to get the same menu (and prices), order their coffee the same way, see the same logo and staff uniform, and have the same WiFi configuration. Some branches might offer a few unique pastries or snacks that others don't, and the seating arrangements must be adjusted to fit the space available for that branch, but at the end of the day, the core Starbucks experience is the same.

With these considerations in mind, in the following sections I've outlined a few products that employ the consistent design approach. For each product example, I will analyze the design similarities and differences across devices, and then discuss the main design lessons we can learn from it.

Discussion: Managing the Device Chaos

Looking at the device flurry around us, anyone could get overwhelmed when faced with the task of multi-device design. Dozens of phones, tablets, and phablets[6]—in various sizes, resolutions, and ratios—all cry for our attention (see Figure 2-6).[7]

The gold standard these days for addressing the myriad of devices, cemented in mid-2012, is *responsive web design* (RWD).[8]

Originally introduced by Ethan Marcotte in 2010, RWD is a technique that enables you to create a single website that adjusts itself seamlessly for any screen.[9]

FIGURE 2-6

Screen sizes of popular mobile devices.[10]

It is based on HTML standards (CSS3) and comprises three main components:

Fluid grids

Percentage-based columns of content that change flexibly with the device size and resolution

Flexible images

Percentage-based image (and video) sizes that are fluid as well

Media queries
> A CSS3 tool that can detect the device characteristics (size, resolution, and more) and target a tailored stylesheet accordingly

Together, these components scale and adapt the web experience across a range of devices. In essence, RWD reduces the multi-device design complexity to a single factor: screen size. And that's both its strength and its weakness.

RWD IS POWERFUL...

On the positive side, RWD offers an effective way to implement a consistent experience across devices, while maintaining a single code base (see Figure 2-7). It relies on setting design breakpoints that define the screen size conditions at which a major design change is needed (like changing a two-column grid to a three-column one).

FIGURE 2-7

Responsive web design for the Big Youth website (via *http://mediaqueri.es/*). Three major layout changes take place as the display gets bigger: going from a one-column display on the smartphone (far left) to a two-column display (second from left), and then a three-column display (third from left). From there (and between those breakpoints), the layout scales to fit bigger screens (far right).

There are different tactics for deciding where to put the breakpoints, and these depend a lot on your website content. One approach you should avoid, though, is going after "common screen sizes" as breakpoint cues.

They don't exist. With the unprecedented pace at which things move in the mobile industry (especially on the Android front), you will find yourself chasing your own tail, fighting broken layouts in new devices. The approach should be a fluid one, a flexible system based on relative measurements. Starting from the smallest screen ("mobile first") and working your way up from there is usually the preferred path. More constraints mean sharper focus on the product's essence, which translates to better experiences across the board.

BUT NOT A SILVER BULLET

Chris Johanesen, VP of Product for social news site BuzzFeed, expresses well the fundamental problem with RWD:

> Responsive design has a lot of buzz right now, but it's not a blanket solution that can be applied everywhere. While it would be nice, in theory, to have one solution that worked everywhere, if you want to ensure everyone has the best experience possible, you need to optimize for many devices and use cases.[11]

Similar to the consistent approach as a whole, RWD assumes one experience for all devices—an experience that can be fully consumed on *any* device. This essentially means a *device-independent* experience. While this might be feasible for certain product offerings, in many cases there's a larger set of interactions, interrelations, contexts, and content flow involved—all of which can fundamentally change people's use modes and needs on different devices. This is where RWD and the consistent approach become somewhat narrow and limiting (conceptually and practically). We will see that with Hulu Plus in this chapter, and will dig deeper into many other use cases and product examples in the following chapters.

Consistency in Minimalist Interfaces: Google Search

A great example of the idea that even with the cleanest, simplest user interface, *good consistent design is not identical across devices* is Google Search. It is available either through the website (which is adapted to the different devices), or as a native app for smartphones and tablets across Android and iOS (see Figure 2-8).

WHAT'S CONSISTENT ACROSS DEVICES?

Google Search keeps two main facets consistent across devices: the layout and visual design, and the core feature set. Together, they make up the core essence of the experience that accompanies users across devices.

FIGURE 2-8

Google Search home page design for web/desktop (top), iPhone app (bottom-left), and iPad app (bottom-right). The layout and visual design are very similar across devices, with a few optimizations for the mobile devices.

Layout and visual design

In terms of its layout, Google Search uses the same basic layout and visual language across all devices, with the Google logo above a search box, a nearby search button, and a similar color palette. At the top of every display, the Google Search home page provides a Sign In button or displays information for the currently signed-in user, like the user's thumbnail photo, profile info, and the Google+ Share button.

When a user runs a search, the consistent design follows through: the results display across all devices offer the same information details (title, description, and URL), organized in the same grid, all following the same visual design. Furthermore, summary information cards that are displayed for selected queries (like "Abraham Lincoln" or "California") persist across devices, keeping the same information and visual design (see Figure 2-9).

FIGURE 2-9

Google Search results screen for "Abraham Lincoln" on desktop/web (top), tablet (bottom left), and smartphone (bottom right). The page content and design elements are consistent—yet not identical—across devices. For example, as the available screen real estate gets smaller, fewer details are surfaced by default in the summary cards.

Core feature set

Regardless of device, you can input your search query using text or voice, and move between all the different search properties (Images, Videos, News, etc.). When signed in, you can check your Google+ notifications, or share a post with your circles from any device.

When you make a search query, you get essentially the same results across all devices (with some adjustments in the location-sensitive mobile use case, discussed shortly).

As mentioned earlier, the at-a-glance summary information card is offered across all devices, as well as the ads component and related search suggestions.

All these commonalities help create a familiar, predictable, and easy-to-use search experience across devices. There's practically no learning curve when you move between devices, and you can immediately pick up any device that is most convenient for you and run the search you need at that moment.

WHAT'S OPTIMIZED FOR EACH DEVICE?

Beyond mild adjustments in the overall arrangement of elements on-screen, Google Search offers a few important optimizations on the mobile devices to accommodate their context of use: alternative input methods, localized results, and Google Now.

Promoting alternative input methods

Google Search's mobile design more prominently surfaces alternative input methods, like voice search and camera. These address some contextual user needs stemming from on-the-go, touch-based devices:

Users struggle to type

> Typing text is a cumbersome, error-prone task on touch-based devices (especially when bundled with a small screen size), so having easy access to search by voice can help facilitate the search action.

Users take their phones everywhere

> People carry their mobile phones everywhere they go. When they're traveling to new places, they often come across interesting landmarks or objects they would like to know more about (e.g., buildings, bridges, artwork in museums, products), which is a

great use case for searching on their phones. However, they don't necessarily recognize the places or know much about them, which makes the traditional keyword-based search somewhat challenging. To streamline this process, Google Search promotes camera input on its mobile apps, offering a simple photo-triggered search: users can just take a picture of the landmark or object of interest, and Google will bring them the information they need. This not only saves typing, but also releases people from having to articulate a query, allowing an easy contextual search on the go.

Localizing (relevant) search results

Google Search adapts the experience for mobile use cases beyond just the visual layer. For relevant queries, it optimizes the search results themselves to consider the user's current location.

For example, when a user makes a search query for a business, the Google Search results deliver information specific to the device's location, such as a map that displays the nearest related businesses with their contact info (see Figure 2-10). For a specific business listing, the result shows a phone and map icon so users can call it or map routes to it from their current location. Each listing also displays the distance to that business from the device's location.

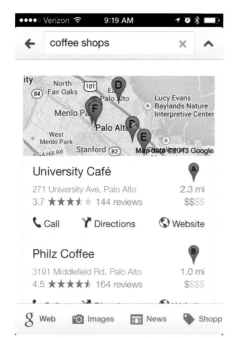

FIGURE 2-10

A Google search result page on a mobile device—searching for coffee shops when in Palo Alto, California. The local businesses are surfaced to the top of the page, along with a map and immediate actions that can be taken from the device.

These small optimizations go as far as the autocomplete search suggestions that appear while a user types a query, even before his finger hits the search button.

Addressing dynamic contexts with Google Now

Google Now offers an intelligent concierge on mobile devices, providing relevant, contextual information for users—before they even ask for it (see Figure 2-11). Through a set of contextual cards that appear automatically in the Google Search application, users can see the weather forecast before they start their day, find out how much traffic to expect before they leave for work, determine when the next train will arrive as they're standing on the platform, or check their favorite team's score during their commute.

FIGURE 2-11

Google Now card examples, along with a screenshot of their integration into the Google Search mobile app. These cards offer contextual information such as weather forecasts, traffic updates, train schedules, and sports scores.

This enhanced functionality demonstrates yet another layer of device-level optimization you can deliver while maintaining a clear, consistent model in users' minds across the ecosystem.

Google Now works in a progressive manner: when users first open the Google Search application, they see the same experience they're already used to from other devices (clean screen, big logo, and a search field). The only difference is a small stack of cards peeking at the bottom of the screen. Then, as they start scrolling down the screen, the UI progressively reveals new content that is personalized for them and mobile-optimized.

Progressive Disclosure in Consistent Design: Trulia

Trulia is an online real estate site for home buyers, sellers, renters, and real estate professionals. It lists properties for sale and rent, as well as neighborhood information and community insights, using a map-based interactive interface.

Trulia's main map view serves as another good example for a consistent approach (see Figure 2-12). In this case, you can clearly see a structured gradual surfacing of content as screens get bigger, keeping a consistent core experience across the board.

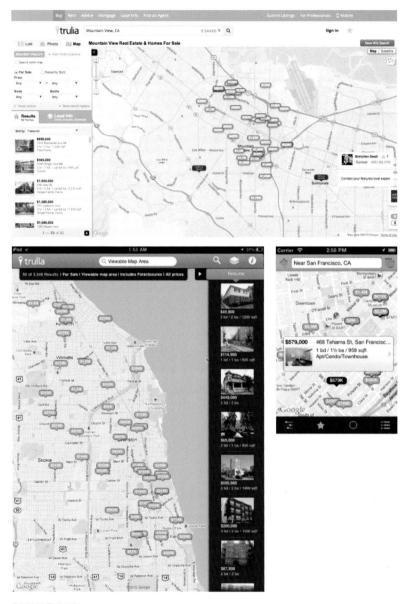

FIGURE 2-12

Trulia's main map view interface across different devices—iPhone, iPad, and desktop. The underlying key elements, like the map background, are consistent across all displays, with some layout adjustments per device.

WHAT'S CONSISTENT ACROSS DEVICES?

Trulia keeps several key experience elements, as well as the main flow and interaction, consistent across devices. Let's take a closer look at each one.

Key experience elements

The underlying interface canvas is a fullscreen map, along with a price distribution layer. This is the foundation of Trulia's design approach, which is applied across all devices. It reflects the simple premise that the primary initial factors guiding real estate choices are location and price.

Three additional key components that persist across devices include:

Content offering
> The entire set of property listings—with all their photos, full profile information, and actions—is available on all devices.

Search bar
> This is consistently placed at the top, enabling users to enter any location as free text (which then adjusts the map below accordingly).

Property details box
> This is offered across all devices, and provides more details about the property in focus.

Main flow and interaction

The overall screen scanning flow is consistent across all devices. The fullscreen map with the price layer gets the primary focus, while supporting information and actions are placed in secondary locations that take up approximately 15–20% of the screen real estate (side strip on desktop and tablet).

In terms of map interaction, the UI follows a consistent pattern whereby users click/tap on the price bubbles to see more info about the property they've selected. In addition, they can pan around to other map locations, double-click/tap to zoom, or use the search to center the map on a specific location.

WHAT'S OPTIMIZED FOR EACH DEVICE?

Trulia optimizes the screen layout and content surfaced for each device. The main map display across devices is a great example of the "mobile first" approach principles. Although the mobile phone wasn't the first device Trulia focused on, its mobile design maintains a sharp focus on what's *really* important by eliminating any elements that are not part of the product's essence.

As screens get bigger and more real estate is available, Trulia gradually enhances the content displayed and adds in elements that support the core experience. Here's a comparison across devices:

Smartphone

> In the smallest device, the display focuses on the product's essence only: a map view with price distribution layer. Everything else is displayed upon interaction.
>
> This simple, clean design reflects clearly Trulia's guiding principle of location and price being the lead decision-making factors in renting or buying a property.

Tablet

> The bigger screen space allows for scaling the display, offering an extended map display with bigger controls. Also, additional elements are included, such as the home listing strip that appears at the right side of the screen and offers quick access to a set of selected homes. This additional content is valuable; it immediately adds "meat" to the display, offering visitors a direct view of actual houses (rather than just displaying the decision-making factors of price and location). Surfacing actual content items that are in line with people's interests usually helps generate more activity on the page, as they serve as concrete anchors from which people can engage in further exploration.

Desktop

> The largest screen display continues in the same direction: scaling the screen elements and enhancing them with more supporting content. It offers not only a home listing strip (with more elaborate property display), but also a set of filters, a local info tab, and other settings. Additionally, the map interaction is adjusted accordingly so that a click on a price bubble in the map automatically scrolls the home listings strip on the left until the selected home is highlighted.

Discussion: Bridging Mobile Platforms

One of the biggest challenges in the mobile market today is its fragmentation. Specifically, when it comes to UX, many design questions arise around the relationship between Android and iOS, the two leading platforms in the market (see Figures 2-13 through 2-15). Some of the most common questions include: *Should Android and iOS apps look exactly the same, or should they be different? Can I port my iOS app to Android? Should I design for each platform separately? Which one should I start with?*

FIGURE 2-13

Trulia's tablet apps for Android (on the left) and iOS (on the right). The design is consistent across platforms, yet it considers the different interaction patterns and layout standard unique to each platform.

These questions are further amplified when you consider a cross-device experience that goes beyond just the smartphone. For example, people might own an Android phone and an iPad tablet that they use in parallel—not a far-fetched scenario, given that Android dominates the smartphone market, while the iPad is still the most popular tablet device.[12] So how do you handle cross-platform consistency?

In many ways, the answer is the same as for multi-device consistency: you need to find the balance between keeping the fundamental experience consistent across platforms, and optimizing the design according to the unique standards and user expectations for each. To accomplish that, here are a few important guidelines to follow:

1. Make sure you know well the Android design guidelines and the iOS human interface guidelines.[13] These provide the nuts and bolts of each platform, as well as the reasoning behind the design standards. Having that understanding helps you apply these guidelines in your own app, which might offer new types of flows and interactions.

2. Adhere to the OS patterns, especially in core UX areas like navigation, basic UI controls (e.g., text field, drop-down, buttons, tabs), and main actions (e.g., sharing). Also, while the gestural UI landscape is still an open field, there are some specific gestures that have formed into habits (like swipe to delete in lists).

   Following these conventions boosts confidence among users, and makes your app easier to use. People are already familiar with these device patterns and know what to expect. Also, it saves you time and effort: you don't need to design and develop these components yourself, and they get updated automatically with every OS release. Furthermore, following the OS guidelines plays an important role in the app quality assessment, which also affects which apps are featured in the app markets.

3. Leverage the core competencies of each platform. Android, for example, offers home screen widgets, enhanced notifications, customized default applications, and automatic UI scaling across devices. iOS provides more built-in animations and transitions that assist in designing slick application experiences.

   While some of these powerful features are unique to a certain platform, others can be implemented on the other one—they just require more work. For example, if you have a certain animation on iOS that you consider critical to the experience, it's probably worth investing the effort to code it for Android. Otherwise, picking an out-of-the-box Android animation could work just as well.

4. Remember that the OS patterns provide only the experience pillars. The real creative juice is in your hands. Application layout, flow, interaction, and visual design are the ingredients that give your product its unique flavor, and the essence you should keep consistent across platforms (as demonstrated in the three following examples: Trulia, Path, and Mint).

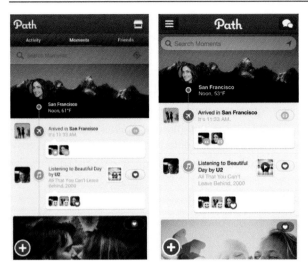

FIGURE 2-14

Path app for an Android phone (left) and for the iPhone (right). The core experience is preserved across platforms, with a few adjustments in navigation and UI controls.

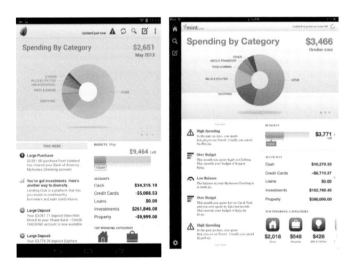

FIGURE 2-15

Mint app for the Android tablet (left) and for an iPad (right). The main layout and flow are consistent across platforms, with several optimizations in terms of navigation and the action bar.

With this in mind, even if your users switch between an Android phone and an iPad tablet, you shouldn't impose one platform's conventions on the other.

Remember, the tablet is very different from the smartphone to begin with, and as such leads to different use habits and expectations. It is used less frequently, considerably bigger in size, held very differently, usually interacted with in a lean-back mode at home, and more commonly used in different orientations. People naturally learn the different devices and contexts they operate in, and adjust their expectations and behavior patterns accordingly.

ALREADY HAVE AN IOS APP?

Here are a few common mistakes you should avoid when building your Android app:

On-screen back button
> Android devices already come with a physical back button on the device itself, which people are accustomed to using.

Tabs on bottom
> Avoid using a bottom tabs strip for navigation, and instead follow the Android top tabs design.

iOS icons
> Android offers its own set of standard icons for common actions such as share, copy, and add. Users are already familiar with these icons and know what they mean.

Right caret in lists
> There's no need to include those.

Beyond Device Accessibility: Hulu Plus

Free on-demand video streaming provider Hulu also offers a paid subscription service, called Hulu Plus (see Figure 2-16). The value proposition of Hulu Plus is offering expanded content library over a wider range of platform accessibility than the free service—its customers can stream on-demand movies, clips, trailers, and other media to Blu-ray players, TiVo, DVRs, TVs, smartphones, tablets, and game consoles.

FIGURE 2-16

Hulu Plus landing screen across four core devices—iPhone, iPad, PC (website), TV—demonstrating a consistent approach in their design.

Hulu Plus, serving as a content provider, is a classic example of where the consistent approach seems to be a natural choice. People want to be able to access and watch their favorite TV shows and movies anywhere, anytime, from any device. To do that, they need to have the entire product experience available on all devices.

As with the previously discussed examples, Hulu Plus offers the same content and feature set across all devices. The experience uses a sign-in model, so a user's personal queue is shared between devices, allowing seamless content consumption between them.

[NOTE]

Hulu Plus currently doesn't have the legal rights to make all shows available to watch on all devices. Still, searching or browsing on any device displays all shows, with relevant disclaimers when required.

In terms of UI, Hulu Plus uses the same information and visual design across all devices, manifested in color palette, typography, styling, prominent top image, visual hierarchy, and grid.

Alongside the commonalities in the design, Hulu Plus makes some necessary device-specific adaptations in terms of navigation hierarchy (adopting a deep hierarchy model on the smartphone) and layout (shifting from a three-column grid on the desktop, to a two-column grid on the portrait tablet display, to a single column on the smartphone). The amount of content items and information surfaced also changes depending on the available screen space (see Figure 2-17).

FIGURE 2-17

Hulu Plus show info page on the iPad (left) and iPhone (right). In the bigger-screen device, the hierarchy is flatter (showing all episodes on the screen), whereas on the small device the user must drill down to access the episode list.

So we have a UI design that is slick, polished, and easy to use; movies and TV shows are available across (almost) all devices, and the consistent experience adjusts nicely to the different devices.

But can it get better? Is there any way we can provide a better experience for people given the ecosystem devices we have?

Well, yes.

Let's put on the user's hat for a moment:

- How often does a user look at her phone while watching TV (for checking emails, surfing the Web, going through a Twitter stream)? And how often do you do these actions yourself?

- Do you think users find themselves watching a TV show and wondering: *What's the name of that actress? Where did I see her before? Isn't she dating that guy from that movie?* Ask yourself, have you thought about things like this?

- Can you imagine how many times users have browsed through the movies catalog and wished to read more about a movie and its cast, check out the trailer, see reviews, and consult friends about it? Does this apply to you?

- Have you ever wanted to start watching a movie on your tablet on the train home and then move it to the big screen later, continuing where you left off?

These questions highlight a key point that brings us to the next step of design.

Devices Are the Means, Not the End

What we really want to focus on with multi-device design is how the different devices *relate to people,* and how these relationships can help better serve their needs and advance them en route to their goals.

Returning to our example of consistent design that travels across devices (Hulu Plus): if you look beyond content accessibility across devices into the specific contexts of use this product supports, you will find important user needs that can greatly benefit from contextual (rather than just consistent) approaches. These include complementary relationships between devices (like the smartphone providing information on what the user is currently watching on TV) and continuous relationships (such as users starting to watch a movie on their tablets, and continuing on their widescreen TVs at home).

Interestingly enough, in the time period during which this book was written, Hulu Plus introduced a new device to its product ecosystem: the WiiU (see Figure 2-18).[14]

This device—as opposed to the other devices in the Hulu Plus ecosystem—prompted a new design approach that takes the user experience past consistency. The WiiU serves as a *complementary* device, offering a second-screen experience for Hulu Plus on TV. I will discuss this in more detail in the next chapters. For now, it's just important to acknowledge that the new device relationship introduced with the WiiU—complementing other devices rather than serving as just another independent access point—provides value to users that goes beyond consistency. In essence, we can do much more with multi-device experiences than just provide access to the entire content offering from any given device.

FIGURE 2-18

Hulu Plus WiiU device demonstrating the complementary relationship between the show on TV (in this case, Nickelodeon's Teenage Mutant Ninja Turtles), and the related content displayed on the WiiU in parallel (info and available actions).

Question to the Reader

Can you think of ways Trulia or Google Search could benefit from contextual design approaches across devices?

A good way to approach this is to go back to the main use cases (e.g., renting a house, looking for a place to eat tonight) and break down each one to its user flow steps. For each step, try to define the context (where is this taking place? when? with whom?), the decision-making process, the required information, and the expected outcome or action. Based on that, think which devices can best support the contextual needs at each step.

Along with changing devices, people's needs, use cases, flows, and behavior patterns also change. To address these new dynamics, you need to understand the set of contexts that arises within your product ecosystem, and adapt the experience on the different devices for each context.

How? In the next two chapters, you'll learn about two other design approaches: continuous and complementary. Both are context-driven in designing multi-device experiences, each handling a different set of use cases. Through these design approaches, you will gain insights into better ways you can use multiple devices to meet people's needs, providing them with more than just multiple access points to the same product.

Summary

- Two key principles of consistent design are:

    ○ Offering the same experience across various devices, porting the same content and core features in a like manner.

    ○ Using informed visual changes and subtle functional adjustments to accommodate the different devices' screen sizes, form factor, and interaction model (not identical experiences).

- Examples of consistent design include Google Search, which demonstrates consistency in minimalistic design; Trulia, which shows the benefits of progressive disclosure among different screen sizes; and Hulu Plus, whose major value offering relies on providing access to all the media content from multiple devices.

- While all of this might make perfect sense (and it does!), it's important to realize that a consistent approach essentially assumes an experience that is device-agnostic. The entire experience can be consumed in the same manner, on *any* device, without much design attention given to the different ways, contexts, and use cases in which these myriad devices are used.

NOTES

1. Display sizes represent the rough ranges of the most common devices.
2. Dean Takahashi, "Qualcom CEO Touts the Ever-Expanding Mobile World," *Venturebeat*, January 10, 2012, *http://bit.ly/18WOR5k*.
3. Luke Wroblewski, *Mobile First* (New York: A Book Apart, 2011), *http://bit.ly/JDXUCk*.
4. Jonah Lehrer, *Imagine: How Creativity Works* (New York: Houghton Mifflin, 2012), *http://amzn.to/1c9NaaL*.
5. Alicia David and Peyton Glore, "The Impact of Design and Aesthetics on Usability, Credibility, and Learning in an Online Environment," *Online Journal of Distance Learning Administration* xiii, no. 4 (2010), *http://bit.ly/1dr2xrU*; Stephen P. Anderson, "In Defense of Eye Candy," A List Apart, April 21, 2009, *http://bit.ly/1deSQuy*.
6. *Phablet* is a smartphone form factor describing devices with a screen between 5 and 6.9 inches in size, designed to combine or straddle the functionalities of a smartphone and a tablet.
7. A detailed list of mobile device viewport sizes can be found at *http://bit.ly/ISZXSt*.
8. Marcelo Ballve, "The Rise Of Responsive Design As A Mobile Strategy—Pros and Cons," (report), *BI Intelligence*, June 2013.
9. Ethan Marcotte, "Responsive Web Design," A List Apart, May 2010, *http://bit.ly/1hZtY1y*.
10. Billy Pyle, "Mobile Device Screen Sizes Resource Guide," Jacobs & Clevenger, May 2013, *http://bit.ly/IT06W5*.
11. David Taintor, "Responsive Design Doesn't Replace Native Apps," *AdWeek*, June 25, 2013, *http://bit.ly/1cbdlxJ*.
12. Harry McCracken, "Who's Winning, iOS or Android? All the Numbers, All in One Place," *Time Tech*, April 16, 2013, *http://techland.time.com/2013/04/16/ios-vs-android/*.
13. Android design guidelines, *http://bit.ly/JxGFlG*; iOS human interface guidelines, *http://bit.ly/1c9TX4b*.
14. *http://bit.ly/1emAi2O*

[3]

The Continuous Design Approach

With continuous design, the second approach in our 3Cs framework, the multi-device experience flows from one device to the next. It is the *experience* that accompanies the user in his set of activities, within different contexts, en route to his information or entertainment goal. In the following set of examples, we'll look at the principles of this approach, as well as its use cases, design lessons, and main benefits to users.

What Is Continuous Design?

Continuous design addresses a user flow that runs along a set of contexts, during which devices "pass the baton" to one another until the user reaches her information goal or completes the desired activity (see Figure 3-1).

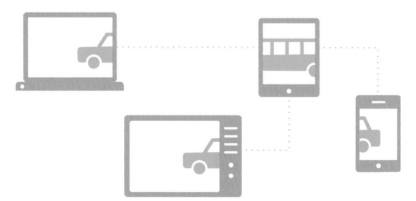

FIGURE 3-1

A continuous approach provides an end-to-end user experience that is distributed across multiple devices. With this "passing of the baton" approach, each device picks up where the previous one left off.

There are two chief experience types that continuous design addresses:

Single activity flow

A single activity—reading a book, watching a movie, or writing a document—typically requires a significant period of time to complete. These kinds of activities, therefore, tend to progress through several contexts (e.g., a laundromat, the airport, or a coffee shop line). And they include the opportunity for a user to use different devices (e.g., an iPad at the laundromat, laptop at the airport, and iPhone in the coffee shop line) and have each pick up the experience where the previous device left off. So, for example, you might start reading *Moby Dick* at home on a Sunday on your tablet and read the next chapter on your smartphone while waiting at the doctor's office.

Sequenced activities flow

Some task flows are composed of sequences of different activities that users need to complete in order to reach the end goal. One good example is cooking. This task is made up of several steps: (1) searching for recipes and deciding on the desired ones, (2) buying the groceries, and (3) cooking. Each step is typically done in a different location, at a different time, with different devices being available and/or most convenient for each activity. Still, all these steps progress the user toward the same end goal. Travel rentals (like with Airbnb) are another good example. They involve pre-trip activities like (1) deciding where to stay, (2) looking for a place, and (3) booking. Then there are multiple activities during the trip itself, such as (1) getting to the apartment, (2) settling down, (3) finding places in the area, and (4) keeping in touch with the property owner. Finally, the flow could also involve post-trip activities, such as (1) leaving a review and (2) possibly listing one's own property for rental. Each activity within this broader end-to-end flow differs from the others in type, location, context, duration, and best (available) device for the task, but they all clearly contribute to accomplishing the overarching task.

It's important to note that activity duration is a key factor in determining the continuity flow across devices. Here are three ways in which it does so:

Multiple sessions

The lengthier the activity, the more likely it is that it won't be completed in a single engagement. Instead, users will complete a lengthy activity in multiple passes (planning a trip, for example). In many cases, this involves the user switching between different devices depending upon the context.

Shifting contexts

The lengthier the activity is, the more likely it is that the contextual environment will change. This happens when users terminate a session and pick it up later (the taxi ride is over, so they close down the website they were browsing), even if they hadn't planned to, either on the same device or a different device more suitable to the new context (e.g., revisiting the website later at the hotel).

Subtasks

The lengthier the activity is, the more likely it is that it can be broken down into a set of granular subtasks. For example, with traveling there's the planning, booking, and the trip itself, and the latter can also be split to subtasks—flying, picking up the rental car, getting to the hotel, visiting attractions, and so on. These subtasks, which can be very different from one another, may take place in different contexts (location, time, social setting, and more), and thus be best served by different devices.

Let's look at some examples to clarify these two forms of continuity using the core user screens: smartphone, tablet, PC/laptop, and TV.

Single Activity Flow

Three good examples of the single activity flow are Apple AirPlay, the Amazon Kindle, and Google Drive, discussed next. They demonstrate how this continuous experience type works well for both consumption and creation of content.

STREAMLINING THE VIEWING EXPERIENCE: APPLE AIRPLAY

With Apple AirPlay and Apple TV, users can wirelessly stream movies, music, and photos from any iOS device—iPhone, iPad, iPod, or MacBook—right to the big screens of their televisions (see Figure 3-2).

In other words, they can "hand off" any content they began consuming on their mobile devices to their TVs, and experience higher-quality images and audio than on a smaller device.

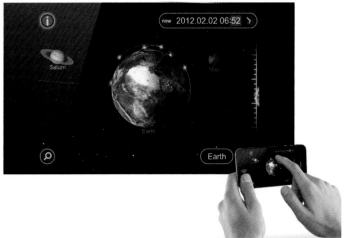

FIGURE 3-2

Apple AirPlay technology enables a continuous watching experience across devices to accommodate changing contexts. Users can begin watching a movie on their iPhones or iPads and continue on the big-screen TV right where they left off.

How is the AirPlay/Apple TV compatibility useful? In many ways:

- A user can start watching her favorite blockbuster on her iPhone during the train commute after work, and continue the movie from the exact point she left off on the big HDTV at home, in a smooth, seamless way.

- Teenagers can start watching a TV show on an iPad in their room while their parents watch the evening news on the living room TV. When the news broadcast is over, the kids can finish watching their show on the TV, taking advantage of the bigger-picture viewing experience. They can hang on to the iPad (or grab their iPhones) and use one of those devices for research while watching TV. (We'll look at this experience flow more closely in Chapter 4, on *complementary* design.)

- Morning-music people can listen to their playlists on their MacBooks as they wake up and start their morning routines. After getting showered and dressed, they can continue listening to their music over breakfast by "passing" the music to the TV downstairs, with better sound.

Question to the Reader

Can you think of other use cases for which being able to start consuming media (movie, music, photos) on one device and continue on another streamlines the experience flow?

Try approaching this question from the following pain points and contexts:

- Not enough devices. What if there's one TV in the house, and each family member wants to watch a different show?

- Not enough time. What if you have just an hour, but the movie you want to watch runs two hours?

- Being on the move. What if you have a busy schedule that requires you to frequently move from one place to the next, like organizing the kids and dropping them off at school, having breakfast with a friend downtown, running a series of work meetings (at the office and outside), and going on an evening run at the gym?

The continuous design approach—in all the aforementioned scenarios, as well as the examples we will see next—improves, streamlines, and facilitates an existing set of behavior patterns and needs people already have. In other words, the strength of continuous design is tied to the variety of new smart devices entering the market, which are available in increasingly more contexts, and it should be used to better support users in their activities.

Watching a movie from start to end, even when changing locations, isn't a new need. The fact is that until technology allowed it, people accommodated the need to finish a movie with suboptimal solutions like:

- Watching the entire movie on the same device, even if there was a better device available at some point during the activity

- Waiting until they got home/until the news broadcast was over to watch the entire movie on their HDTVs

- Starting to watch a movie on DVD on their laptops, and then continuing at home using their DVD players, after manually setting the movie to the point where they left off

The new smart devices that people increasingly have within reach give designers the opportunity to rethink existing user flows and use cases, and improve the activity flow among different contexts. We need to start asking ourselves how these new connected devices, especially mobile ones (tablets and smartphones today, and watches, glasses, bracelets, shoes, and many more tomorrow), can be used to help people accomplish their tasks. How can these devices optimize quality, speed, ease of use, and user delight?

Offering the entire or an identical UI on each and every device (i.e., consistent design) is not only suboptimal, but also becoming practically impossible as devices diversify in size (specifically, getting smaller and smaller—up to not having a screen at all), form factor (like wearables), ergonomics, and technological capabilities. The need to define the roles of different devices along the user flow, understand the use patterns around multiple devices, and identify the contexts, actions, and use cases where certain devices are more suitable or convenient than others is now a necessity as we design for multi-device experiences. Remember that down the road, when the Internet of Things disseminates with connected walls, ceilings, desks, bus stations, and whatnot—we will need to consider (again) the following questions:

1. How will these developments impact people's behaviors?

2. How will these new capabilities change the definition of "best available device (or display)" per context?

3. How can we further optimize users' experience along varying contexts using the connected devices?

SEAMLESS CONTENT CONSUMPTION EXPERIENCE: AMAZON KINDLE

The Amazon Kindle ecosystem (Figure 3-3) is another example of a continuous single activity flow. It takes this concept one step further, though, with its Audible.com integration.

FIGURE 3-3

The Amazon Kindle product ecosystem, which enables a continuous reading experience across a variety of devices.

At its core, the Kindle ecosystem allows users a seamless reading experience across multiple Kindles and Kindle apps by way of its Whispersync technology. It automatically syncs books across apps (including bookmarks and annotations), so users can begin reading on one device and pick up where they left off on another device.

This is great for a user sitting at a café waiting for a friend without having the Kindle device at hand—the user can simply pull out her smartphone and continue reading a novel from where she left off while she waits.

But, as I said, the Kindle ecosystem takes things a step further.

By partnering with Audible.com, Amazon expanded the range of contexts that make up the Kindle's continuous experience. Audible's Whispersync for Voice integration allows users to switch between reading and listening seamlessly, so that there's no need to put the book down even when on the move (running, cooking), or lying in bed at night with the lights turned off. This example shows that a single activity flow doesn't necessarily need to be limited to the same exact continuous action (reading), but it can include additional related actions (like listening) that are all part of the underlying user's activity goal—consuming content. Not only that, but extending the set of contexts in which the product can be used, as demonstrated through the Kindle/Audible integration, enables greater, more frequent use of the product by users, which in turn enhances habit formation.

The Kindle ecosystem exemplifies two important principles:

- **Rethink what's possible.** The constant technological progress continuously affects people's behaviors, forming new needs and habits. Over time, these changes flex the contexts and ways people already use (or can use) your product. Keeping a finger on the pulse and stepping back to reassess the product landscape are instrumental in tapping into these trends and extending the product's use. In this example, the Kindle was able to break out of the (still) ingrained perception of "books = reading," broadening the scope to content consumption. Framing it this way immediately surfaced new opportunities—like audio—that support a richer, more "sticky" product ecosystem.

- **Together, everyone achieves more.** We designers and product creators don't necessarily need to build the entire ecosystem on our own. Powerful multi-device experiences can be the result of integrated solutions, which usually benefit both product owners and consumers. (More about this topic in Chapter 8.)

CONTENT CREATION AND EDITING FLOW: GOOGLE DRIVE

So far we've seen examples of content consumption flows. However, the single-activity continuous experience can also be applied in content creation and editing flows. Google Drive (Figure 3-4) is a helpful model for this functionality. It provides free online storage for a variety of file types—documents, photos, and videos—and enables users to access them from any device.

FIGURE 3-4

Google Drive design on three main devices: desktop (top), tablet (bottom-left), and smartphone (bottom-right). All users' files are accessible across all devices, enabling a continuous content creation process between them.

In addition to being able to access content across devices, users can create and edit content across their devices as well. A user can begin writing a document on his home computer, for example, and continue editing it on a tablet right where he left off during his train ride to work. Cloud computing and real-time synchronization between devices are the key enablers of continuous flow of content creation.

THE LINK BETWEEN CONTINUOUS AND CONSISTENT EXPERIENCES

If you look carefully at the three examples just discussed, you'll notice that across the devices, the user can consume the entire span of content on *any* device.

This should sound familiar, as it follows the consistent design approach discussed in Chapter 2.

The difference between those consistent experiences and the continuous experiences discussed in this chapter is that the latter incorporate an additional layer—a context-sensitive one—that adds continuity to the experience. By saving the "last visited" point for content items, users can resume their activity from the point at which they left off (on multiple devices). This can take place automatically upon the user's entering the app (jumping the user right to the last visited spot), or be triggered manually by user action; this is a design decision that depends on the use case at hand.

This consistency/continuity combination in the single activity flow highlights two important fundamentals of the 3Cs framework:

- The 3Cs are design approaches that should be treated as experience building blocks. You can have an experience that is based solely on one of them, or you can integrate several approaches within the same ecosystem experience. In fact, most multi-device experiences follow the latter line, as we will discuss in more depth in Chapter 5.

- The 3Cs framework is focused on the way *people relate to the task flow* and how the different devices support them in achieving their goals—meaning you could argue that the single activity flow is actually a consistent experience. The UI design is practically the same across all devices, with one functional difference in the behavior of content items visited before. You might ask, couldn't that be regarded as merely a consistency adjustment between devices?

While they might seem similar on the surface, from the user's perspective there is actually a world of difference between the consistent experience flow and the single activity one. In the consistent experience, design adjustments aim to accommodate *device characteristics* (mainly screen size and input method). In the continuous experience, the difference in behavior has nothing to do with the form factor. It's a flow change that accommodates *people's needs*, supporting them in a continuous activity. The fact that it ends up manifesting in a similar way in the UI layer doesn't mean it stems from the same root—just like a computer failing to load can be the result of hardware malfunction, a software configuration problem, or a virus, for example. This distinction is important, as it affects the way you approach the situation to begin with. So, while the single activity flow relies on consistent design at its core, it's still a distinct experience that provides a continuous flow for users.

Discussion: The Importance of Sign-in

Knowing your users is the most valuable asset you can have for designing powerful, engaging, easy-to-use products. The more you learn about what they do, want, and need—what matters to them and what doesn't; what their preferences, interests, habits, and behavior patterns are; and how all these are affected across different contexts—the better, more personalized experiences you can deliver.

When you're designing multi-device experiences, this need to know your users skyrockets, especially given the dynamic nature of these experiences and the key role context plays. In this ever-more-complex connected world, there are many unknowns and hardly any proven best practices, and use patterns among devices are still in early formation stages. Both designers and users are still figuring out their way through all these connected devices, and there's a whole lot of learning to do in order to create meaningful experiences that advance people to their goals in an optimal way.

Until we get to the stage where we can easily identify the individuals using devices through implicit signals that don't require user action (like individual use patterns, physical/biometric signals, proximity, and leveraging multi-device connections and leveraging multi-device connections—like SlickLogin and Knock), getting them to sign in is an extremely important step in building knowledge around who they are and their usage profile across devices.

The sign-in process (let alone registration) is still a significant conversion roadblock. Users abandon products when they are confronted with a sign-in prompt—whether because they've forgotten their usernames or passwords (or both), they've gotten stuck trying to recover those components, or they're just reluctant to identify themselves due to privacy or security concerns. Add to that enhanced security measures (like two-factor authentication), and getting over the sign-in hurdle becomes even more challenging. Having users do that multiple times across several devices makes the task much, much harder.

And yet, given the critical value of the sign-in step in product flow, sign-in design is one area of the experience design pillars you shouldn't overlook. Here are a few good things to start thinking about sign-in design:

Consider single sign-on (SSO)

This simplifies the sign-in process by using a single account (e.g., Facebook, Google+, or Twitter) to access many different applications (see Figure 3-5). SSO offers several advantages:

- Shortens the sign-up process by requiring fewer details and clicks

- Reduces the number of usernames and passwords people need to maintain

- Gives you access as a product developer to information about users, their friends, and their activity on that service. They will need to approve this access, of course, and in some cases the information might be basic (e.g., name, age, and profile picture), but it's still valuable data that you won't need to collect yourself.[1]

An important design consideration to keep in mind is that with every account login option you add to the form, you complicate your design in terms of decision junctions and visual load.

Furthermore, the more login options are offered, the harder it is for users to remember which of the accounts they used to log in to your service.

FIGURE 3-5

Foursquare sign-up form promoting SSO with two services, Facebook and Google+. Users can still choose to sign up using their email.

Use simple, engaging forms

Whether you offer SSO and/or your own sign-up process, simplify the form as much as possible:

- Ask for the minimum necessary information (usually email/ username and password). Even if you really want to get users' birthdays or genders, wait and ask for that later, after they get a better grasp of the value you're giving them. Users will be more inclined to share information with you at that point.

- Don't make users re-enter information (password, email, or any other field).

- Include a "Stay logged in" option, and have it checked by default.

- Offer a "Forgot?" gateway if people can't remember their usernames/passwords.

- Provide useful, actionable feedback. For example:

  ◦ If a username is taken, offer similar available usernames for people to choose from.

  ◦ Don't overcomplicate the password restrictions, and explain them clearly from the beginning. If people get it wrong, specify the exact error. If all goes well, indicate that as well and make them a little bit happier.

  ◦ Give clear, focused error messages rather than generic ones.

- Be clear about privacy and other conditions.

- Pay attention to tone of voice and copywriting; they matter. The text you supply can provide useful assistance throughout the process, as well as making the experience more fun and light-weight (see Figure 3-6). If you're contemplating several alternatives, try running A/B testing to see which performs best.

FIGURE 3-6

The Polar mobile app sign-up form, which uses a clear and conversational tone of voice.

Incorporate gradual engagement

An effective strategy to encourage people to take action in your product is to let them get a feel for its benefits before asking them to invest effort (or provide personal data)—similar to how movie producers release trailers to attract viewers to "invest the effort" (and money) and come to the theater. Giving a little teaser to users can help get them on board more easily (see Figure 3-7). I find this approach very useful as a general UX principle, and it definitely applies to sign-in specifically. Luke Wroblewski calls this sign-in flow approach *gradual engagement*—get people to engage with a product and try out its core features before asking them to sign up. This way, people see the benefits of the product through hands-on interaction, following which they are more willing to join in and provide personal information. The activity and information recorded during this interaction can be added to the user's account later, once she signs in.

FIGURE 3-7

Sugru lets you look at the most recent issue of its newsletter before you actually join (via stepoffthis-utlingmachine, littlebigdetails.com).

The challenge with giving away something while asking users to sign in is finding the sweet spots in the product flow to trigger the sign-in request. These spots vary depending on your product type.

For example, in the Polar app (shown in Figure 3-6), you can vote on polls without signing up, but to access your activity log, create a poll, or see your profile, you must be signed in. On many ecommerce sites, users are asked to provide sign-in details during checkout (after they've browsed the site and found items of interest). For utility tools, such as design software, asking users to sign in when they're trying to save the work is usually a good practice.

In any case, gradual engagement can—and should—be combined with the previous guidelines as part of your sign-in design strategy. They handle different aspects of the flow, and together can make for a better, more streamlined experience.

Promote the advantages of being signed in in a clear, concise, and attractive manner

> Make sure to incorporate the multi-device experience in your message so that people get educated about the broader ecosystem value early on (more on ecosystem education below). You can do this as part of an introductory experience: a marketing page, a warm welcome tour, or some other introduction method. Another approach is to integrate the advantages of sign-in as part of the in-product experience flow, highlighting contextually the benefits of signing in when certain features are used (like "signed-in users enjoy...and can do..."). Another method is to display an "incomplete" UI: greyed-out elements or other visual distinctions in certain areas to encourage people to sign in and "fix it."

As a last note, you've probably noticed there's diverse terminology around the call-to-action label: Sign in, Login, Log in, Sign up, Register, Join, and others. While all these terms are valid, you should avoid using "Sign up" and "Sign in" together in the same product, as the similarity between these terms can be confusing to many users. If you go for "Sign up," combine it with "Log in," for example; and if you prefer "Sign in," then use "Register" or "Join" for the complementary action.

Sequenced Activities Flow

The continuous design approach can be used not only for supporting the continutation of a single action, but also to encompass a variety of user activities—all within a single experience.

In a sequenced activities flow, the experience design addresses broader user needs and goals that involve a series of activities and contexts, and aims to optimize these flows with the help of the multiple connected devices people now have within reach.

As part of the design process, the overarching experience (for example, going out to dinner with friends) is broken down to the user steps that it comprises (like looking for a restaurant, coordinating with friends, booking a table, arriving at the restaurant, etc.). Each step is then analyzed in terms of activity flow, contextual landscape, and the device(s) that can best advance people through that activity on to the next ones and finally to successful completion.

The following examples involve a series of activities that users perform across different contexts in order to accomplish a certain task or goal.

ADAPTING THE EXPERIENCE TO DEVICES' STRENGTHS: ALLRECIPES

Allrecipes (Figure 3-8) is a good example of exploiting the continuous approach by encompassing a broader, multi-step use case like cooking. It demonstrates how multiple devices can support the user every step of the way in a tailored, contextual fashion.

FIGURE 3-8

Allrecipes apps for iPad (Your Kitchen Inspiration) and iPhone (Dinner Spinner), demonstrating a continuous cooking flow made up of sequential activities taking place on different devices: (1) looking for recipes, (2) getting the groceries, and (3) cooking.

Under the hood: Examine the user's workflow

First, let's look at the "cooking" workflow and break it down into the discrete steps that it comprises. For each step, we'll identify the contextual elements involved and see how certain devices are more suitable aids for different portions of the experience. The steps are:

1. Decide what to cook.

   Often, the story begins with a user's basic need to cook dinner for friends. The first step is for the user to decide what to cook. This is where he takes the time to explore recipes—what is usually called the "research" or "seeking information" phase. This research is often done in front of bigger-screen devices like a PC or a tablet, which allow for better content consumption and information scanning while the user engages with the device in a relaxed way.

   For this, Allrecipes provides a desktop interface as well as an iPad app where the user can conveniently look for recipes. What's convenient about it? The bigger layout, easy navigation, search functionality, and easy-to-read recipe display provide all the details he needs: ingredients, dish type, time and ease of preparation, and ratings.

2. Shop for groceries.

   Once a user finds the recipes he'd like to make, he can add them to a "recipe box." This fires up the continuous experience torch: adding recipes to the recipe box automatically extracts the ingredients from all the recipes, syncs the list with his iPhone, and creates a nicely designed shopping list already grouped by dairy, produce, and so on (aligned with most grocery store aisles).

   This activity automatically shifts the experience to the smartphone, which is the device the user is probably going to have on him at the grocery store. There's no need for him to write down all the ingredients or worry about forgetting anything once he's at the store, as the experience seamlessly flows between the relevant devices, with all the content he needs.

3. Cook the meal.

The user has done his shopping and returned home. When it's time to start the actual cooking, he'll switch from his smartphone to, very likely, a tablet (tablets have become popular as a cooking aid in the kitchen).[2]

The Allrecipes iPad app provides a very comfortable UI for that—a nice, clear layout with the list of ingredients, the directions to follow (including highlighting the current step the user's on), and even a built-in timer to use during the cooking process. All that's left is for him to follow the instructions and not burn anything!

Design lesson: Rethink user flows

Allrecipes introduced a new way to approach the flow of cooking, taking into consideration the various steps involved and customizing the experience by leveraging the particular strengths and use modes of each device—from searching on the PC or tablet, to shopping for required ingredients with the smartphone, to the actual cooking using the tablet.

Throughout the last several years that I've been researching and working in this multi-device space, I have found that the Allrecipes example is the strongest generator of "aha!" moments from people to whom I'm explaining the continuous design approach. Its emphasis on a fluid, innovative user experience (supported by a strong active community) has paid off. In November 2011, Allrecipes surpassed the 10 million downloads mark. Its two apps—Dinner Spinner (for smartphone) and Your Kitchen Inspiration (for tablet)—continue to be the world's most downloaded recipe apps.[3]

Design lesson: Break down the continuous experience steps even more

When I came across the pioneering work Allrecipes had done with the cooking use case, it got me thinking about additional possibilities for how this product ecosystem can grow further in the near future. Here are a few examples for additional use cases at each of the different cooking steps, which can benefit from dedicated multi-device attention:

I want to be a master chef!

Cooking fans don't just browse the Internet for hot new recipes: they also get inspired by cooking shows on TV. Recently, some of the most popular ones have been reality shows like *MasterChef, Top Chef,* and *Hell's Kitchen.* What if Allrecipes could integrate with such shows, so that while watching *MasterChef* on TV, users could save the full recipe for a dish they really want to make? With one tap in the Allrecipes app on a smartphone, they could send the full recipe details automatically to the recipe list on Allrecipes. This could fulfill that immediate gratification desire and allow people to act on the spot, while they're engaged and excited about a delicious-looking pie.

Remember the milk

As we saw, Allrecipes generates a shopping list containing all the ingredients needed for the selected recipes. That's great. However, what it *doesn't* take into account are the ingredients users already have at home. Thus, one might not need to buy all the things on the list, or at least not the entire quantity appearing in the recipe. What if the fridge and kitchen cabinets could be equipped with sensors and network capability (a scenario that is not so far-fetched, as we'll discuss in Chapter 6),[4] so they could inform the Allrecipes shopping list what users already have? The list could adjust itself accordingly and truly represent what users need to buy at the grocery store. And hey, if it could also connect to the grocery store systems, we could inject some more continuity here by having the shopping list ordered and delivered to people's homes or available for them to pick up at the store.

Show me the money

Another enhancement Allrecipes could add to its smartphone app is support for in-store product comparison. We already see today that smartphone owners rely on their devices in-store to make the most of their shopping choices: 73.9% compare prices among retailers, 61% research the items, 39% claim mobile coupons, and 80% want more mobile product information in stores.[5] Wouldn't it be nice if people had a one-stop shop for that? They would just need to fire up the Allrecipes app on their phones to get access to all the price-comparison information they need.

Who moved my cheese?

If we break down the actual cooking process to more granular steps, we get the following cycle of actions:

a. Read the current step's instructions.

b. Get the required ingredients for it.

c. Complete the step's instructions.

d. Move to the next step.

Expanding on the notion of connected devices like refrigerators and cabinets, wouldn't it be useful if those compartments could communicate with a tablet, learn which cooking step a user is on, and shuffle around the items they contain so that the ones the user needs at any given moment are most accessible? Imagine yourself in the following user scenario: you're baking a cake and you get to step 4, where you need to whip the cream. You open the fridge door and—ta-da!—the cream is just in front of you, top shelf, within reach. This interaction could actually change people's behavior because they would no longer need to first take out *all* the ingredients involved in the baking in order to avoid the stressful moments of "where did that bag of cacao disappear to?"

Once we start playing with the idea of all these devices being able to talk to and inform one another, the resolution of user flow steps we can optimize gets finer and finer. This enables us to rethink behaviors and flows we might have taken for granted, dissect them to their most basic components, and really make the best, most tailored user experience for each.

ADAPTING THE EXPERIENCE TO CHANGING NEEDS: EVENTBRITE

Eventbrite (Figure 3-9) is another good example of contextual thinking through a continuous use case. This product, focused on organizing and attending events, shifts the experience across devices as users progress through time. Put more accurately, *the user's contextual needs change* through the sequence of an event.

FIGURE 3-9

Eventbrite's example event page—at left on the desktop (before the user signs up to an event), and at right on the mobile app (after sign-up).

Eventbrite actually offers two sets of continuous experience flows—one for event organizers and one for event attendees. As most people more often belong to the second group, we'll examine that particular flow.

Under the hood: Examining the user's workflow

Let's follow the same process as we did for Allrecipes, and break down the broad events use case to the different steps that compose it:

1. Register for an event.

   The event flow is often triggered from an event invite over email, or casual browsing (through social networks, the Eventbrite website, blogs, etc.) that surfaces events of interest. At that point, the "research" or "information seeking" stage starts (similarly to Allrecipes), where the user reads more on the event, checks the agenda and attendees, and possibly browses through other events while she's at it. This activity is more suitable for bigger-screen devices like the tablet or desktop, which can accommodate more information in a convenient layout. The desktop is also likely to be where the user acts upon the invite (especially if the event is professional), as she does most of her email activity on this device during the week.[6]

The need for a comfortable display for browsing event details intensifies as the event increases in length.[7] For example, a conference that spans a few days—offering multiple sessions per day with many taking place in parallel—requires much more exploration and research time. People need to review many more sessions, pick the ones they would like to attend (especially when sessions are scheduled simultaneously), and go over a longer list of attendees, identifying people they would like to connect with. In the case of a professional conference, the latter is of special importance since networking plays a very important role in going to the event. In fact, for many people, the opportunity to meet and get a conversation going with key people relevant to their work *is* the main goal of attending an event—a point I'll talk more about later.

2. Attend the event.

Sign-up is complete, and the day of the event has finally arrived: the user is all set, ready to go on her way, and the device she most likely carries is her mobile phone. Understanding this context of use, Eventbrite offers a mobile app that picks up the flow of events:

   a. **Getting to the event.** The mobile app provides quick access to the event the user has signed up for, including the event information along with the location of the event. She can immediately pull up directions on her phone, and have the GPS navigate every step of the way.

   b. **Checking in.** When arriving at an event venue, users often need to register at the entrance. For that, Eventbrite offers a barcode that is easily scanned for check-in to the event. The user doesn't need to go through the hassle of printing the event invitation beforehand and remembering to bring it along—she just uses her phone, which is already there with her, and smoothly slides into the flow of it all.

Eventbrite is another example of a multi-step activity that ranges across different contexts. Across these contexts, peoples' needs change and the devices they use change, so designing an experience that admits these variations and adapts to them can provide much higher value.

Design exercise: Expanding the continuous flow

I've talked in this chapter about how the continuous design approach provides designers with the opportunity to rethink user flows, dissect them to component steps, and explore new ways to help people achieve their goals—all by leveraging the set of connected user devices. Now, I'd like to use our Eventbrite example to do a deep dive into rethinking *process*. Let's now explore the ways multi-device experiences can better meet user needs. Taking this deep dive doesn't mean all the ideas we generate are implementation-worthy (that would require more data, research, and assessments). Yet this is still an important design exercise that will help us to redefine the product landscape, identify areas for innovation, and prepare early for what's ahead.

We will do this exercise on two key types of events: conferences and concerts. Despite the different nature of these event types, there's still a unified theme between them: the social- and people-centered experience at their core. With conferences, for example, the events are aimed at bringing people with shared interests together, facilitating conversations among them, and hopefully taking some of these conversations beyond the geography of the conference venue. There is a lot of potential in addressing ways we can promote this social scene at events—and the multi-device ecosystem can play an important role in enhancing that.

Conferences. Let's look first at the conference event type and break it down into the main set of contexts involved. For each, we'll try to categorize user needs based on the following dimensions (see Table 3-1):

Agenda-centered
What are the users' needs in terms of event logistics, facilities, and schedule?

People-centered
What are the users' needs in terms of social interactions and networking?

Multi-device focus
What are the dominant devices for this context?

TABLE 3-1. Analyzing the conference experience flow across shifting contexts and multiple devices along the agenda-centered and people-centered dimensions

	AGENDA-CENTERED	PEOPLE-CENTERED
Pre-event	**Big screens (mostly desktops)**	

	• Finding events
	• Exploring event info
	• Registering for an event
	• Choosing sessions (if relevant)
		• Sharing event with peers/friends and encouraging them to join
		  • Reviewing attendee list
		  • Getting a sense of the crowd and noting people to meet (possibly even contacting them in advance to set up a chat during the event)

Arriving at the venue on day 1	**Mobile devices (mostly smartphones)**	
	• Checking the event schedule • Getting to the event on time (transportation, directions, traffic, parking) • Checking in • Getting coffee to start the day	• Determining who's here • Anyone I already know? • Any of the people I noted?
During event[8]	**Mixed devices (stationary = laptop/tablet; on the go = mobile)**	

	• Checking the event schedule
	• Exploring events info
	• Attending sessions:
	  • When, where, and how to get there
	  • Session and speaker info
	  • Taking session notes
	• Taking breaks:
	  • Options (cafeterias, exhibitions)
	  • Time left until breaks/"break about to end" alerts
	• Attending social events:
	  • What, when, and where
	  • How to get there
		• Making new connections (many contexts):
		  • Meeting new people, especially those I want to talk with
		  • Catching up with people I already know
		  • Exchanging business cards
		  • Taking quick notes about people I spoke with for later use
		• Attending sessions/social events:
		  • Who's going?
		  • Who's here? (Can impact seat choice.)
		  • Basic professional info
		  • Conversation starters (e.g., common interests, background, recent articles published, recent updates)

Post-event	All devices as a starting point (data analytics can help determine which devices are needed)[9]	
	• Organizing event materials (slides, videos, books) • Posting photos/videos from the event (best moments, the event at a glance) • Researching related events	• Following up with people

Table 3-1 demonstrates how, by stepping back and taking a fresh look at end-to-end user journeys through the lens of multi-device experiences, you can identify important themes about your experience flows and rates and functions along the following scale:

- Well supported

- Supported, but can be improved

- Not supported at all

For example, two prominent design themes that arise in Eventbrite's conference experience are:

- It mostly focuses on the pre-event and event-day parts of the flow. Some features are well supported, while others could possibly be further optimized.

- It mainly supports the agenda-centered activities along the flow. The social needs receiving attention are only the pre-event needs (ability to see attendees list and share the event on social networks).

Identifying these gaps and opportunities is an important first step in setting the product's direction going forward. This doesn't necessarily mean that Eventbrite needs to deepen its design efforts in the social scene, or add other features just highlighted. However, it is important to make these decisions when you have all the information in front of you, after reassessing the product landscape given the new technological developments, and specifically the new multi-device opportunities. Next, we'll look at concerts.

Concerts. At a very basic level, concerts are similar to conferences in the sense that they involve both "logistical" needs and social needs that accompany the main set of contexts involved. However, concerts have an additional emotional layer to the event experience: individuals listen to songs performed right in front of them by the artist, while absorbing the energy of the crowd around them, dancing, singing along, taking photos, and more. It's a powerful experience. Capturing that emotional connection, and finding ways to allow people to extend that just a little bit longer, can be very impactful. Let's break down the concert experience as we did the conferences (Table 3-2).

TABLE 3-2. Analyzing the concert experience flow across shifting contexts and multiple devices along the agenda-centered and people-centered dimensions

	AGENDA-CENTERED	PEOPLE-CENTERED
Pre-event	**Big screens (mostly desktops)** • Finding concerts • Exploring concert info • Buying tickets	• Determining which of my friends are going • Organizing a group to go together • Sharing concert with peers/friends, encouraging them to join, showing off

Event day—we're on our way!	**Mobile devices (mostly smartphones)**
	• Getting directions
	• Parking:
	  • Help finding a spot is cool.
	  • Finding a cheap one is even cooler.
	  • Saving my location to take me back there later is legendary.	

Arriving at the venue and during the event	Mobile devices (mostly smartphones)	

	• While in line:
	  • How much longer will I be in line? (Will I miss the beginning of the concert?)
	  • I'm bored and somewhat anxious, but trying to keep my energy up. (How about a second-screen experience while waiting—fun facts, artist videos, stuff to keep that energy pumped up?)
	• Getting through the ticket check
	• Showing me a detailed concert lineup
	• Setting a five-minute alert before artists go on stage
	• Inside the venue:
	  • Help me find my seat
	  • Food (what, how much, and where?)
	  • Restroom location
	  • Merchandise (what and how much?)
	  • I already have my phone up to take pictures/videos during the song; wouldn't it be cool to see the song lyrics too so I can sing along confidently?
		• Determining whether my friends are here (even if our seats are far apart, we could at least meet later for a beer and a hot dog)
		• Tweeting and checking tweets about the concert
		• Adding people I meet to my social networks

Post-event	All devices as a starting point (data analytics can help determine which devices are needed)	
	• Posting photos/videos taken during the event (best moments, concert at a glance) • Receiving a special thank-you note from the artist, along with a video from the concert • Leveraging post-concert excitement to promote the artist's CDs, merchandise, and online presence • Sharing recommendations for related events	• Contacting new people I've met • Creating shared memories with my friends[10]

As with the conference analysis, in a concert there are clearly experience areas that can benefit from a more granular multi-device treatment, mainly in the social space, but also in some agenda-centered aspects. For example, providing a second-screen experience while people are waiting in line can be a very interesting avenue to explore. The smartphone has already become a time filler for people standing in line, so why not leverage this behavior pattern to get them even more excited about and engaged with the concert that's about to start?

Not only that, but second-screen experiences can (and already often do) incorporate a social layer to encourage group engagements. In the case of concerts, an app can be used to enhance connections between people standing in line together, who are already sharing a real-life experience—even if just for a few hours.

There is always room for pushing continuity a step further, reinforcing the idea that if we step back and expand our design lens to encompass the end-to-end user flow and acknowledge the range of connected devices people use, we can find new ways to optimize their experiences. This kind of optimization can stem from dissecting the existing flow into smaller pieces, or expanding its boundaries to include more activities that couldn't have been supported as well before all these devices came into users' lives.

Discussion: Educating for Continuity

Multi-device continuous experiences introduce new types and granularity of flows and use patterns. Most people are not yet familiar with them; their mental models are still anchored in consistent experiences that focus on access anywhere rather than contextual continuity, and they might not even have clear use cases in mind for these device relay races.

To tap into the potential of the new connected world, as designers we need to help people make the cognitive leap and expand—or even break—the existing mental models around multi-device experiences. Our responsibility is not only to build awesome, innovative ecosystems for our users, but also so they equip them with the tools and guidance to engage with these experiences, to feel empowered and in control.

This is where product education plays an important role. In researching for this book, I found myself doing *a lot* of active work to identify continuous product examples out in the market. Current ecosystem experiences do not offer descriptions in the app markets, multi-device tutorials, or in-product guidance; people are left to decipher the multi-device experience layers on their own.

To get our users onto the multi-device–experience bandwagon, we need to first make them aware of it, and—better yet—help them understand and get excited about the value it provides. How do we get them on board?

SEEDING THE ECOSYSTEM NOTION: FIRST-TIME EXPERIENCE, APP MARKETS, AND PROMOTIONS

A good opportunity to make people aware of the multi-device ecosystem and its very basic flow is the first-time experience. Whether you implement it through a marketing landing page, an introductory splash page, or a quick welcome tour, you can use the first to introduce people to the idea of your multi-device structure. A few important principles to remember:

- Users have a lot of experience using other products and services. So even when they start using yours, they have more experience with all the others. Their expectations about the experience you offer will be shaped by that.

- At the point of entry, users know very little about your product (if anything). They probably haven't used it yet and don't have a feel for the use cases and the value it offers, and thus there's a lot they can absorb and internalize at this initial stage.

- Users skip copy and instead scan for meaningful headings, high-lighted words, bullet lists, and short paragraphs.[11]

Given these facts, it's important to keep your ecosystem messages short, simple, and concise. Incorporating meaningful visuals (e.g., a visual flow of devices with their roles as headings, or just a group of devices as part of a bigger message) can help you convey the message (see Figures 3-10 and 3-11).

FIGURE 3-10

TripIt website landing page, incorporating devices in a prominent manner. This visual introduces (part of) the ecosystem, demonstrates the value of the continuous experience, and shows a glimpse of the role each device plays.

FIGURE 3-11

Evernote website landing page, incorporating a multi-device image as part of a broader product message. The image, along with the accompanying text, clearly indicates that this product spans multiple devices.

Taking a step back in the setup flow, you can already utilize the app markets (subject to their specific terms) as part of the user education process. In all the continuous products I came across, however, there was no indication in the app description about other devices taking part in the experience.

For example, Allrecipes simply released two separate apps to the market (Dinner Spinner and Your Kitchen Inspiration) without any messaging about their relationship to each other. It missed an opportunity to wrap users' minds around the ecosystem flow and continuity value before they download the products. Not only could this encourage people to get the apps, but it could also frame their product perception beyond just a specific device. Explaining the cross-device relationships from the very beginning (in each of the device pages, along with a link to the corresponding device) can help establish expectations and use patterns around multi-device experiences.

You can also seed the ecosystem concept through occasional promotional messages that bring product features to the surface. For example, you can display a promotional modal dialog at a certain frequency when the user enters the app (or accesses some other activity-related trigger). These can be integrated alongside the product content, such as in the notifications area or content stream. You can also use common gestures—such as shake—to trigger product education messages, as Google Maps does (see Figure 3-12). Make sure you select a gesture that is not too complex (undiscoverable) or too easy (triggered unintentionally too often).

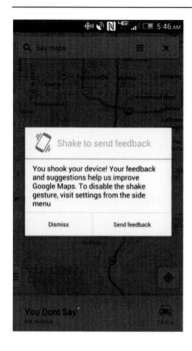

FIGURE 3-12
"Shake to send feedback" message triggered in Google Maps when the user shakes the phone.

INGRAINING THE MULTI-DEVICE VALUE: IN-PRODUCT FLOW

After the first-time experience, which seeds the idea of device continuity, the next (and more important) part is integrating continuity cues within the product flows.

In many ways, the challenge here is similar to that of gradual engagement in your sign-in strategy (discussed earlier in this chapter): it's all about finding those sweet spots during the flow where it makes sense to notify the user about "passing the baton" to the next device. When it's done contextually, after the user has just completed a certain relevant action that reflects a clear intent or state of mind, it is much easier for the user to understand the value of the cross-device continuity, as he's already engaged with the experience.

For example, if we go back to the Allrecipes cooking use case, the first time the user adds recipes to his recipe box on a desktop or tablet, we could show a modal dialog notifying him about the option of (and benefits to) automatically creating a shopping list on his phone. This dialog can ask for missing user details needed to complete the operation (gradual engage-ment). Also, incorporating an option to send a text message or email with a direct link to download the app to his phone would shorten the path to con-version even more. Finally, offering a checkbox to "Always create shopping list on my phone" could help streamline the flow for future cases, prevent-ing recurring pop-ups from breaking the user flow.

In other cases, like with TripIt (shown in Figure 3-10), delivering a pop-up message following a trip booking might not be the optimal timing. When it comes to traveling, there might be a significant time gap between when the user books her trip via her tablet, and when she actually departs for the trip (with her phone). In this case, alerting the user one to two days before the trip about the mobile phone app and its advantages would better suit her state of mind. Also, on the trip day itself (assuming she has the app), triggering a phone notification a few hours before her flight with its details and status would be useful. As the trip progresses and different needs arise (hotel, car, attractions, etc.), it would be useful to balance phone alerts (for the highest-priority issues) with in-app UI notifications (which can wait until the next time the user logs in to the app).

A relevant example for contextual in-app notifications comes from Pocket. After copying a URL and opening the Pocket app, the user will automatically be prompted to save the content (see Figure 3-13).

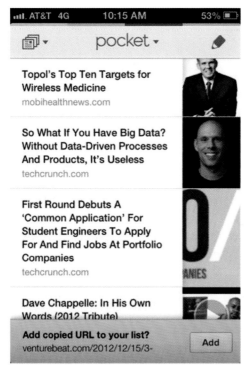

FIGURE 3-13

Pocket mobile app notification after a user copies a URL (via Myles Tan, littlebigdetails. com).

Contextual triggering can also take place based on additional signals, like location and time. For example, in the Allrecipes case, when the user finishes shopping at the grocery store using the mobile app (app usage + time + location) and returns home (location), the phone app can trigger a notification recommending that he switches to the tablet app for cooking. Given that tablets are not yet as widespread as mobile phones, it might be useful to offer an option of "Thanks, but I don't have a tablet," so that users are not annoyed with repeated tablet-related messages.

The important takeaway here is that we must think carefully about how to approach users *while they're engaging* with a task-related activity (cooking) in order to increase the value of helping them very tangibly with the next step in that task flow (grocery shopping). The benefit is not only educating users about the continuity flow as they go, but also encouraging them to engage with additional devices (possibilities they might not be aware of) and thereby advancing them toward their goals.

BRIDGING PHYSICAL AND DIGITAL: POP

POP (Prototyping on Paper) offers designers an ecosystem experience that aims to simplify and accelerate app prototyping in order to make the overall design process quicker and more effective. It enables users to more easily make the leap from wireframes on paper to a live prototype on the actual mobile device, providing a better feel for the interactions and overall flow across the app.

POP's continuous experience introduces a flow that differs from what we've seen so far. While this chapter's previous examples relied solely on wireless connections to generate the ecosystem flow, this product is different: it uses the smartphone camera as a key player in driving the sequence of activities forward.

The sequence starts with paper sketching and then moves into the digital space, where the dynamic prototyping is applied (see Figure 3-14).

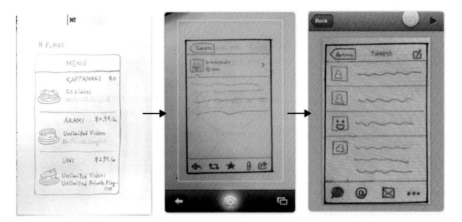

FIGURE 3-14

POP app continuous flow: from pen and paper to the mobile device, connected through the camera.

Under the hood: Examining the user's workflow

As with the previous examples, we will break down the experience flow into the user steps that compose it:

1. Design on paper.

   The first step of the process doesn't involve any ecosystem device or special technology: it's all about the designer following his regular workflow, starting off with creating the initial wireframes using pen and paper—a much faster process than using a software tool.

2. Create a prototype.

   The second step is to create a live prototype out of the sketches, composed of a full storyboard that shows the interaction and flow.

   To do that, the POP app lets you import the paper sketches into your phone by taking a picture of each of them. The app automatically adjusts the brightness and contrast to improve the sketch legibility and ensure the clarity of the simulation.

   Once the sketches are on the phone, you can easily create a storyboard by linking the sketches together through "hot spots" definition. When all the sketches are properly linked and ready to go, you can hit Play and simulate the UI flow from start to end.

3. Share for feedback.

The last part in the process is sharing the prototype with friends or colleagues to collect feedback early on in the process and discuss it collaboratively. This capability is also incorporated into the app, which provides a built-in sharing mechanism that supports collaborative review across the three core devices: iPhone, iPad, and desktop (through the web browser).

This entire process can then repeat itself iteratively—based on feedback received, you can create new paper sketches, get them on the device, link them together, and share new prototypes with your reviewers.

Once the experience is ready for the next step, you can use more advanced software design tools like Photoshop, Fireworks, or Illustrator to build detailed, polished experience screens.

Design lesson: Continuous experience can start offline

What I like so much about the POP app—beyond the fluid continuous experience—is that it admits to the power of the oldest tools around, pen and paper. Instead of trying to come up with ways to beat them, it joins them. POP acknowledges that sophisticated technology is not always needed every step of the way; at times it's better to just stick to what we already do well offline (like sketching on paper), and leverage that. This allows us to really focus on the parts of the process that *don't* work as well (such as the difficulty involved in setting up a live prototype), and mitigate the effort and resources involved in getting those tasks done.

Note that in the case of transferring the experience from the physical world to the digital one, an explicit user action is required (in this case, taking a photo) to clearly connect the experience flow between the different touchpoints. Thus, the continuity between devices, embedded in the usage flow and done on the spot, doesn't require additional user education in this respect.

In the following chapters, we will see more examples of contextual experiences (continuous and complementary) where the multi-device design combines and helps to bridge the physical and digital spheres.

EXPANDING CONTINUITY WITH AN OPEN PLATFORM: POCKET

Pocket (formerly Read It Later) is another interesting example of a continuous experience that addresses a more focused, iterative flow of sequenced activities (see Figure 3-15). It demonstrates a close attention to the varying contexts in which people consume content across different devices, and shows that this kind of attention can really matter when you're creating a seamless, fluid experience tailored to user behavior patterns.

FIGURE 3-15

Pocket product ecosystem—desktop, tablet, and smartphone—across iOS and Android.

The basic premise of Pocket is to help people save interesting articles, videos, and more from the Web for later enjoyment. When Pocket users come across interesting content (articles, videos, or web pages) but don't have time to read or watch it at that moment, they can save the URL. Pocket makes clever use of continuity by tailoring the UI across the different devices, splitting the content discovery and content consumption roles between them. Let's take a closer look at the flow.

Under the hood: Examining the user's workflow

Pocket's experience flow can be broken down to two main steps:

1. Find interesting content.

During the course of a day, people use their computers for long periods of time—doing work, reading emails, checking favorite news sites, visiting their social networks, and searching content. As part of these activities, they often come across interesting content they would like to take a deeper look at, but cannot at the moment for one reason or another (e.g., they're at the office, running from one meeting to the other; they are at a break between classes at school; or they simply don't have the peace and quiet required to sit back and focus on the article or video from start to end).

A similar scenario can take place on the smartphone as well. While doing some quick phone browsing in the lunch line, a user might spot an interesting article that has been retweeted; she can't read it right then and there, so she adds the article to her list on Pocket.

Pocket's solution is to help users save content for later—with a single click. They do this using an online "pocket" icon integrated into the browser toolbar (Figure 3-16).

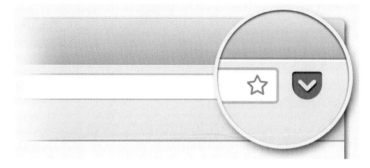

FIGURE 3-16
The "Save to Pocket" button integrated into the desktop browser.

Also, Pocket is integrated into many content apps such as Twitter, Flipboard, Zite, and gReader, and this allows for an easy save from many contexts (Figure 3-17).

FIGURE 3-17

"Save to Pocket" buttons integrated into popular content-based mobile apps.

In the background, all the saved content items are synced across all devices that have the Pocket app installed.

2. Read the saved content.

Whenever users have some quiet time to catch up on all the stuff they didn't have time for during the day—at the end of the workday, during the train ride home, or maybe as bedtime reading— the tablet or smartphone takes over the experience, continuing the flow started during the day.

Pocket's app design for both devices is tailored to the context of content consumption (see Figure 3-18). With a digital magazine design, composed of all the content items saved previously, Pocket offers users an easy way to catch up on the content collected during the day and consume it comfortably when it's convenient for them.

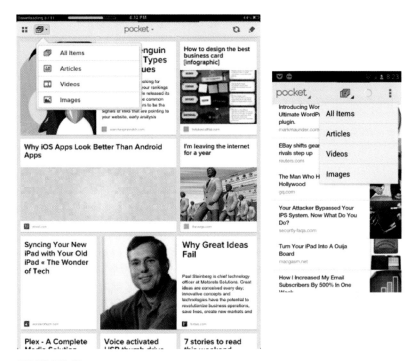

FIGURE 3-18

Pocket's mobile apps (for smartphone and tablet) are designed in a digital magazine format presenting the content saved during the day. This design acknowledges the strong role mobile devices (especially tablets) play as content consumption devices.

Design lesson: Divide and conquer

Pocket makes a very clear separation in its UI treatment between the context in which a user saves URL information (mostly the desktop browser, along with specific app integrations on other devices) and the one he uses to consume it (which is comprehensively handled in Pocket's own native app). The first merely offers a button to save the content the user runs into, and the latter is a fully designed, personalized, magazine-like experience made up of the personal saved content.

This workflow—aligned with the contextual behavioral patterns of Pocket's target audience—establishes a fluid, almost transparent experience. People don't really think about the different UIs; they just use them contextually, and it works.

Design lesson: The power of openness

Pocket has an open API that allows developers to create their own Pocket applications, integrate them into their existing apps, and share them with other Pocket users.

This capability has a couple of important advantages:

Increased distribution channels

The open API provides a more scalable solution for getting Pocket into many more entry points (or "saving" points) for users to access. Pocket is already integrated into over 500 applications, across many platforms people already use.

More channels feeding into the continuous experience

Users can trigger the experience from a growing number of channels, hassle-free, after installing the app once. While in many other ecosystem experiences, the continuous experience is limited to the specific product's website/native apps (Allrecipes and Eventbrite arc two examples), in Pocket's case, any of the integrated apps is a starting point that can feed the continuous Pocket experience.

Open platforms carry many advantages in a multi-device world, as we'll see in Chapter 8.

Summary

- With a continuous approach, the multi-device experience flows from one device to the next, within different contexts, supporting users every step of the way through their task flow in two forms:

  - *Single activity flow*, where the same activity flows between devices, like watching a movie (Apple AirPlay), reading a book (Amazon Kindle), or composing a document (Google Drive).

  - *Sequenced activities flow*, which handles broader use cases composed of a sequence of different activities that all lead to the end goal—for example, cooking (Allrecipes), events management (Eventbrite), prototyping (POP), and content management (Pocket).

- Having users sign in to the product across all devices is significant in multi-device experiences—especially continuous ones. The increased complexity involved in these experiences, along with the constantly shifting contexts, requires building a robust knowledge base of the users completing these activities so that their experiences can be personalized and improved over time. Sign-in is still the most prevalent way to identify the people using the product.

When building your authentication strategy, you should consider:

- ○ Offering SSO
- ○ Simplifying registration/sign-in flow and forms
- ○ Incorporating gradual engagement
- ○ Promoting the ecosystem benefits when users are signed in

- Continuous design, supported by multiple connected devices, enables us to rethink user flows we might have taken for granted, break them down into smaller steps, and then reconstruct them to create better, richer, more tailored user experiences.

NOTES

1. Facebook login (*http://bit.ly/1eon4SU*); Twitter sign-in (*http://bit.ly/1eon8lS*); Google+ sign-in (*https://developers.google.com/+/*).

2. Hendrik Muller, Jennifer L. Gove, and John S. Webb, "Understanding Tablet Use: A Multi-Method Exploration," *Proceedings of the 14th Conference on Human-Computer Interaction with Mobile Devices and Services (Mobile HCI 2012)*, ACM, *http://bit.ly/1eop0Lp*.

3. "Allrecipes' Mobile Apps on Fire—Surpassing 10 Million Downloads," *Fresh Bites blog*, November 17, 2011, *http://freshbitesblog.com/2011/11/allrecipes-mobile-apps-on.html*.

4. Samsung has already launched a fridge with a built-in Android tablet and aWiFi-enabled washing machine (*http://bit.ly/1cQWnTS*).

5. Bill Siwicki, "Smartphone Owners Want More Mobile Information in Stores," Internet Retailer, December 31, 2012, *http://bit.ly/1ji1IJc;* "Mobile Devices Empower Today's Shoppers In-Store and Online," Nielsen, December 4, 2012, *http://bit.ly/JBNdQ5*.

6. "Email in Motion: Mobile Is Leading the Email Revolution" (infographic), *http://bit.ly/18ReaWu*.

7. Most of the events currently offered on Eventbrite are still primarily on the small, local, one-day scale. Still, if we're touching the events space, we might as well talk about it broadly, especially since Eventbrite has already started supporting more complex events—from classes to concerts and festivals, where it provides ticketing solutions for 20,000–80,000 attendees.

8. This is a significant change in context compared to the pre-event phase. Laptops or tablets are useful for stationary contexts (lokike taking notes during sessions), and smartphones are best for on-the-go situations (during breaks between sessions). The event UI on these devices can change accordingly.

9. A conference is often perceived as somewhere between business and pleasure; thus, participants can engage in post-event activities either during working hours (usually in front of the PC), or after (where the mobile devices are more prominent). Tracking your device usage with data analytics—discussed in Chapter 8—can help you determine how the different devices serve post-event needs.

10. Flayvr (*http://www.flayvr.com*) is a great example of an app that generates such an emotional experience.

11. "Myth #1: People read on the web," UX Myths, *http://bit.ly/1i6NkSX*.

[4]

The Complementary
Design Approach

The third approach in the 3Cs framework—complementary
design—involves collaboration among multiple devices operating
together as a group. While in the previous two approaches (consistent and continuous), user interaction at any given point takes
place with a single device, the complementary approach involves
interaction with multiple devices as a connected group, which
together create a complete experience.

What Is Complementary Design?

The complementary design approach introduces a new multi-device
experience, where different devices complement one another, either by
collaborating as a connected group, controlling one another, or both
(see Figure 4-1). This means that the full experience involves interaction with at least two devices—usually simultaneously—at any given
moment. Up to now we've focused on experiences based on interaction
with a single device, either throughout the entire experience (consistent) or before the user moves on to the next device in the sequence
(continuous). With complementary design, we are entering a new space
of concurrent multi-device usage. While there are use cases in which
the user interacts with the devices asynchronously (as we'll see), the
essence of a complementary approach remains that of devices that work
in concert.

FIGURE 4-1

With the complementary approach, the different devices work together as a group, complementing one another to create the full experience.

Achieving a complementary approach involves two types of device relationships:

Collaboration

Different devices, each with its own distinct role, work together collaboratively (and usually simultaneously) to construct the whole experience—for example, playing *Scrabble,* where the tablet is used as a game board and smartphones hold the tiles.

Control

The user's primary experience takes place with a particular device, while other devices control aspects of that experience, usually remotely (e.g., a smartphone that serves as a remote control for a television).

Additionally, devices can carry different weight in the overall ecosystem experience:

Must-have

Participating devices are an integral part of the experience, and the experience cannot exist without each device contributing its part. One example is the racetrack game Pad Racer, in which the iPhone serves as the steering wheel and the iPad displays the racetrack; in this case, each of the two devices is a *must-have* for the gaming experience.

Nice to have

> A *nice-to-have* device is an added device that can deepen the user's experience, enriching it in content or functionality, but isn't essential to accomplishing the fundamental task. For example, in the case of the Pad Racer app, users can connect two iPads to have a richer set of tracks. In this case, the second tablet is *nice to have*, as it is not essential for the gaming experience.

As we progress through the examples that follow, you will see that this *must-have* and *nice-to-have* distinction is actually an evolving, fluid one; what is considered nice to have today may become a must have tomorrow, as the industry develops and new standards emerge.

Think, for example, about Internet connectivity in mobile phones. In the early days of the mobile industry, when the phone was still perceived as a communication tool focused on call management, having an Internet connection was a nice-to-have feature. However, as technology developed and mobile phones became small computers offering a wide variety of services well, Internet connectivity became a must have. The story was the same for phone cameras—a nice-to-have feature became a must have. We will see similar potential pathways in some of the multi-device experiences available today.

The set of product experiences outlined in Table 4-2 will accompany us in this chapter as we dig into the complementary approach.

TABLE 4-1. Product examples discussed in this chapter, organized along the complementary approach dimensions: collaboration versus control, and must-have versus nice-to-have

	Collaboration	Control
Must have	Real Racing 2 - Party Play Scrabble - Party Play KL Dartboard	
	Pad Racer	Slingbox
Nice to have	Heineken Star Player IntoNow Avengers	
		Xbox SmartGlass

Table 4-2 maps the product examples reviewed in this chapter along the two main complementary design dimensions: device relationship type (collaboration/control), and the weight devices carry in the ecosystem experience (must-have/nice-to-have). As you can already see, some products (like Xbox SmartGlass) incorporate both relationship types in their experience. In a similar manner, products can integrate both must-have and nice-to-have devices (as indicated with Pad Racer and Slingbox).

Before we start, bear in mind that there is no single combination in the Table 4-2 matrix that is arguably the best. Each product addresses different use cases and carries its own set of characteristics and flows. The "right" combination for you really depends on your product offering and the user needs on which you focus. You will understand that better once we review some examples and discuss the principles behind them.

Collaboration: Must-Have

The following examples demonstrate that collaborative design can be particularly powerful in bringing people together and enhancing social interactions—online and offline—through game play.

PLAYING WITH FRIENDS: REAL RACING 2—PARTY PLAY

Real Racing 2 is a racing video game (by Firemint, Ltd.). With its Party Play mode, two to four friends can play together in a split screen on the HD TV, using an iPad 2 or iPhone 4S as the host. This capability takes advantage of iOS devices people already own and carry with them to offer an enriched social gaming experience (see Figure 4-2).

FIGURE 4-2

Real Racing 2—Party Play, showing a collaborative game involving an iPad 2, three iPhones, and an Apple TV (split-screen experience).

The gaming experience flow is beautifully simple.[1] Friends meet up at someone's place, pull out their phones (which they have with them anyway) or grab a nearby tablet, and spread comfortably throughout the living room, playing together in front of the split-screen TV.

If you compare this experience to a traditional video gaming experience, you can see how much more streamlined this one is; users simply use the devices they already know and have with them in a modular way. Their devices are repurposed contextually for new use scenarios. It is low cost in that it's unnecessary to buy a proprietary game console with a dedicated set of controllers; it's convenient in that players can gather anywhere, not just at the friend's house with the game console; and it's uncluttered in that there are no cords and cables.

Design Lesson: Extending the game experience

People carry their phones with them everywhere, all day long. Once these devices become part of the game, they can also be used "off-game time" to extend the experience and enhance it. Here are a few examples of how smart devices partaking in the game experience can be used pre- and post-game. Users can:

- Set up group gaming events, which can take place at anyone's house.

- Receive alerts about friends playing nearby and/or invite friends to join (before or during the game).

- Manage personal and group leaderboards, and share achievements on social networks.

- Keep a score history across multiple games (with analysis over time).

- Save memorable moments from games (so they can always go back and see how a certain player pulled off a crazy turn and won the race).

- Extend the game experience to other spaces (who said it has to remain within the walls of the house?). If you consider our movement toward the Internet of Things (a topic Chapter 6 is dedicated to), having connected things everywhere introduces new opportunities for continuing the game play in the street, in a store, while waiting at the bus station, and elsewhere.

- Enhance the core game with a broader gamification layer for ongoing engagement. In that respect, Foursquare did many things right with its points and badges mechanics (up to the point of relying too heavily on them). Still, its rules and rewards strategy encouraged hundreds of thousands of people to pursue the desired behavior (that is, to check in) repeatedly, frequently, and across a variety of places and contexts, creating a healthy competitive drive.

Creating these kinds of games takes a lot of work, but when done right, it can significantly engage users and encourage behaviors.

Design lesson: A new species of game controllers

Traditionally, game console controllers serve as peripheral accessories that provide only input to a video game, in order to control an object or a character (see Figure 4-3). They don't have screens, memory, or processing power and cannot operate as independent devices when not being used in a game. During game play, there's a predefined set of actions players can perform with the controllers using the tactile buttons.

FIGURE 4-3
Proprietary game controllers for popular game consoles.

Smart devices like phones and tablets offer the opportunity for players to use smart-device game controllers in new ways—not only pre- and post-game, as just discussed, but also during the game play itself.

While smart devices can't equal some of the specialized game controllers (in terms of industrial design, ergonomics, convenience of grip and operation, robustness of the tactile keys, etc.), they offer other advantages:

- Motion and orientation sensors built into these devices, such as the accelerometer, can be used for fun, natural user interface control. Touch gestures can be leveraged as well for game maneuvers.

- The basic shape and functionality of the smartphone can be somewhat optimized for game play through smart accessories (like covers, readers, and other devices that plug into the phone). Coupled with a corresponding app, this allows for enhanced game controllers that are still smartphone-based, but tailored for more serious gamers or specific types of games. We will see several examples of such modular smart-device ecosystems in the next chapters.

- Repurposing existing devices for different use cases could help with reducing electronic waste (e-waste)—a fast-growing problem worldwide, due to the rapid changes in technology and media. An estimated 50 million tons of e-waste are produced each year. In the United States, an estimated 70% of heavy metals in landfills comes from discarded electronics.[2]

But the advantages of smart-device game controllers go beyond hardware. The stronger value offering smartphones bring to the table lies in their software, which has a significant effect on the user experience:

Personalization

Games that know who the players are and what their preferences are (through ongoing data collection) could save players the hassle of a lot of the pregame configuration. For example, user input—like choosing the number of players, entering their details, choosing their preferred car models and colors, and more—can be automated through connected devices that record players' preferences (remember the importance of sign-in?), and detect who's around them.

Multi-tasking

Even if there is some setup flow to go through, when each player has a personal screen, everyone can complete it at the same time instead of sitting in front of one screen (the TV) and doing the setup serially.

Augmentation

Smart devices can do much more than just serve as game controllers. For example, they could augment the game, adding new layers of information or display when users are looking at the TV through their smartphones. Additionally, when you have multiple players using their devices to play a collaborative game, you could potentially design a game experience that is distributed along these devices. In other words, instead of having everyone getting the same experience—each on his own device—different users can play different roles in the game, thereby experiencing a different game UI. As a group, the players establish the full game experience.

Question to the Reader

Can you think of any other experiences—digital or physical—where smartphones and/or tablets could potentially serve as replacements for traditional tools, offering an enhanced complementary experience?

Try to think about this question from the following angles:

- Product experiences that are based on a set of physical components that can be replaced with digital ones

- Collaborative social experiences, incorporating a group of individuals interacting with one another

- Situations or contexts in which users are already interacting with multiple devices at the same time

- Day-to-day scenarios where the variety of devices that need to be operated becomes confusing and daunting

DIGITALIZING SOCIAL GAMES: SCRABBLE FOR IPAD— PARTY PLAY

Scrabble for iPad (by Electronic Arts) is a virtual version of the highly popular game *Scrabble*. One of the options offered in this version is Party Play support for two to four players. Here, the iPad serves as the board, and players can use their iPhones or iPod touches as tile racks (see Figure 4-4).

Whereas Apple AirPlay takes a digital experience based on proprietary devices and ports it to our day-to-day ones, Scrabble for iPad takes an offline board game experience and brings it to the digital sphere.

FIGURE 4-4

Scrabble for iPad—Party Play in action, with the iPad as the board game and the players' iPhones holding the tiles (source: YouTube).

The combination of the tablet and smartphone in this game does a good job of preserving the classic game experience of a group of people gathering around a board and interacting through a game (as opposed to playing on a website, for example). From a design perspective, that familiar social experience is facilitated through gestures like "flicking" tiles from the iPhone rack to the main iPad board, and "shaking" your smartphone in order to shuffle the letters. All in all, the Scrabble app demonstrates how a multi-device experience that is based on the highest-end devices can be leveraged to encourage "traditional" face-to-face social interactions.

You might ask yourself, why do we even need to bring such games to devices? Why not simply continue playing *Scrabble* on the good old board? It's true that a physical board game does have its advantages (for example, it's more tactile, you can spread it out over a larger space, and it doesn't need batteries or software upgrades). At the same time, there are several important design considerations that make the digital version an attractive route.

Data, data, data

Playing through devices allows you to collect valuable data about your users and their use habits: who they are (demographics), when they play, how long they play, how many people (and possibly whom) they play with, and how frequently they play. This allows you to better understand game play patterns, response times, exit points, areas of difficulty, feature usage, and more.

This data is invaluable in continuously learning what works well in your product and what needs improvement. Furthermore, if you offer several related products, or can correlate the data with other usage data you have available, you can learn even more about your users, which is the key to designing successful experiences. I will talk in depth about data analysis and why it is critical in a multi-device world in Chapter 7.

Richer, more streamlined game experiences

In our discussion of the Real Racing 2 Party Play example, considered how multiple devices can extend the game experience beyond just the actual game time and place. These opportunities apply in the Scrabble for iPad use case as well. In addition, the Scrabble use case demonstrates ways in which the digitalized version of an offline game can streamline the experience and improve it. The most prominent example is the electronic dictionary feature. During the game, users can access the dictionary to verify that the word they're about to play actually exists. In real life (using the board game), that would require either using a smartphone to search for the word, keeping an online dictionary open, or maybe even having a physical one within reach—three solutions that are hardly as streamlined or effective as verifying the word in-app, on the spot.

The dictionary integration is yet another example of how designing a multi-device experience opens up new opportunities to improve a traditional, familiar experience. Reassessing the game experience flows in light of the new devices' capabilities allows for reconstructing it in ways that better support people's needs.

Lower barriers for entry

Scrabble for iPad relies on devices many players already have (and these continue to disseminate at a fast pace). Downloading the app is still an easier, shorter, and often cheaper process than going to the store or buying the game online. Furthermore, as opposed to physical board games—where cards, tiles, and other pieces tend to get lost, torn, or broken—digital experiences don't wear.

INTEGRATING MUST-HAVE AND NICE-TO-HAVE DESIGNS: PAD RACER

As with Scrabble for iPad, the experience in Pad Racer (from SMHK Funlab) is split between two devices. The iPhone becomes a steering wheel and the iPad becomes a racetrack (see Figure 4-5). Clearly, one must have both devices in order to play the game.

FIGURE 4-5
Pad Racer in action—the iPhone serves as a steering wheel for racing on the iPad track (source: YouTube).

However, one interesting design aspect in Pad Racer is how it incorporates a nice-to-have component in the game. Pad Racer enables users to link two iPads together to create a much larger racetrack, enriching the game experience by offering more track adventures and challenges (see Figure 4-6).

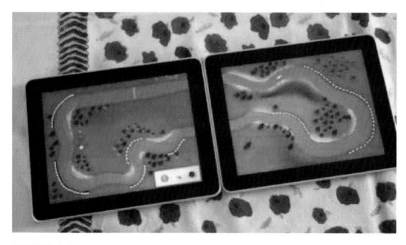

FIGURE 4-6

Pad Racer nice-to-have feature—connecting two iPads together for more track variations (source: YouTube).

With this enhancement, Pad Racer takes into account its ongoing, more advanced users in order to foster the longevity of the game. Being able to step up the game by connecting another iPad (or two, or three) introduces new racing challenges and difficulty levels, boosting the players' excitement and confidence in their improving skills.

Discussion: Designing for Beginner versus Advanced Users

A key principle in any product design—especially when you're focusing on the *minimum viable product* (MVP) for launch—is to keep it simple. You want people to get it quickly, jump on board, and start using your product. A lot of thought is usually invested in the first-time experience and helping new users develop an understanding of the core value, functionality, and flow of the product.

Getting users up to speed and gaining traction is indeed essential. At the same time, however, you shouldn't lose sight of these new users as they gradually learn the interface and features, become power users, and develop advanced product literacy, needs, and actions.

Power-user features can take various forms, like keyboard shortcuts, gestures, or long-press–triggered actions, that are not immediately visible in the UI (see Figure 4-7). They can include actions offered behind menus (rather than surfaced on the screen), extended information displayed behind "more" prompts, advanced search capabilities (for example, searching in Gmail for an email you sent using the syntax "From: me To: *email address*" instead of browsing through your sent items), and more.

FIGURE 4-7

In Tumblr for Android, a long press on the Create button offers users immediate access to posting photos or text (via tex-el, littlebigdetails.com).

When it comes to games, bridging the novice and power-user levels is practically a necessity—especially in genres like action, adventure, role playing, and strategy games. A well-known game design principle from Nolan Bushnell, the founder of Atari (also known as "the father of video games") is that "All the best games are easy to learn and difficult to master." In other words, to keep players interested in the game, you must introduce an increasing level of difficulty—preferably building upon their past experience to ease the transition. You can achieve this through new challenges, routes, tools, obstacles, enemies, and other game mechanics.

With multi-device experiences, which are only in their infancy, there's a strong need to invest in onboarding users at this stage. As discussed in Chapter 3, educating people about the multi-device value and familiarizing them with the main flows are critical to gaining traction, engaging users, and gathering data—which in turn drives more and better experiences.

At the same time, keep in mind that as we go deeper into the connected world (with movements like the Internet of Things, discussed in Chapter 6), ecosystem experiences become more extensive, involving many more types of devices. In these cases, the users to first engage with such products are early adopters, and tech-savvy by nature.

This doesn't mean you should loosen up your focus on simplicity, ease of use, or clear product flows and guidance. However, you should make sure to empower your audience of early adopters by offering channels for more advanced actions and configurations. For example, in a home automation product ecosystem, it is useful to offer predefined configurations to start from, like "Turn off the lights when I leave home." It's also important, however, to allow users to define their own custom configurations. These early adopters are the users who will fill your product with content (e.g., a user-supplied pool of home automation configurations that others can use off the shelf), along with usage data you can track and learn from.

NOT JUST FOR MULTI-PARTY GAMES: KL DARTBOARD

The last example in this collection comprises two apps, from Key Lime 314, LLC: KL Dartboard for the iPad, which transforms the device into a dartboard, and KL Darts for the iPhone, which "holds" the darts (see Figure 4-8). Once they are both installed, the user can aim her iPhone at her new iPad dartboard, give it a quick shake, and watch as the dart is "thrown" from the iPhone onto the iPad.

FIGURE 4-8

Dartboard apps for the iPhone (KL Darts) and iPad (KL Dartboard); the first provides the darts, while the latter serves as the board.

The apps share a Bluetooth connection, and the iPhone determines the dart's location on the board using accelerometer data. Clearly, this experience is strongly collaborative in design—each device plays its own role, and the magic happens when they are used together.

This example shows that collaborative must-have experiences are not necessarily multi-player ones. This product can definitely benefit from several people playing together, but one person can also enjoy the core multi-device experience.

Additionally, the focused, easy-to-use, fun design of this experience is a great example of the power of simplicity. I wouldn't be surprised if soon enough the traditional dartboards in local pubs will be replaced with digital ones. It might actually encourage more people to take part, as many people will already have the darts in their pockets, and the fear of being hit by a stray sharp projectile is completely removed.

Collaboration: Nice to Have

We saw in Chapter 1 that tablets and smartphones are used widely for multi-tasking with other media, especially as an interactive part of regular TV viewership. The traditionally passive act of watching television is steadily becoming far more interactive, offering new opportunities for contextually enhanced TV watching experiences. This type of experience is known as the *second-screen experience*.

In this next group of examples, we'll look at how the complementary approach enhances the traditional experience of watching movies or sports by taking advantage of additional devices in order to offer complementary content and actions. The end result is a truly enhanced entertainment experience, one that offers new design opportunities.

SOCIAL LAYER ATOP TELEVISION VIEWING: HEINEKEN STAR PLAYER

Heineken Star Player (Figure 4-9) offers an engaging game-watching companion during a live soccer match from the UEFA Champions League.

FIGURE 4-9

The Heineken Star Player app becomes active only during the live game, and complements the viewing experience with real-time activities.

The app works in real time, allowing viewers to log in only 10 minutes prior to the big match. During the match, users are engaged with various real-time activities tied to the game's progress: they are invited to anticipate the outcome of corners, free kicks, and penalties, as well as to predict when goals will take place. During the game's quieter moments, the app engages viewers with trivia questions related to the UEFA Champions League. All of this is wrapped in a thick social layer, including a points system, badges, leaderboards, the ability to form leagues with friends, and the ability to share scores on Facebook.

A comparison between this type of complementary approach and the examples we looked at earlier in the chapter reveals a few important differences in the role the complementary device plays:

The mobile device is not mandatory (yet)

While the basic complementary approach principle holds in the Heineken example—all the devices operating together to provide the full experience—the second screen is merely a nice-to-have component. It enhances the TV watching experience, but isn't essential to the primary experience (at least not yet).

If and when the second-screen experience reaches the critical adoption point, becoming a robust standard in the TV industry, it could actually transform from a nice-to-have to a must-have device.

An ecosystem experience was developed from a single device

While the previous examples required developing apps across all participating devices in order to establish a product ecosystem, Heineken Star Player developed an app only on a single device: the smartphone. In this case, Heineken Star Player created an ecosystem by leveraging an existing device—the TV—and encouraging new behavior patterns across devices through a live event. Its creators still offered an ecosystem experience from the users' perspective, despite the users' actively controlling only one touchpoint.

This might sound like the dream ecosystem from a developer's standpoint: just build a single mobile app, tie it to a live TV event, and—*voilà!*—you have an instant ecosystem experience. You save a lot of design and development resources, you launch more quickly, and people enjoy a fun, engaging ecosystem experience. So far, so good, right?

But there's a catch.

What's easy for you is easy for others as well, leading to second-screen experiences becoming almost *too easy* to build—and a market flooded with apps. Somrat Niyogi, CEO of Miso, talks about this challenge in his article "Please Don't Ruin The Second Screen":

> Take three engineers from a top-tier school and after writing some Objective-C and doing some simplistic design...there you go, an app is launched. Since we started Miso, there have been more than 100 second-screen apps developed (and this doesn't even include the one-off iPhone apps that have been created by the networks)... [L]ook at the Super Bowl. I think I could have downloaded at least 15 apps just to experience that one-time event.[3]

The race to produce second-screen experiences enhances fragmentation in the mobile market. Startups, companies, TV networks, and other players are all building proprietary second-screen apps, trying to win consumers' attention—sometimes for the same event. Don't get me wrong: competition in a market is important and beneficial. It encourages creativity, growth, effectiveness, progress, and focus on the consumer (who holds the power to choose). The question, however, is always one of magnitude.

Right now—as usually happens with emerging revolutionary technologies—there's chaos out there. There's no data trajectory, structure, best practices, or standards to use. We are in the process of establishing those. However, the huge potential such ecosystems embody is staggering, driving many companies and developers to jump into this new territory and try to conquer it.

From networks and advertisers to production companies and even TV manufacturers, they all get one thing: the audience is no longer focused on the TV screen alone. Whether for live events like the Oscars or the Super Bowl, reality shows like *Iron Chef* or *The X Factor*, or even presidential debates, the second screen has become a major player in the TV viewing experience (see Figure 4-10)—let alone the third screen, fourth screen...soon enough, I'm sure, these will join in, too.

36% of Super Bowl 2013 viewers reported they would use a second screen to supplement the game-viewing experience.

FIGURE 4-10
According to a Century 21 survey, 36% of viewers reported they would use a second screen during the Super Bowl last year.[4]

When we look at the heated social TV market, it seems it's only a matter of time until we will start seeing even richer groups of even more layered shared TV watching experiences. What might this look like? Different family members could use the same TV device on different occasions, each person having an individual second-screen experience tailored to his preferences and interests. Or it could look like a group of friends watching TV together at the same time, each getting different content on her second-screen device—and, together, they've created a *super-power* experience (à la *Captain Planet and the Planeteers*).[5]

SECOND-SCREEN EXPERIENCE AS A PLATFORM: INTONOW

IntoNow, bought by Yahoo! only three months after launching its first app version, adds a rich social layer to TV watching (Figure 4-11). The app listens to what people are watching on TV, identifies the program, and unlocks a companion experience.

FIGURE 4-11

IntoNow app with two different TV shows: The Next Iron Chef (Food Network)
and The X Factor (Fox). The app complements the viewing experience with
additional information and relevant activities.

This experience offers a wide set of complementary elements:

- Captures and shares "did you see that?" moments with a user's
  friends by pulling up screenshots of the show the user is watching

- Identifies music playing in the show as it happens (song titles and
  artists)

- Retrieves related articles, people, live stats, behind-the-scenes photos, and additional information during the show

- Lets users see what their friends are watching, chat with them, and
  start groups around a show

- Provides trivia, discussions, and polls

- Displays live tweets from actors, athletes, and celebrities related to
  the show currently being watched

These elements provide real-time accompaniment to the TV shows,
resulting in a much richer viewing experience in terms of both content
and social networking.

Design lesson: A second-screen experience can go beyond a specific show

Whereas Heineken's Star Player and the plethora of Super Bowl
second-screen experiences all focus on a single type of TV event with
limited frequency, which makes scaling difficult, IntoNow provides
a second-screen platform that serves many different TV shows. As a
result, it not only accompanies the TV watching experience, but also

helps users discover TV content through their social circles and their own TV watching habits. This also means that the second-screen app becomes useful not only during showtime, but also between shows, extending the usage potential beyond the limited time when a show is aired.

Design lesson: A second-screen experience doesn't have to be associated with a predetermined broadcast time

While Heineken Star Player was inherently tied to the *broadcasting time* of the event (which is not in the user's control), the IntoNow experience is associated with the *user's own viewing time*. Accordingly, it provides much more flexibility in terms of the time, place, and frequency at which the product can be consumed. The second-screen experience in this case does not rely on a specific live broadcast time, but rather on the time(s) the user chooses to watch a show, at his leisure.

This is an important aspect given the radical shift in the way people have come to consume TV content over the last decade. Previously reliant on a given program guide, schedule, and channel selection provided by the broadcasting company, viewers can now create their own personalized viewing experiences based on their preferences. Services like Video on Demand (VOD), Netflix, Hulu, and Aereo—along with products such as Apple TV, Slingbox, Roku, and Google's Chromecast—significantly expand and completely change the contexts, touchpoints, and ways in which people watch TV.

Design lesson: A second-screen experience can complement TV watching continuously

Continuing with the theme of usage potential, the second-screen experience has strong use cases ranging along a broad timeline:

- TV show engagement is not bound to the time a show is aired. Viewers anticipate and prepare for it ahead of time, and talk about it after. The second-screen experience can accommodate these needs, providing both relevant, fresh content and a social communication platform to interact with friends.

- If the TV show airs weekly, even more opportunities open up, as the TV watching experience can be viewed as a continuous one, from one week to the next. The second-screen experience can tap into that flow and create a longer-term narrative between episodes, keeping the viewers engaged. Opportunities include running polls among viewers about what they think will happen with a certain character or event in the next episode, sharing episode trailers, providing fresh news on the show's stars or exclusive interviews, and recommending similar shows.

Case Study: Bites.TV—Building a Second-Screen Experience

EYAL BAUMEL, CEO, BITES.TV

Eyal holds a BA in communication and media studies from the Interdisciplinary Center (IDC). Eyal is also a graduate of the Zell Entrepreneurship Program (cum laude) at the IDC and the Merage Executive Leadership Program at the University of California Irvine's Paul Merage School of Business.

Bites[6] is a cross-platform, turnkey solution that facilitates and rewards live fan interaction and participation with their favorite shows, events, brands, and personalities.

Using Bites, content owners can enhance, gamify, and monetize their content, allowing fans to play along; discover contextual info and merchandise; and express themselves through polls, ratings, and moods.

HOW WE STARTED

The first thing we did when we decided to develop a second-screen app was to learn the behavior, habits, and needs of our potential users. We literally joined viewing parties (e.g., groups of friends watching football) and observed their behavior as they watched these shows together, as well as when they watched alone. At the end of the show, we followed up with deep-dive interviews to get their in-depth perspective on their needs, the group interaction, and how to improve their viewing experience.

We saw, for example, that females like to talk, rate, and share clothes they see in shows, while males like to predict what will happen in sporting events and brag about it on social networks.

The data we collected from our few dozen observations helped us define the product features and prioritize them. That was our starting point.

OUR FIRST MILESTONE: AMERICAN MUSIC AWARDS

As part of our ongoing marketing activities, we met with Dick Clark Productions (DCP) to explore opportunities to enhance the viewing experience for one of its premiere live events—the American Music Awards (AMAs).

We kicked off by identifying some of DCP's needs. (We later learned that these needs represent the TV industry as a whole.) Our key areas of focus for the AMAs were as follows:

- Drive tune-in and engage viewers for the duration of the show.

- Increase real-time viewership for real-time engagement and impact of the event.

- Create deeper engagement and interaction with the content.

- Improve social media measurement. While social networks are definitely spreading the hype about the AMA events, the only way to measure social engagement with promotions is through the amount of tweets and status updates.

- Get in-depth data on viewers' behavior patterns and engagement triggers, per DCP.

- Find new ways to increase revenues, drive more tune-in/viewers (to increase ratings), and create measurable buzz around the event, per DCP.

We took these inputs into consideration and enhanced the app offering accordingly, with additions like unique advertisement interactions, tune-ins, and comprehensive data analytics capabilities. We then presented a demo of Bites based on a copy of the previous year's AMAs. Sold!

Once we got the event schedule from DCP, we created a second-screen experience tailored to the AMAs (Figure 4-12). The Bites experience included features like rating dresses on the red carpet; predicting the winners for each category (e.g., artist of the year, album of the year); asking trivia questions about the presenters, performers, and past events; making entertaining predictions such as who would be Justin Bieber's date (following his breakup with his girlfriend the week before the event); fun facts; additional related info; and much more.

FIGURE 4-12

The Bites iPhone app for the AMA ceremony.

We used the opportunity to test several monetization strategies, like selling a song while the band sang it in real time (via iTunes), or asking users to indicate their favorite pizza topping while a pizza promotion was on air.

From the very beginning, we saw huge value in the data we collected—qualitative and especially quantitative—tracking and carefully analyzing actual app usage. In fact, we see the Bites ecosystem as a Google Analytics for live TV (and live events), and one of our main goals was to simply learn the engagement rate and patterns of the viewers. Through this partnership, we not only got to go on the red carpet and chat with Taylor Swift, but we also learned more about how viewers engage with the second screen, how they use the OMG button (described shortly), and the correlation between what the viewers predicted and what actually happened (a positive correlation).

The event report, along with a nice infographic, can be found at *http://bit. ly/1et4TvB*.

OUR THREE TOP LESSONS AND HOW THEY AFFECTED THE PRODUCT

We learned several important lessons along the way through the data we collected during various television events (AMA and others).

Live events trigger more complementary activity

In terms of second-screen experiences, TV content is divided between two primary types: scripted shows and live TV (sporting events, real-time reality shows, and award shows). The latter has the highest frequency of "dead" moments, triggers the highest amount of conversation on social networks, and gets the highest television ratings.

We realized that live event shows are more suited to second-screen enhancement, where it is not perceived by viewers as disruptive. We do believe that scripted shows can and should be enhanced and gamified, but mainly between shows and not during the show.

There's great value in facilitating fan participation beyond social conversations

There is a lot of "conversation" around TV shows, and it happens mainly on Twitter and Facebook. Content owners use these channels to communicate and engage the fans, yet these platforms are not optimized for second-screen experiences, participation activities, and fan rewards.

- Viewers show a high interest in taking an active part in the show through voting and rating. These activities generated a big part of the engagement throughout our TV shows. As a result, we kept enriching our content in these areas (such as live polls, play-along features, and ratings), offering more opportunities to engage in these activities, more frequently.

- Viewers want to be able to speak with their friends and other fans during the show. To address that need, we developed a chat feature for the viewers before and during the show.

- Viewers want to express their feelings about the content in real time, "like" moments, and share big moments. Facebook gives users the option to "like" a show or an actor, a team, or a player, but they can't "like" a specific moment in time. Inspired by so many "OMG" reactions we saw in our observations, we came up with our real-time OMG button, which captures that moment and allows users to publish it to social networks along with a short description.

Viewers want more than just a real-time, second-screen companion

Our data showed that viewers are not ready (yet) to use an app for a specific show/channel/network while they watch TV. We saw our users checking the app repeatedly for several days before and after the event, and when there was no new content to show, they were disappointed. We learned that fans want more than an amplified experience while they watch—they look to consume more of the content they like around the clock.

Through our ongoing testing and data collection, we realized that our core product offering was valuable, but the content strategy had to change. Consequentially, we decided to break away from the concept of "events" to the broader notion of "channels" as part of a participation platform, where fans can interact, participate, and get rewarded on an ongoing basis.

Recently, we formed a strategic partnership with WME, the largest talent agency in Hollywood, and we're continuously trying to find new ways to get people more engaged with TV-related content. Stay tuned for more exciting TV experiences on a channel near you.

TYING TOGETHER WATCHING EXPERIENCES: AVENGERS

The Avengers second-screen app (Marvel's *The Avengers*: A Second-Screen Experience) is a companion experience for the blockbuster movie *The Avengers* (see Figure 4-13). You might be scratching your head right now (as I was), wondering if Marvel was expecting people to take out their phones and use the app at the theater during the movie. The answer is no. This second-screen app targets the movie fans who bought it on Blu-ray or DVD, and is meant to accompany the movie-watching experience at home.

FIGURE 4-13

Marvel's The Avengers second-screen app for iPad, accompanying the movie-watching experience (source: Marvel.com).

The user experience starts after the user completes the required Blu-Ray and WiFi configurations to sync mobile devices with the movie; then, when the user presses Play, the second-screen app comes to life with rich content streaming in.

The app is themed around the S.H.I.E.L.D. database, which offers access to personnel files, comic book origins, and exclusive interactive content, as well as the option to become a S.H.I.E.L.D. agent. Users can explore rich content about the film and its cast, behind-the-scenes footage, storyboards, videos, photos, and more.

A unique feature offered in this app is a button to sync the app to the movie, which immediately injects relevant interactive content for exploration that is tied to the currently playing scene—for example, loading the visual effects labs to explore the special effects layer by layer. Syncing the movie to the app is also available.

From a design perspective, this feature offers interaction flexibility that we haven't seen before: you can wander around the app freely, exploring any movie content you want (without being bound to the movie playing), and at the same time, anytime you wish, with a click of a button you can sync the app immediately with the movie and get contextually relevant content.

An additional feature this app offers is that viewers can use their mobile devices as remote controls for the movie. This means they can pause the movie, for example, using simply the devices they already have in their hands.

This brings us to the second type of device relationship in the complementary approach—control, which we'll look at next.

Question to the Reader

The sync flexibility offered by the Avengers second-screen app raises interesting questions related to its design affordance.

On the one hand, this flexibility puts the steering wheel in the hands of users, giving them much more control over the content they consume (when and how).

On the other hand, this flexibility could get in the way of actually watching the movie (which is the main activity in this scenario). Could this be overly distracting in the context of movie watching? How much complexity does this add to the app usage? Does it justify the added value?

Then there are the actual usage patterns. How many users use the sync button, and how often? Do they engage with synchronous and asynchronous content while the movie is playing, or do they separate between them?

Is there another way to approach this design challenge? Can contextual signals help in the content management here?

What do you think?

Control: Nice to Have

In this last set of examples, we are faced with a dominant device, usually the TV (at least today), where the main experience takes place. The other ecosystem devices—once installed with the required apps—can control different aspects of this experience, extending its reach beyond traditional time and space limitations.

Let's have a closer look.

NOT NECESSARILY A SIMULTANEOUS EXPERIENCE: SLINGBOX

Slingbox is a TV streaming media device focused on ensuring that viewers don't miss their favorite TV shows and events when they're away from home (Figure 4-14). It's accompanied by a proprietary SlingPlayer app for mobile devices.

FIGURE 4-14

The Slingbox ecosystem on Android. The smartphone, tablet, and PC can all control the TV, either by serving as a direct remote control or by changing TV settings remotely (such as recording).

With Slingbox, users can control their home TVs remotely in several ways—from a laptop, tablet, smartphone, or any other connected device. First, viewers can use a mobile phone as a TV remote control to change channels, adjust the volume, and so on. In addition, Slingbox provides an even more powerful feature: any of the ecosystem devices can be used to remotely choose a program for Slingbox to record. This means that when people are out having drinks with friends and suddenly remember that their favorite TV show starts in 10 minutes, all they need to do is pull out their mobile phones or tablets (whatever is at hand at that moment) and set their TVs to record that show.

So is the Slingbox example really that different from what we've seen so far?

The answer is *yes*.

Slingbox demonstrates for the first time an ecosystem experience in which devices can interact with one another—complement one another—without necessarily having to operate simultaneously. They don't even have to be in the same room. This is a first.

This expands the ecosystem possibilities beyond time and space to a world of asynchronous ecosystem relationships, which theoretically can continue indefinitely. By comparison, collaborative games or second-screen experiences require all the devices to play together at the same time and in the same place, and the experience lasts only as long as the devices are active. With the Slingbox design approach, the experience is not bound to these space/time limitations.

WHEN COLLABORATION AND CONTROL MEET: XBOX SMARTGLASS

Xbox SmartGlass (Figure 4-15) allows for various devices and the TV to connect with one another to enhance the overall Xbox experience for TV shows, movies, music, sports, and games. As with the previous second-screen experience examples, the added devices are all considered nice to have, as they aren't strictly necessary to the core Xbox experience taking place on the TV.

FIGURE 4-15

The Xbox SmartGlass ecosystem—the tablet enriches the Xbox experience with complementary information, interactive guides, and more. In this example, while watching Snow White and the Huntsman from Universal Pictures on the big screen, users can use their tablets to control the movie play (pause, change volume, etc.) as well as get related content.

Xbox SmartGlass demonstrates how the two types of complementary device relationships—control *and* collaboration—can be incorporated into a single experience:

Control

The smartphone, tablet, and PC can all control the living room Xbox experience. Players can use a mobile device to navigate to the Xbox dashboard; pause and rewind movies; swipe, pinch, and tap to surf the Web on the TV; and use the device's keyboard for text input and search on the go.

Collaboration

A smartphone or tablet can transform into a second-screen companion by automatically serving up extended-experience TV shows, movies, music, games, and sports. For example, Xbox collaboration provides relevant immersive details about a movie, TV show, or game; interactive guides; behind-the scenes commentary; real-time game strategy; and more.

In other words, the Xbox SmartGlass experience offers an interesting *universal* complementary experience. Not only does the second-screen device enrich the viewing experience, but it also releases users from the need to maintain and operate yet another device (the TV remote control). All TV-related activities are merged into a single device.

Is integrating both collaboration and control activities on one device a problem?

Not necessarily.

These two relationship types—collaboration and control—represent alternative activities on a single device that do not actually conflict or overlap. Either users' attention is focused on consuming content on the current channel, or they're flipping through channels or adjusting the volume. In fact, the relationship types can be perceived as compatible and potentially facilitate the overall TV experience.

To clarify, I'll share a story from my days as a senior UX designer at a design consultancy several years ago. One of my biggest projects at the time was to redesign the entire TV interface for a leading cable television provider. When we started working on the EPG (electronic program guide), a key guideline (based on a lot of user research and A/B testing) was to maintain the context of the current channel being watched, even when viewers browsed through the channel guide. For that reason, we made sure to allocate space for an on-screen TV window in all our design explorations.

Now, if you take into account the design challenges with TV, the amount of content the EPG contains, the one-quarter-screen TV window that needs to fit in, *and* the sacred goal of keeping it all simple, clean, and light, you'll quickly realize that this was quite a challenging task. Any design option involved significant compromises.

If I had the same project today in our multi-device world, I could approach the design challenges from many new directions. For example, if we go back to the Xbox SmartGlass, the second-screen device has already leveraged the functionality of the remote control, so it already includes the "button" to trigger the program guide. And if we can already call the EPG from the device, why can't its content be displayed on that same device as well? This provides a seamless flow (i.e., there's no need to switch focus between devices) and allows increased design flexibility on the second-screen device—all while maintaining the TV's current context. Furthermore, the EPG could naturally link to extended information about each show—another feature that belongs under the jurisdiction of the complementary Xbox SmartGlass.

With that said, we would probably still need to come up with a design solution for the TV only, as not all Xbox users necessarily own a device that serves as a second screen. Still, the second screen opens up new design opportunities for creativity and innovation by exploring how the experience can be distributed between the TV as the activity center, and the second screen devices that complement it.

Fascinating Use Cases: What Do They Mean for My Work?

Collaborative games, second-screen experiences, and the other complementary experiences are beyond interesting examples; they could not *exist* with only a consistent design approach. These experiences come to life when an ensemble of devices play together, complementing one another to create a bigger, better experience.

In fact, almost any user activity is worth exploring in terms of everyday experiences that could benefit from complementary enhancement. For example, someone who is exercising might want to also watch a TV show or listen to music, and in this case those activities are complementary to the main activity. Once you have this realization, you find yourself looking at every product design from a new perspective—a context-sensitive one. This inevitably leads to examining the problem through the lens of the broader relationships between users and their devices; reassessing user flows, needs, and tasks; and constructing them anew in a more streamlined way.

Once we are able to create these collaborative experiences, we can begin to gain speed and move into some very promising opportunities. The benefits include:

Lower barrier to entry

> The mere fact that all these experiences are built upon devices people already own and carry with them significantly lowers the barrier to joining in. *Anyone* with a connected device can now play these games, or enjoy an enhanced viewing experience. There's no need to buy a special controller or dedicated accessories; just download the app, sit back, and enjoy.

Increased reach and accessibility

Being able to use only the ecosystem devices to partake in the full experience increases its reach to new audiences, new locations, new contexts, and potentially new settings (playing *Monopoly* remotely, for example).

In addition, these experiences are accessible *anytime, anywhere*. All users need to do is pull out their connected devices and get started. They are no longer bound to a specific place where the game console, TV, or game board is located.

Accumulating knowledge

Having people shift their offline experience (physical board game, isolated game console, or living room chats during a TV show) to the connected ecosystem opens a window for an increased understanding of viewer/player behavior. A digital ecosystem can potentially provide usage data on each device, as well as on the overall ecosystem connections. This can then help us continue to optimize the experience. Furthermore, if we can correlate and analyze this data with other ecosystem data, we can derive even deeper insights.

Enhanced social connections

The complementary experience is very much suited to supporting social engagements between people, like the previously discussed collaborative game play. As a new game is now just a tap away—easily accessible and readily available for party play with friends—it enhances social engagements and helps strengthen group ties.

Enforced habits

The more users engage and interact with devices, the stronger their use habits become, which triggers a positive feedback loop that encourages them to continue using the devices.

Complementary experiences contribute to this mechanism, helping to enforce habits around the overall usage of multiple devices.

With consistent design, there's no imminent incentive to use more devices, since the entire experience can be consumed on any device. When people use complementary design, the use across all these devices is reinforced and strengthens both the whole ecosystem and each device individually.

Summary

Complementary design involves interaction with at least two devices—usually at the same time and place—and is based on two types of device relationships:

- *Collaboration*, where the different devices work together as a connected group to create the full experience

- *Control*, where the primary experience takes place on a certain device and other devices control aspects of it, usually remotely

You've seen a diverse set of examples demonstrating different combinations of device relationships and weights—all of which convey the idea of an experience whole that is greater than its parts:

- Multi-player game experiences (like *Real Racing 2* and the Scrabble for iPad and Pad Racer apps) show how complementary design fits social activities nicely, and allows users to extend the experience beyond the game time and location.

- Second-screen experiences (such as with Heineken Star Player, IntoNow, the Avengers app, and Xbox SmartGlass) illustrate the radical shift in the TV watching experience, from a passive experience to an active one involving multiple screens that complement one another. While this experience is still considered "nice to have," we might not be far from the day it is established as a standard, becoming a "must have."

- The control relationship (like with Slingbox) demonstrates that complementary experiences can serve asynchronous contexts, extending the experience beyond specific time and place constraints.

Through these examples, you also saw that different device relationships can be integrated in the same experience (as in the Xbox SmartGlass case), as well as different device weights (as in Pad Racer).

A Summary of the 3Cs

This concludes the discussion of the 3Cs framework for addressing multi-device experience design. To summarize, the framework includes three main design approaches:

Consistent

Each device acts as a solo player, creating the entire experience on its own.

Continuous

Multiple devices handle different pieces sequentially, advancing the user toward a common goal.

Complementary

Multiple devices play together as an ensemble to create the experience.

Table 4-2 gives a comparison view of these three approaches, summarizing their main characteristics.

TABLE 4-2. Comparison view of the 3Cs

	CONSISTENT	COMPLEMENTARY		CONTINUOUS	
		Collaborative	Control	Same activity	Sequenced activities
Pattern type					
Description	Same experiences is offered independently in each device (with minor adjustments to fit device traits)	Experience is split simultaneously between devices. They complement each other, to collaboratively create the full experience	Primary experience takes place on a single device, whereas others can control aspects of it (usually remotely)	Experience is split simultaneously between devices. They complement each other to collaboratively create the full experience	
Devices need to be at the same place?	No	Yes	No	No	No
Devices need to work together at the same time?	No	Yes	Depends	No	No

	CONSISTENT	COMPLEMENTARY		CONTINUOUS	
		Collaborative	Control	Same activity	Sequenced activities
Number of devices engaged with at a given moment	1	At least 2	At least 2	1	1
Examples	• Google Search • Trulia • Hulu Plus	• Real Racing 2 • Scrabble • Pad Racer • KL Dartboard • Heineken Star Player • IntoNow • Avengers	Slingbox	• Apple AirPlay • Amazon Kindle • Google Drive	• Allrecipes • Eventbrite • PDP • Pocket
		Xbox SmartGlass			

Most of the examples we examined in the last three chapters illustrated one approach in isolation. However, we've also started to see how some products combine more than one approach in their multi-device experiences in order to meet more use cases, or engage users across the various contexts in which they use the product.

In the next chapter, I will dive deeper into the topic of integrated design approaches, as in actuality *most* products integrate more than one design approach in their experiences. Let's explore why and how the 3Cs framework supports that.

NOTES

1. Here, I'm focusing on the conceptual design of this product (putting aside the limitations of the iOS walled garden).
2. *http://en.wikipedia.org/wiki/Electronic_waste*
3. "Please Don't Ruin The Second Screen," TechCrunch, May 27, 2012, *http://tcrn.ch/1cRHRqP*.
4. "Big Game Survey," Century 21, December 2012, *http://www.century21.com/superbowl*.
5. In the TV show *Captain Planet and the Planeteers*, when the Planeteers came across situations they couldn't resolve alone, they'd combine their powers to summon Captain Planet, a superhero, who possessed all of their powers magnified, symbolizing the premise that the combined efforts of a team are stronger than those of its individual parts (source: *http://bit.ly/1hzDmsQ*).
6. Author note: in the interest of full disclosure, Bites was one of the startup I worked with as part of my role as UX mentor on the UpWest Labs accelerator.

[5]

Integrated Design Approaches

> This chapter describes how the three approaches act as building blocks for constructing a multi-device user experience. In most product ecosystems, it's necessary to integrate more than just a single approach in order to meet people's new and diverse needs across distributed contexts.

Now that you have a basic understanding of the 3Cs framework, let's take things a step further. In the previous three chapters, we examined the three design approaches—consistent, continuous, and complementary—in an isolated fashion; in this chapter, we'll take a bigger-picture look at some of the different approaches working together in varied and integrated ways. When you begin designing multi-device experiences, you shouldn't treat the three approaches as a crossroads from which you must choose one of three paths. The three approaches are actually a set of building blocks available for you to construct the experience that best fits your users. Each approach defines different types of relationships and task flows between devices. Together, as part of a greater ecosystem, they can help people achieve their goals across different contexts.

We saw in Chapter 3, for example, how single-activity continuous experiences, like with the Amazon Kindle and Google Drive, are actually a combination of consistent and continuous approaches. These products provide access to all the content anywhere, and at the same time support a continuous flow of reading and editing across devices, when relevant. In Chapter 4, we saw that second-screen experiences like Xbox SmartGlass combine both control and collaboration device relationships in their flow to provide a universal TV watching experience. In this chapter, we will see more examples of integrated approaches and how they address user needs.

3Cs as Building Blocks

I like to think of the 3Cs as a LEGO® kit (Figure 5-1). The bricks are the devices we have available, such as smartphones, tablets, PCs, and TVs. Note that the list doesn't actually end here—there are many other devices, accessories, and "things" we can use (these will be discussed in Chapter 6).[1]

FIGURE 5-1

LEGO brick pile, representing the set of connected devices we have available to use as part of our multi-device experiences.

As shown in Figure 5-2, these bricks can connect to one another in different ways and relationship patterns (i.e., consistent, continuous, and complementary—including their subtypes).

FIGURE 5-2

LEGO bricks connect in different ways, representing the different design approaches.

You don't necessarily need to use all the bricks you have available, and you don't have to connect them in all possible forms. Putting together consistent, continuous, and complementary design is really about building a clear, simple ecosystem that is truly focused on the user context. The magic happens when you use these bricks to tell a product story that is meaningful and useful for people (Figure 5-3).

FIGURE 5-3

A castle book made of LEGO bricks, representing the overarching ecosystem narrative we need to convey (artwork by artist Nathan Sawaya; photo courtesy of www.brickartist.com).

Before we analyze a set of examples that illustrate integrating multiple approaches, let's first consider why we need integration. Understanding the reasons behind combining several design approaches can help you frame your product ecosystem when you plan the multi-device flow. Let's break it down here, and later we'll apply these reasons to our use cases.

MULTI-DEVICE EXPERIENCES ARE IN THEIR INFANCY

The multi-device era is just starting. Use patterns among different devices are in the early stages, and development too is gradually taking shape. There are some initial, common behaviors we already see happening among users (like the emerging co-usage of tablets and TVs, and the use of the smartphone as a shopping assistant), but these situations are a small sample, aren't 100% clear-cut, and may not entirely reflect what the future holds. Users' behavior may change, especially as more devices join the ecosystem. Designers and users alike are still exploring this new playground—trying out all these different devices— and formulating new habits. Designers are smart to be both sensitive to these dynamics and tentative about them, making sure we design for an experience that leaves room for variation.

For instance, the tablet as a "babysitter" for the kids is a use pattern that emerged organically as people started using the device and discovered how much their kids became engaged with it (even at a very early age). Parents started sharing the devices with their children, utilizing their unexpected benefit as a digital babysitter. This use pattern fostered a prosperous market for kids' games on the tablet—geared toward kids as young as two.

[NOTE]

A bigger question that such a phenomenon immediately raises is whether using tablets (or other digital devices, for that matter) at such a young age promotes or hinders learning abilities and the development of certain skills among kids.[2] This is a very important question, one that touches many disciplines—psychological, sociological, and educational, to name a few— and should continue to be researched. As one would expect, there are currently arguments supporting both sides. However, this discussion is out of scope for this book, which is focused on providing design frameworks and principles for multi-device experiences without associating them with a specific type of audience.

2

A similar course of events took place with the tablet as a cooking aid, as discussed in the Allrecipes example in Chapter 3. When the iPad and its successors were launched, their main design premise revolved around a superior browsing experience and digital media consumption (videos, books, and magazines). Nobody marketed this device as the next cookbook, and yet it gradually grew into this role as people started exploring different use contexts and found its benefits in the kitchen especially appealing (Figure 5-4).

FIGURE 5-4
iPad as cooking aid.

USER NEEDS AREN'T BLACK AND WHITE

When you start breaking down your product flow into different contexts, diving into each one and analyzing which devices are best suited to serve each context, you might find that overlapping needs arise across several devices. This means you'll probably want to offer some features and flows that address them on multiple devices (i.e., apply consistent design in this part of the experience). At the same time, you might also discover unique needs for specific contexts that require integrating one or more of the other design approaches into the experience. For instance, in the Allrecipes example in Chapter 3, we talked about the role of the smartphone as *shopping list carrier* within the flow of actions. While this is definitely a prominent need while a user is in the grocery store, it's not necessarily the only one for the mobile context. There are additional needs that might arise and should be mapped as part of the design analysis. For example:

- The user is still planning the menu for Friday's dinner, and during the train ride home he has some time on his hands, so he wants to review what he's chosen so far, or maybe browse through additional recipes. He might even want to recheck the ingredients for a few of the recipes, or how long it takes to make each one, so he can plan his cooking schedule. For that, he would need access to the recipe list on his mobile device(s) as well.

- During shopping, he might feel that there's not enough food, or get the urge to add another fruit dessert after seeing those nice juicy strawberries at the store. Having all the recipes accessible on the mobile phone as well can support these spontaneous needs in the store.

These two example use cases demonstrate the need for a certain level of consistency across different devices to support overlapping needs across contexts. In addition, some complementary needs might arise in-store: more in-depth information about products, price comparisons, healthier substitutes, or coupons for the different ingredients. To support these needs, you might want to consider enhancing the smartphone app with additional features that complement the shopping use case.

Keep in mind that you don't necessarily have to support all these needs across all contexts. However, it's still a good exercise to try to identify all that you can within each context, and from that view make an informed decision about your focus, adjusting the feature set (and experience flow) to the different devices accordingly.

GREAT DEVICES LEAD TO GREAT EXPECTATIONS

The more connected devices people have (particularly mobile ones) and the smarter these devices get, the richer and more diverse the usage patterns will be, and users' expectations will also change as a result. Here are two examples:

- Users expect more data and features to be accessible anytime, anywhere. This demands both consistent and continuous design.

  > I want to be able to read (or continue reading) my book from any device I carry at any time!

- Users want more of their needs (or a finer granularity of needs) to be met. This demands both complementary and continuous design.

  > I'm watching the Oscars on TV with my smartphone and hey!—why can't it control the TV?

  > Scarlett Johansson looks gorgeous. Where did she get that dress? Has she won an Oscar before? I have to search...

  > I wonder what my friends are saying about Meryl Streep winning Best Actress!

  > I'm so tired. If only I could get the full list of winners delivered to my phone tomorrow morning...

The more experienced and literate people become with multiple devices, especially when embracing the devices' connectivity potential, the more sophisticated their needs, goals, and expectations become.

Until five or six years ago, most people didn't think their little mobile phones could ever become powerful computers. For the most part, a contact list, SMS and call capability, a media player, and an alarm clock were sufficient. Today, a smartphone without a camera, WiFi, a media player, photos, maps, a browser, and email doesn't even meet the baseline expectations of users. Add to the mix the dozens of apps people download to enhance their phones' functionality, and the whole situation creates increased use and higher expectations and encourages the development of better, more tailored experiences.

It's important to remember, though, that this multi-device space is a world in the making. This puts a lot of power and responsibility in our hands to determine its direction and set expectations. The types of experiences we design for people, the use cases we choose to address, the contexts we tailor the designs for—they all impact the way people perceive these ecosystems. This, in turn, affects their behavioral and use patterns across these connected devices.

APPROACHING MULTI-DEVICE EXPERIENCES: DOS AND DON'TS

When approaching multi-device experience design, don't start by asking questions such as:

- Are we doing responsive design so we can launch on tablets as well?

- Can we support that feature we already have on our website on mobile as well?

- Should we start from the tablet, or do the smartphone first?

Even a question like "Which approach out of the three should we go for?" is not the place to start your multi-device design. All these questions have a place in the design process, but they shouldn't be the ones driving the decision making; rather, they should themselves be driven by the user needs and goals you're focusing on.

The 3Cs are your toolbox for approaching multi-device experience design. But before you can choose which tools to use, you need to understand the problem space and what you're trying to solve. For this, as with any good UX design, you need to start with the user.

This means you need to start by asking the following questions:

- What are the *users' needs and goals* that this product ecosystem tries to address?

- What are the *main flows and use contexts* involved in this product ecosystem?

- Which *experience approaches* can best accommodate these needs within each flow, and between use contexts?

- Which *devices* should be used, and what are their roles in each context?

Before you think about devices, you need to focus on the *core user needs and goals,* map the *contextual landscape along the user task flow,* and think about how the different *experience approaches* can address them. Only then should you optimize the way you *distribute the experience elements across different devices,* taking into consideration people's use patterns, the available devices they have, and which one(s) are the best fit along the varying contexts.

Keep adhering to the basic principles of user-centered design, and beware of getting too device-enchanted, which can pull you into the tempting yet risky technology-driven approach—especially with the pace at which connected technology is developing and new, exciting devices are proliferating, offering people new means to reach a goal. Think, for example, about directions and navigation—what started with paper fold-out maps transitioned into map-based websites and GPS devices, then moved into smartphones and tablets, and is now going into wearables. While each technological progression improved the user experience in aspects like precision, speed, mobility, visual display, accessibility, geo information, and navigation options, the core user need remained the same: getting from point A to point B. That core need is what should continue being the focus of the design. Our task as designers is to continuously rethink how we can better serve it.

Integrated Approaches: Another Look at Our Examples

Let's take another look at some of the examples used in previous chapters, this time with an eye toward integrated approaches. As these examples are already familiar to you, it will be easier to look at them through this new lens and see how combining several design approaches can enhance a user's experience.

COMPLEMENTARY AND CONSISTENT: SLINGBOX

In Chapter 4, we saw how Slingbox enables users to control and track their TV content from almost anywhere, using a smartphone, tablet, or PC. Now we're going to see that this is not the *whole* story. Here are Slingbox's core objectives, as posted on its website:

> Don't miss your favorite TV shows and events when you're away from home. On the road, at work, or on vacation, a Slingbox makes it easy to watch and control your home TV from virtually anywhere, anytime on your laptop, tablet, smartphone, or connected device.[3]

In other words, the two main value propositions of this product are *watching* and *controlling* the home TV from anywhere, anytime, on any connected device.

In this case, it's pretty clear from the product message alone that the design will have to incorporate *consistency*—which will provide the basic layer of TV content access across all devices. On top of that, *complementary* design is needed in order to provide the remote control functionalities.

Let's clarify that further in order to suit a design perspective, breaking down these objectives into a set of more concrete user needs or use cases:

1. Watch favorite shows when traveling abroad.

2. Watch a movie in the bedroom, which doesn't have a TV.

3. Watch a TV show recorded last night during the train ride to the office.

4. While out with friends, remember that an interesting TV show is about to start, and make sure not to miss it.

5. Keep track of live sporting events while waiting in line at the doctor's office.

6. Want to watch some TV and, as usual, can't find the remote.

With these use cases, you can see that the basic ability to watch shows from any device, whether the user is out of the country (#1), on the way to work (#3), out of the house (#5), or simply in a different room (#2) requires *consistent* design.

To use a smartphone as a remote control (#6), as well as remotely set a TV show to record (#4, and possibly also #1 in case there are time zone/schedule conflicts), you need to add *complementary* design (with the control relationship type between the devices). The user can decide later which device to use to watch the recorded show (going back to consistency).

Design lesson: Design approaches can complete each other

A question that immediately arises is: how do these two approaches work together and enhance the same multi-device experience?

Well, they actually complete each other nicely. The consistent approach, which allows people to use any device at hand to watch the shows they want, releases them from any *space constraints* related to the physical location of the TV. The complementary approach also frees them from the *time constraints* of having to watch a show when it is being broadcasted. Together, these approaches establish a highly flexible watching experience.

In terms of ecosystem experience distribution between devices, you may notice that a few basic guidelines emerge:

Consistent design (TV, PC, tablet, and smartphone)

- The TV content library should be available across all devices. Not only that, but accessing this content is the main need across all devices.

- Preferably, as a starting point, you should organize the content in the same way in terms of information architecture across all devices for easy browsing and orientation. If usage data analysis later suggests different content consumption patterns along different devices, then it's worth considering tailoring the content organization and prioritization to each device.

- Sign-in should be available across all devices, to allow easy access to personalized preferences (recently viewed, favorites, etc.).

Complementary design (smartphone, tablet)

- Control functions are not relevant for the TV, as they are applied on this device.

- The TV control features are relevant for mobile devices that are always on and readily available for use. Following that, prioritize the smartphone first, and the tablet next (across the two main platforms—Android and iOS).

- The PC—due to its size, stationary mode, and use patterns—is more suited for content consumption (similarly to the TV), rather than as a remote control.

Design lesson: Design approaches should be prioritized within an experience

As indicated before, accessing and watching TV content is the main use case for Slingbox, across all devices. Thus, this part of the experience should get the most attention in terms of prominence, flow, and interaction across all devices—for example, promoting TV content when a user enters the app, implementing smart search, and allowing quick access to favorite content and especially items that the user has recorded or has already started watching.

On top of this, complementary features are added to the mobile devices. The specific detailed design can take many forms: adding items to the main menu, allocating a certain screen space in the main landing screen, providing a separate view that can slide in, and implementing many other design solutions. Deciding on these details depends on the overall design of the app, such as its interaction model, navigation system, screen layout, flow, and visual language.

But it doesn't necessarily end there.

Design lesson: Context awareness can take us far

Thinking more closely about different use contexts opens up additional opportunities to better tailor the Slingbox experience. Take, for example, the experience of a user opening the Slingbox app on her smartphone while watching a show on TV. Clearly, this is a very different use case than that of a user accessing the Slingbox app via her smartphone on the train to work. Although in both cases the action is the same—accessing the smartphone app—the context is very different. The different context signals that the user may actually have a different intent when using the app in each context.

Subsequently, making informed dynamic UI changes based on (strong enough) contextual signals can help shorten the distance between user intent and need fulfillment. For instance, you could provide faster access to the remote control UI if the user opens the app while watching a show on TV. Alternatively, you could offer complementary content related to the show currently being watched (a feature that is currently not included in Slingbox). Either way, taking into consideration these contextual differences, understanding what users are trying to do, and, if possible, saving them the need to do it themselves can provide a much more streamlined, delightful experience. It's important to make sure, though, that such UI changes are done thoughtfully, and with clear communication and user consent, so that your users don't become confused or feel out of control.

Fab (Figure 5-5) is a great example of such an approach: it analyzes users' behavior (*Do they read the emails we send?*), based on which the experience is automatically optimized (*They haven't in a while? Let's stop sending the emails then.*). The change is communicated to the user, with an explanation and a way to undo it.

FIGURE 5-5

Fab opts you out of emails when it discovers that you don't read them.

CONTINUOUS AND CONSISTENT: ALLRECIPES

Allrecipes offers an interesting (even if not immediately obvious) integration of the continuous and consistent approaches.

We saw in Chapter 3 that the Allrecipes continuous experience supports a set of separate tasks that are all strung together in the larger cooking narrative: (1) finding the recipe, (2) buying ingredients, and (3) cooking.

However, if you take a closer look at the Allrecipes experience on each device (Figure 5-6), you'll see that some core use cases—as mentioned at the beginning of this chapter—require certain components to be available across multiple devices.

FIGURE 5-6

Allrecipes offers its recipe list across the three core devices: PC (allrecipes.com), tablet (Your Kitchen Inspiration app), and smartphone (Dinner Spinner app).

These include, for example, the recipe list (shown in Figure 5-6), along with rich information about each recipe, like reviews, images, ingredients, and cooking time. Other common features are the search functionality and the personal recipe box that are available across all devices.

Design lesson: Different design approaches promote people to their goals in different ways

As you can see, Allrecipes didn't rigidly split the experience components across the different devices—there's a consistent motif across all devices, on top of which each device gets a special treatment best suited to its usage mode and context.

Going back to the recipe list feature, if Allrecipes hadn't made the list available on the smartphone device, it would have missed out on important contexts of use where people would find the feature useful. For example, during on-the-go scenarios, where people have time to burn (such as during a bus ride, or while waiting for a friend or standing in line), being able to use the smartphone to search for recipes is highly valuable. It allows people to gradually make progress on their to-do tasks by utilizing spare time slots during the day.

At the same time, Allrecipes enhances the smartphone with unique components, like a shopping list (as discussed before) and ingredient scanning at the store, which fit the device's use context and feature set.

These unique components also play an important role in advancing people toward task completion, but in a different way: while the consistent components across devices open up more time slots during the day for users to engage with an activity (thus allowing them to finish it sooner), the continuous components cut down the time it takes to complete it in the first place. Think about the shopping list feature. Instead of people having to prepare a handwritten shopping list (i.e., go through all the recipes, sum up the ingredients across them, and then write everything down on paper), the grocery list is generated automatically in seconds, and already offered on the smartphone.

Design lesson: Optimize the design for the most suitable device for the task

The Allrecipe shopping list feature is offered both on the smartphone and on the tablet, providing a similar feature set. At the same time, comparing the design between these devices highlights a few interesting differences (see Figure 5-7).

 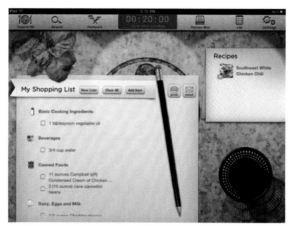

FIGURE 5-7

The Allrecipes shopping list design on the smartphone (left) and tablet (right) apps.

The shopping list design on the mobile phone is much tighter, clearer, and easier to scan—the screen focuses just on the ingredients list, with no redundant spacing or big, distracting visuals.

The tablet, on the other hand, offers a more widespread screen layout, with generous spacing and prominent visual elements. These visual elements (the pencil, the sprig of basil, the basket) do not carry any functional or educational role and are mostly there for atmosphere, emulating the physical environment. Also, interestingly enough, the tablet interface offers two prominent action buttons on the right—Print and Email—which seem to further imply that the tablet is an intermediate device on the way to the one the user will actually carry while grocery shopping.

From a naïve perspective (since we're not privy to complete information about the design considerations), it seems that more design attention was put into the smartphone UI, which is the device more likely to be used for grocery shopping. Accordingly, perfecting the design on this device is much more important compared to the tablet design.

Discussion: What If My Users Don't Have All the Devices?

OK, so you go about designing your multi-device experience, and invest the time thinking about ways you can weave the different devices into the varying contexts along the experience flow. But what if, after all this effort, users are missing one of the devices along the way? Does that break the entire chain? Is the ecosystem experience ruined?

Not so fast.

While it would definitely be ideal for everyone to own all your ecosystem devices, there are a few things working in your favor:

- You don't need to worry about smartphones. Your users most probably have at least one.

  Moreover, the smartphone is the device most people cannot detach themselves from; it's on them all the time, in all their daily contexts. As such, this device usually plays a key role in multi-device experiences, and you can rest assured that your users have it.

- Device roles overlap. The split isn't a clear-cut one.

  Most multi-device experiences involve a certain level of consistency between devices. This means that multiple devices can fill the same role, and act as substitutes for one another (for that consistent feature). In many cases, this helps ensure that fundamental functionalities are supported broadly. We've seen several examples where a smartphone and the tablet play the same (or very similar) roles in the ecosystem, so even if users have just the smartphone, they should be able to complete the core tasks.

- Technological innovations are embraced first by innovators and early adopters. These groups usually hold financial resources, advanced technical knowledge, and also the latest and greatest gadgets, devices, and things. If you're launching a product ecosystem that involves an innovative device or disruptive concept, chances are good that your initial audience, at least, is already equipped with the devices you need them to have (and probably a few more).

BUT WHAT IF SOME PEOPLE ARE MISSING A DEVICE?

Obviously, the user experience will be affected—to different extents—if users don't have all the required devices. The impact will depend on your product, the design approaches you use, and the way you integrate the devices:

- Consistent parts will probably be least affected. These are offered across all devices, so even if people are missing a device, they can get the entire functionality on another. It might not be the most convenient device to perform that action, but it is still possible. For example, watching a movie or having a video chat is much more convenient on bigger displays, which offer a superior viewing experience. At the same time, even if users have only a smartphone available, they can still accomplish both tasks fully.

- With continuous design, missing a device carries a greater effect, but you can still ensure that the core experience—the part that offers the strongest value—is available in the devices your users have. For example, people who use Allrecipes and don't own a tablet cannot follow the continuous experience through to the cooking step, leveraging the tablet as a cookbook. But they can still engage in the core experience along the first two steps of the cooking use case: planning the meal and getting the required groceries. It doesn't capture the full experience sequence, but going two-thirds of the way is a significant step in the right direction.

  Theoretically, an alternative approach here could be to offer the cookbook interface on the smartphone as well in order to make it available for the large majority of users. However, this is where you need to consider design trade-offs like:

  - What are the usability implications of designing this feature on the smartphone? How good of an experience will it provide to users? Will it be usable on such a small display?

  - What would be the broader implications of adding more features to the mobile device (in terms of information architecture, flow, and overall experience complexity across the app)?

    You must weigh these questions against the expected benefit of the feature to users and the business in order to decide which path to choose.

- Complementary experiences are the ones that often suffer most from users not having all the required devices. For example, with a product like IntoNow, people who don't have a second-screen device cannot get any of the product offering.

  However, there are still ways to mitigate this effect. Most people have smartphones, so taking an integrated approach here and designing a complementary experience to the TV while offering consistent design between the smartphone and the tablet ensures that most users can consume the product. This way, people who don't have tablets can still use the product on their smartphones. Bear in mind that the design trade-offs just discussed apply here as well as you decide which ecosystem devices offer which experiences (if any).

MORE DESIGN DIRECTIONS

Looking at the longer term, there are additional measures you can take to address the missing device's hurdle:

- In-product education like onboarding assistance and contextual help along the product flow can promote the benefits of having more of the ecosystem devices. One product would probably not make consumers buy more devices, but over time, with more products offering useful multi-device experiences, the benefits can add up to the point that people see a strong enough value in expanding their device set.

- Promoting the value behind the entire ecosystem can begin with the first-time experience. Also, surfacing relevant tips and encouragements contextually—for example, informing users about the tablet cookbook feature after they add recipes to their recipe list or return from grocery shopping—can be an effective way to clarify the benefits right at their moment of need.

  The Google Maps app on iOS is a good example of applying these strategies (see Figure 5-8).

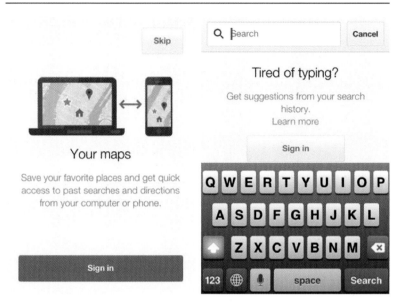

FIGURE 5-8

The Google Maps iPhone app promotes sign-in as part of the welcome tour (left), and contextually during use (right), approaching the user exactly at the point of "pain" of having to type in a query using the touch-based keyboard.

- For some products (particularly those that involve a social activity), you can try using the power of social connections to help users complete "the missing piece of the puzzle." One way to go about it is to create the experiences with group interactions in mind, so that people can gather together, each "contributing" a certain device to the joint ecosystem that everyone can then benefit from. Alternatively, you could just let users know which of their friends have the device they're missing (under the appropriate privacy settings, of course), as a channel through which they can try out the device firsthand and learn its benefits, as part of a real-life context.

At a more macro level, device prices are constantly dropping, and worldwide unit shipments are on the rise. So even if people don't have a certain device today, it's probably just a matter of time until they do. Tapping into these trends, coming up with an innovative vision, and executing on it early can help set a first mover advantage, as well as serving as a valuable learning experience about users' needs, goals, and habits.

ARTICULATING THE ECOSYSTEM NARRATIVE

Conveying the ecosystem experience to users requires a very clear definition of the role each device plays in the ensemble within different contexts—and that should then lend itself to the design. This requires you to be an even more guarded gatekeeper for which features go into which devices. The more functionality you distribute across all devices, the harder it becomes to distinguish between the devices' roles and identify the unique value each contributes to the overall narrative. Also, as we already know, more functionality means more complexity—which now accompanies users with every device they pick up.

Deciding what should be assigned where gets back to the four basic questions you need to answer:

- What are the *users' needs and goals* that this product ecosystem tries to address?

- What are the *main flows and use contexts* involved in this product ecosystem?

- Which *experience approaches* can best accommodate these needs within each flow, and between use contexts?

- Which *devices* should be used, and what are their roles in each context?

After you answer the first three questions as they apply to your product, the following guidelines can help you determine the answer for the fourth one:

- Tasks that are highly likely to take place on multiple devices (serving as parallel, alternative channels) should be supported across all these devices—preferably in a consistent manner. For example, in a second-screen experience, the smartphone and the tablet serve as alternative companions for the TV watching experience, and thus they should both offer related content and activities.

- Tasks that are a strong fit for a specific device should be offered only on that device. A shopping app, for example, should offer product scanning only on the smartphone, as this is the device that will most certainly be with people while they're shopping at the store. It is also more convenient for this purpose (even if they happen to have their tablets in their bags).

- You can address tasks that you're not really sure about and that are somewhat unclear in several ways:

Take no chances

> Include features related to these tasks in *all* the devices you think might be used for them (even if to different extents). The downside to this approach, however, is more clutter and less product clarity, as explained previously.
>
> Allrecipes seemed to take that approach with its shopping list feature, offered across its mobile devices (even though it's probably much less used on the tablet). As we saw, however, Allrecipes still optimized the design for the specific device that is most commonly used in this context: the smartphone.
>
> It's not necessarily ideal, but knowing how organizational dynamics can sometimes work, you might not be able to get an agreement on taking out a feature completely. In these cases, and especially as timelines get tight and trade-offs need to be made, it's better to focus your design efforts on the main device you expect most people to use a feature on (rather than compromising all of them).

Take a leap of faith

> Apply more selective gatekeeping, supporting the "question-able" tasks *only* in the specific device(s) where you think this is absolutely necessary. You might end up with some users missing out on some features (because they're using a different device, for example). However, even if they had a feature there, it doesn't mean they'd use it (it's less of a fit anyway). In addition, you can use other methods to expose users to additional features through product education practices, as discussed previously.

Balance chances and faith

> A third approach is a hybrid of the preceding two. The basic idea is that you offer the relevant features across all the devices you think might be a fit, but you prioritize and treat them differently in each device UI. Using a strawberry cake as a metaphor, strawberries (the feature at hand) can carry different weight in the cake (the overall experience), based on how they are baked in:

You can put whole strawberries as the icing on the cake.

 You can cut the strawberries into slices and integrate them as a layer in the middle.

 Or you can grind and blend them in the cake mix, so they are practically everywhere.

Each recipe reflects a different role the strawberries play, which in turn has a significant impact on their dominance in the overall cake flavor.

Returning to our multi-device experiences, the Nike+ Running app is an example where the hybrid approach can apply well. This app aims to track users' runs and keep them motivated, so its main target device is the smartphone. Still, it works on tablets as well, and the devices share the same design—it is merely scaled between the different screen sizes.

When we examine the app modules, it's clear that the run-tracking features belong on the smartphone only. People are not likely to go running with their tablets. However, features like activity analysis and the Nike Shop could be useful on both. This is where the hybrid solution could work well:

- *On the smartphone*, where the main focus is the running activity, the main app screens (including the home screen) should be dedicated to that. Other features should be treated as secondary, having less prominence in the UI and possibly being accessible only via an entry in the main menu.

- *On the tablet*, however, the activity analysis over time is the primary use case (as with the desktop), and it is much more comfortable to consume and interact with this content on a bigger display. Thus, the UI treatment for these elements should be much more prominent—for example, the home screen should already display a dashboard of the user's activity status, possibly also with comparison to his friends. Similarly, the Nike Shop on the tablet can be surfaced more prominently and provide a convenient shopping experience.

COMPLEMENTARY, CONSISTENT, AND CONTINUOUS:
HULU PLUS, WII U, AND XBOX SMARTGLASS

The last example for integrated approaches demonstrates how all three can live in a single multi-device experience.

I mentioned in Chapter 2 how I came across a new product offering from Hulu Plus while I was writing this book. Up to that point, the Hulu Plus ecosystem focused completely on a consistent experience—making the content available across different devices. Through a new integration with the Nintendo Wii U, Hulu Plus introduced two additional design approaches:

Complementary

> The Wii U game pad serves as a second-screen experience for Hulu Plus, allowing users to quickly discover more information about shows while watching them on the big screen.

Continuous

> The console's controller also enables people to easily move what they're watching from the big screen to the Wii U game pad. As we saw with other similar products, this is very useful when people want to move the viewing experience away from the TV to somewhere else.

With Wii U, Hulu Plus practically expanded its ecosystem offering to include all three approaches, thus meeting a varying set of user needs. I wouldn't be surprised if soon enough we see these additional two approaches spread into the other Hulu ecosystem devices.

Xbox SmartGlass offers a similar combination of patterns. While we've discussed the complementary and continuous roles that SmartGlass introduces as part of the Xbox ecosystem, it's good to see how it incorporates some consistent pattern elements as well:

- The entire Xbox catalog is accessible through all devices.

- All purchased movies and TV shows can move easily between the tablet, PC, and Xbox 360, offering access to this media on all devices.

Design lesson: A new TV ecosystem experience standard?

Looking through these examples, there seems to be an emerging trend toward a new ecosystem standard for consuming TV and entertainment content. This experience incorporates consistent, complementary, and continuous designs together to provide a comprehensive viewing experience across location, time, and social contexts.

Having these three approaches combined together gives profound flexibility to people in their TV watching experience, allowing them to:

- Watch any TV content, from any device, anywhere, anytime. People are not bound to the physical location of the TV set, nor to the time a show is aired.

- Enjoy a streamlined TV watching experience along varying contexts during their day. In essence, in any given context (on the bus, waiting for the train, at home, or at a friend's place), people can choose the best available device to "serve" them the content they'd like to watch, right from the point they left off.

- Enhance their TV watching experience with a second screen that offers complementary content, activities, and social engagements in real time, in accordance with the show being watched.

  Not only that, but the second-screen device can also be used as a remote control for the TV, releasing users from the need to find (and operate) the proprietary remote.

The fact that this ecosystem experience is quickly becoming a standard signifies the leading role the TV industry takes in the diffusion of multi-device innovations. Being at the forefront of exploring the benefits of cross-device experiences, and offering continuously richer interactive experiences for consuming media and entertainment, the TV industry pushes its traditional boundaries and inspires others to follow. The TV ecosystem demonstrates nicely how the three patterns can be used effectively to drive innovation and accelerate consumer adoption, which in turn helps extend the reach and impact of multi-device experiences altogether.

Discussion: More Screens, Stronger Habits

NIR EYAL, NIRANDFAR.COM

Nir is a two-time entrepreneur and blogs about the intersection of psychology, technology, and business at NirAndFar.com. He has taught consumer psychology and design at both the Stanford Graduate School of Business and the Design School.

Allow me to take liberties with a philosophical question reworked for our digital age. If an app fails in the App Store and no one is around to use it, does it make a difference? Unlike the age-old thought experiment involving trees in forests, the answer to this riddle is easy. *No!*

Without engagement, your product might as well not exist. No matter how tastefully designed or ingeniously viral, without users coming back, your app is toast.

ENGAGEMENT IN A MULTI-SCREEN WORLD

How, then, to design for engagement? And as if that were not challenging enough, how should products that touch users across multiple devices, like smartphones, tablets, and laptops, keep people coming back?

The answer is *habits*. For the past several years, I have studied, lectured, and consulted on how products form habits, and my work has uncovered some startling conclusions.

To be clear, not every product requires user habituation; plenty of businesses drive traffic through emails, search engine optimization, and advertising. However, if the company's business model requires users to come back on their own accord, unprompted by calls to action, a habit must be formed.

The good news is that in today's multi-screen world, the ability to interact with multiple devices has the potential to increase the odds of forming lasting user habits. By designing across devices, developers have a unique opportunity to leverage an ecosystem approach to drive higher engagement.

Through my research, I have found a recurring pattern endemic to these products, which I call "the Hook." This simple four-phase model is intended to help designers build more engaging products.

Building for habits boils down to the four fundamental elements of the Hook: a trigger, an action, a reward, and an investment. This pattern can be found in any number of products we use automatically, almost without thinking.

TRIGGER

Designing for multiple interfaces means your product is more readily accessible throughout the day. The more often the user chooses a particular solution to meet her needs, the faster a habit is formed. A trigger is the event in the user's life that prompts her to use the product.

Sometimes the trigger can be external, such as when a user receives a notification with a call to action. Other times, the trigger is internal and the information for what to do next is imprinted in the users' memory through an association. For example, many products cue off of emotions as internal triggers. We use Facebook when we're lonely and check ESPN or Pinterest when we're bored.

It is important that companies understand the users' internal triggers so they can build the product to meet those needs. Designers should be able to fill in the blank for the phrase, "Every time the user (_____), they use my app." The blank should be the internal trigger.

Take, for example, the experience Nike has constructed for its aspiring athlete customers. Nike's suite of products includes wearable monitors, which track physical activity throughout the day, as well as a host of smartphone apps to be used while running, playing basketball, or golfing.

For Nike, it is critical that users attach the company's products to a discrete moment in their lives. To succeed, Nike has to own the instant just before the user heads out the door to work out. Athletes want to know their effort matters, and Nike helps them meet that need. By digitally recording the workout, Nike's apps tap into a deeper emotional need to feel that all that sweating is not going to waste, that the amateur athlete is making progress.

By creating an association with a moment in time—in this case, every time the user exercises—Nike begins the process of creating a habit.

ACTION

When it comes to multi-screen experiences, it is important to design a narrative for how the product is actually used. Knowing the sequence of behaviors leading up to using the products, as well as the deeper emotional user needs, is critical for successfully executing the next step of the Hook, the action phase.

The action is the simplest behavior the user can take in anticipation of reward. Minimizing the effort to get to the payoff is a critical aspect of habit-forming design. The sooner users can get to the reward, the faster they can form automatic behaviors.

In Nike's case, simply opening the app or wearing one of their body-mounted devices alleviates the user's fear that his exercise will be in vain. Clicking a button marked Run in the Nike+ running app, for example, begins tracking the workout and gives the user the relief he was looking for.

Finding ways to minimize the effort, be it by eliminating unnecessary logins or distracting functionality, improves the experience both on mobile and web interfaces. Nike makes the action of tracking exercise easier by building products designed to make recording even easier—for example, shoe-mounted devices that passively collect information.

Designers should consider how many steps they put in the way of users getting what they came for. The more complex the actions, the less likely users are to complete the intended behavior.

REWARD

The reward phase of the Hook is the where the user finally finds relief. After being triggered and taking the intended action, the user expects to have the internal trigger satisfied. If the user came to relieve boredom, she should be entertained. If the trigger was curiosity, she expects to find answers.

Thus, the reward phase gives the user what she came for, and quickly! When the athlete uses the Nike app, for example, a 3-2-1 countdown displays to signify that the workout is about to begin. The user can get on with her run, knowing it is being recorded. But the Nike suite of products layers on more rewards. The apps not only record the workout, they also motivate it.

To boost their habit-forming effects, many products utilize what psychologists call *intermittent rewards*. When products have an element of variability or surprise, they become more interesting and engaging. For example, scrolling on Twitter or Pinterest offers the allure of what might be found with the next flick of the thumb.

In Nike's case, the element of variability can be found in various forms throughout its product ecosystem. For example, when athletes connect to Facebook, the app posts to the social network and runners hear the sound of a cheering crowd every time one of their friends "likes" their update. Nike also implements a point system called NikeFuel, which is meant to be a quantification of physical activity. However, the mechanics of how rapidly points are earned is intentionally opaque, giving it an element of variability. Finally, exercising itself has an element of surprise, which Nike's products accentuate by encouraging users to complete new and increasingly challenging goals.

INVESTMENT

Lastly, a critical aspect of products that keep users coming back is their ability to ask for an investment. This phase of the Hook involves inviting the user to do a bit of work to personalize the experience. By asking the user to add some effort into the app, the product increases in value with use, getting better the more the user commits to it. Investments are actions that increase the likelihood of the next pass through the Hook by loading the next trigger, storing value, and creating preference for using the product. It is important that the four phases of the Hook are followed in sequential order for maximum impact.

Every time the user exercises with a Nike app or body monitor, he accrues a history of performance. The product becomes his digital logbook, which becomes more valuable as a way of tracking progress the more entries he makes. Additionally, each purchase of a Nike+ device—like a FuelBand, for example—is a further financial and psychological investment in the ecosystem.

While not yet a feature of the Nike app, other exercise training apps, like Strava, allow athletes to follow other athletes to compare performance. The action of selecting and following other users is a form of investment; it improves the product experience with use and increases the user's likelihood of using the product again.

In the future, products like Nike+ could automatically collect information from multiple touchpoints to create an individualized workout plan. The product could improve and adapt the more the user invests in using it.

AN ENGAGEMENT ADVANTAGE

For multi-interface products that rely upon repeated user engagement, understanding the fundamentals of engagement is critical. By following the Hook framework of a trigger, an action, a reward, and finally an investment, product designers can ensure they have the requisite components of a habit-forming technology.

By building products that follow users throughout their day, on smartphones, tablets, and, more recently, wearable devices, companies have an opportunity to cycle users through the four phases of the Hook more frequently and increase the odds of creating products people can't put down.

Integrated Approaches: A Fresh Look at New Examples

Let's now examine two fresh product examples that will give us new insights into how design approaches can be integrated. Additionally, these product ecosystems go beyond just the core devices, setting the scene for the next chapter, which expands multi-device experiences into the world of the Internet of Things, where any physical object (from the lights in your home to your sneakers, from roads to gas meters) can connect to the Internet and be part of a networked environment.

COMPLEMENTARY AND CONSISTENT: WITHINGS SMART BABY MONITOR

The Withings Smart Baby Monitor (Figure 5-9) lets parents keep an eye on their baby remotely, wirelessly, via a mobile device. The ecosystem is composed of the following components:

- A smart monitor device—WiFi enabled and camera equipped—that can be attached to the crib rail with a clip. It not only tracks the baby's movements and sounds, but also measures the temperature and humidity of the room.

- A set of compatible mobile devices (Android device, iPhone, iPad, and iPod touch) that can connect to the monitor and interact with it remotely.

These devices offer multiple alternative touchpoints for communicating with the smart monitor device, providing the same features and thus contributing to the consistent part of the experience.

FIGURE 5-9

The Withings Smart Baby Monitor system, demonstrating consistency among the mobile devices, which control the monitor device.

The main interaction between the smart monitor and any of the mobile devices is complementary by design. The monitor device serves as a "second pair of eyes," monitoring the baby at all times, from anywhere (as long as it's connected to the Internet). The mobile device provides a remote panel to view and control what the smart monitor captures. This video recorder captures both audio and high-resolution video (complete with pan, tilt, and zoom functions), including a special night-vision mode. In addition, parents can talk to their baby through the system using the mobile device, play a preloaded lullaby remotely, and even turn on a nightlight.

Not only that, but even while closed, the app continues running in the background, so users can either keep it in nonstop listening mode or rely on alerts that can be set for crying, sleep disruptions, extensive fidgeting or motion, or even changes in room temperature and humidity. This background activity is a powerful one—as you will also see in the Square example in the next chapter—because it signifies the first step toward truly seamless experiences, where no user intervention is needed in order to trigger the right thing, at the right time.

Smart contextual triggers initiate the relevant actions, establishing a more streamlined experience on the users' part and releasing them from having to allocate cognitive resources (attention, memory) for these tasks.

COMPLEMENTARY AND CONSISTENT: BITPONICS

Bitponics (Figure 5-10) is a Kickstarter-funded startup that offers a complete, cloud-based, hydroponic garden ecosystem, demonstrating an innovative way to help people keep their plants alive, healthy, and blooming.

FIGURE 5-10
How Bitponics works (source: Bitponics.com).

Bitponics simplifies and automates the plant's growing process through a set of sensors and automated accessories that continuously monitor and adjust the garden's environment (gathering data like the pH level of the soil, temperature, and light and moisture levels). These are directly powered by the Bitponics Base Station, which is connected to the WiFi network. The data is then presented in a web-based dashboard that's accessible anywhere, from any connected device, and can control every aspect of the garden environment, as well as sending alerts whenever sensor data deviates from the plan and an action is required (see Figure 5-11).

FIGURE 5-11
A view of the Bitponics
ecosystem in action.

In addition, the product integrates a social layer through the ability to share plant care tips, plans, and results with the Bitponics community of growers, building a knowledge center for growing plants (and pains).

Similarly to the Withings Smart Baby Monitor, the multi-device experience combines:

Complementary design

> The main experience part allows people to control any aspect of the garden environment (pH level, temperature, light, and more) via the complementary relationship between the core devices and the base station. Additionally, alerts are sent whenever sensor data deviates from the plan and an action is required.

Consistent design

> Bitponics incorporates consistent design by offering access to the plant ecosystem dashboard via any of the core devices (mobile, tablet, PC).

WHEN COMPLEMENTARY AND CONSISTENT DESIGN MEET

Looking across the different examples of ecosystems that offer complementary and consistent integration (Slingbox, IntoNow, Xbox SmartGlass, Withings Smart Baby Monitor, Bitponics, and others), we see a clear design pattern emerge in constructing these experiences:

- There's a single main device (TV or smart monitor) being complemented remotely by other devices, like the TV being controlled by the smartphone.

- Those other devices (smartphone, tablet, PC) have a consistent design applied across all of them, enabling each one to be the controlling or second-screen device. In other words, consistency is used to provide multiple access points to the main complementary interaction.

- In most cases, several devices can complement the main one at the same time, providing access for multiple actors to the main device. One main use case is social—enabling multiple people to engage in an activity as a group (either with all of them in the same room, or remotely). Another use case can be to simply share the experience with others—not necessarily synchronously. The Withings Smart Baby Monitor, for example, offers multiple account support, which allows parents, grandparents, and the nanny to all monitor the baby, each from their own device. In addition, access can be shared with family from afar, giving them the opportunity to see the baby more often.

This repeated pattern demonstrates a clear, useful way to address integrated design approaches involving complementarity and consistency. As ecosystems advance and expand to more devices (as discussed in the next chapters), you can think of ways (and reasons) to contextualize the experience even between the collaborating devices, so they're not all following the same design. As a starting point, though, using the aforementioned framework of relationships is an effective reference.

Question to the Reader

Can you think of ways that integrating complementary and consistent design approaches can take a different form?

A good way to approach this is to think about cases where the different complementary devices need to (or can) play different roles in the multi-device experience (rather than serving as merely alternative access points). Try to explore, for example, whether in such cases consistency can be implemented only for specific portions of the experience, while the rest is customized per context.

Summary

- Multi-device experiences are often composed of more than a single design approach. The 3Cs should be regarded as building blocks, useful to you in constructing experiences that best fit your users.

- Integrating approaches enables you to support more diverse and granular use cases, within varying contexts, and offer your users a richer experience adapted to context. Such integration also provides more flexibility in supporting the constantly developing and changing behavior patterns—which characterize the early stage we're in—around multi-device experiences.

- Integrated approaches can also be used to mitigate the challenge of users not having all the ecosystem devices (i.e., the integration between complementary and consistent approaches, as seen in products like Hulu Plus, Xbox SmartGlass, and the Withings Smart Baby Monitor).

- When approaching multi-device experience design, start by answering these questions:

  - What are the *users' needs and goals* that this product ecosystem tries to address?

  - What are the *main flows and use contexts* involved in this product ecosystem?

  - Which *experience approaches* can best accommodate these needs within each flow, and between use contexts?

  - Which *devices* should be used, and what are their roles in each context?

- Articulating to users the ecosystem narrative is very important in order to help them understand how your multi-device experience advances them toward their goals. This requires you to find the right balance between defining a clear role for each device in the experience ensemble, and refraining from doing that in a rigid, straining manner that leaves no room for variation, diversity, and exploration.

NOTES

1. *Things* as in the *Internet of Things*: the idea that any object—from smartphones, fridges, and cars to animals or people—can connect to the Internet (and thus to one another), transfer data, and interact in a seamless, transparent way.

2. See, for example: Kit Eaton, "The iPad Mini Will Be Bad for Your Kids. Discuss," *Fast Company*, October 16, 2012, *http://bit.ly/1jiHqiK*; Philippa Roxby, "Does Technology Hinder or Help Toddlers' Learning?" *BBC News*, April 19, 2013, *http://bbc.in/1hlLwlJ*; Nick Bilton, "The Child, the Tablet and the Developing Mind," *The New York Times Bits*, March 31, 2013, *http://nyti.ms/1cRs6Ef*.

3. *http://www.slingbox.com/go/products*

[6]

Beyond the Core Devices

This chapter expands the 3Cs framework beyond the four core devices into the realm of the Internet of Things. We'll look at even broader user scenarios in which the 3Cs—consistent, continuous, and complementary—can be applied, across the physical and digital spheres, in an ecosystem of fully connected devices.

Up until now we've established the foundations of multi-device experiences by focusing on the nuclear family of devices, comprising the four core members: smartphone, tablet, PC, and TV. We explored each of the design approaches and saw that in many cases, the experiences these devices create together involve multiple approaches that intertwine to strengthen and expand the scope of use cases.

Now it's time to look beyond those devices and at the grand scale of (the Internet of) things.

The Internet of Things

As powerful as the Internet seems today—with always-on WiFi at home, and mobile broadband connections standard in many mobile devices—the true power of the Internet is yet to be realized.

Consider this: the Internet today connects anywhere from 10 to 15 billion devices.[1] That is *six times* the number of people connected to the Internet. Yet that figure still represents less than 1% of the 1.5 trillion things that have the capacity to be connected to the Internet (see Figure 6-1).

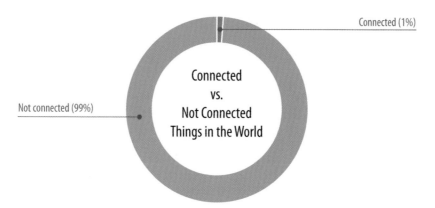

FIGURE 6-1

The share of connected vs. not connected things in the world (source: Cisco).

From an individual perspective, this means there are approximately 200 connectable things per person in the world today, with 99% remaining unconnected. These *things* can be any physical objects, from home appliances and medical devices, to roads and bridges, to toasters, coffee machines, and milk cartons, and even microchipped pets—and people. It's the Internet connection that defines a *thing* being part of this system: anything that can be networked (through embedded RFID chips, barcodes, sensors, or other means) can become part of the grand ecosystem of things that have the power to transform our daily lives.

The phrase *Internet of Things* (IoT) was coined by Kevin Ashton back in 1999. It expresses the following idea:

> Today computers—and, therefore, the Internet—are almost wholly dependent on human beings for information... If we had computers that knew everything there was to know about things—using data they gathered without any help from us—we would be able to track and count everything, and greatly reduce waste, loss, and cost. We would know when things needed replacing, repairing, or recalling, and whether they were fresh or past their best. The Internet of Things has the potential to change the world, just as the Internet did. Maybe even more so.[2]

The IoT is also described by some as one step on the path to the *Internet of Everything* (IoE; see Figure 6-2), which:

...brings together people, process, data, and things to make networked connections more relevant and valuable than ever before—turning information into actions that create new capabilities, richer experiences, and unprecedented economic opportunity for businesses, individuals, and countries.[3]

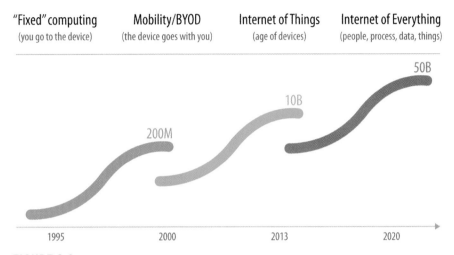

"Fixed" computing (you go to the device) | Mobility/BYOD (the device goes with you) | Internet of Things (age of devices) | Internet of Everything (people, process, data, things)

200M · 10B · 50B

1995 · 2000 · 2013 · 2020

FIGURE 6-2

Growth of the number of things connected to the Internet (source: Cisco).

The IoT and IoE do not seem to be significantly different concepts. They both refer to the combination of things, people, and data—along with the processes required to integrate them intelligently, and in a way that is meaningful and valuable to us as a society. As IoT is still the more common term used to describe these notions of a connected world, I'll use it going forward.

Is the Internet of Things Already Here?

If you look around, you will see that the IoT is no longer a futuristic notion found in the science fiction genre. It has already begun, and is already gradually entering our lives and our homes. And it spreads beyond those bounds.

In this chapter, we'll walk through a set of examples that show the first signs of ecosystem experiences in a networked world, where any device can be connected—to the Internet and to other devices. These examples are important for a few reasons:

Knowledge

The more we know about the IoT, both in theory and practice, the sooner and more easily we can control, shape, and anticipate what's coming next.

Inspiration

It's almost impossible at this point to imagine what a "smart" world—where everything is connected and able to interact anytime, anywhere—could even look like. But we can try to approach it by breaking the question down into smaller bites that are easier to digest, and build upon that foundation. Simple, clear, and powerful examples help make highly complex notions more tangible and accessible, and serve as a mental springboard for jumping even higher. As you will see, those bite-size examples already provide a broad canvas for creativity and innovation, and demonstrate the vast potential embodied in a connected world.

Toolbox

This book aims not only to inform you about the future, but also to provide you with a useful set of tools to work your way there. The 3Cs framework that has been instrumental in approaching multi-device experiences so far will continue to serve us as our ecosystems evolve past the four core devices. In essence, *people's core needs, goals, and task models do not change as a function of the number of available devices.* The consistent, complementary, and continuous building blocks remain the core components of our experiences. At the same time, given the diversity of things entering the space, we need to enhance our 3Cs framework with a few more accessories that support the new types of connections we now face.

Expanding the 3Cs

The IoT stretches the multi-device notion into a new world of connected things, expanding our family of devices to include a diversified range of gadgets, appliances, and accessories of any shape, size, or form factor. These devices are not necessarily equipped with a screen or computing power. To continue the LEGO analogy from Chapter 5, we now have a new array of LEGO bricks, gears, and various other parts that get added to the playground. Accordingly, they introduce new ways to assemble an ecosystem experience and interact with it.

We still need the oxygen flow provided by the wireless connection, transferring data between things across all experiences. But we can augment these digital connections with physical ones. Things can be physically attached or plugged into other things, and by doing so we augment their capabilities in various ways.

In this new playground, an ecosystem experience doesn't necessarily need to incorporate *any* of our core devices. However, as you will soon see, most of them still do—especially the smartphone, as the one device that most people carry with them everywhere (see Table 6-1).

TABLE 6-1. Comparison between ecosystem experiences based on core devices versus Internet of Things

	CORE DEVICES	INTERNET OF THINGS
Things (What can we play with?)	Smartphone, tablet, PC, TV	Smartphone, tablet, PC, TV, wearables, appliances, accessories, and other things
Device communication (How do they play together?)	Digital (WiFi, Bluetooth)	Digital, physical
Device relationships (How do they relate to each other?)	Consistent, continuous, complementary	Consistent, continuous, complementary

Table 6-1 will guide us through the variety of examples in this chapter, where we will see how multi-device experiences can be approached in very diverse ways in a connected world. These examples are ones I find compelling in terms of creativity, innovation, design thinking, and value offering—and they carry broader design insights from which we can learn.

For each example, I will introduce the product objectives, describe the ecosystem experience design, and then discuss the main design takeaways.

ADAPTIVE DESIGN: NEST—THE LEARNING THERMOSTAT

Nest (Figure 6-3) is *the* most beautiful thermostat you've ever seen. What makes it absolutely spectacular is the fact that it doesn't just have the looks: it also has the brains. A Nest thermostat "learns" the temperature change patterns over time and automatically programs itself accordingly, so people don't need to remember to do that (or get frustrated when they forget). Consequently, it saves energy and can lower heating and cooling costs to boot.

Users can also control the Nest thermostat remotely with any of the core devices (smartphone, tablet, or PC): turn it on or off, change the temperature, and access other settings (see Figure 6-4). In addition, Nest provides a detailed energy usage history (data it collects anyway as part of the learning process), so people can stay informed and in control of their use patterns.

The ecosystem experience

THINGS	Home appliance, electronic devices (smartphone, tablet, PC)
DEVICE COMMUNICATION	Digital
DEVICE RELATIONSHIPS	Complementary and consistent

As you've probably noticed, Nest combines the following two approaches in its design:

- *Complementary design*, which establishes the connection between the thermostat and the smartphone, tablet, or computer so people can control it remotely.

- *Consistent design*, which is incorporated through Nest's having three devices—PC, tablet, and smartphone—that offer the same experience design, serving as substitute devices. These devices enable people to engage in the complementary flow in a variety of contexts, at home as well as on the go.

Design lesson: The control relationship between devices is not bound to the TV

Up until now, we've discussed only *TV-based* ecosystems that utilize a control relationship between devices. Adding Nest to the mix highlights the idea that essentially *any product that is already operated by remote control* (or can benefit from having one) is a promising candidate for a complementary ecosystem. Just replace the traditional remote control with a smart device (mainly the smartphone), build an app for that, and—ta-da!—a new ecosystem is born. The Phillips smart lighting product HUE—"personal, wireless lighting"—is another example of a nontelevision ecosystem, in which users manipulate the intensity and color of the lighting in their environment (and what time the lights go on) from a phone or tablet once they've installed the lighting in their homes and the app on their handheld devices.

Design lesson: Extracting (actionable) knowledge from data

Nest is an example of a product that relies on *adaptive design*, in which a system "gets to know" its users over time—collecting and analyzing data about users' behavior patterns, preferences, actions, and contexts of use. Then, based on the intelligence extracted, it can adapt itself accordingly, tailoring the experience and refining it continuously to fit a specific user's needs across contexts. This context awareness, along with progressive learning, is a key part of the IoT vision; this approach reflects an important leap from merely collecting raw data across devices to extracting useful information out of it, so that the system can act upon it and empower people to perform better on life's stage.

While the next chapter will discuss data collection and analysis in a multi-device world, which is an important challenge on its own, it's important to remember that data is just a means to the goal. The Holy Grail lies in making that data *actionable* for people, preferably in an intelligent and seamless way, so that it actively helps them achieve their goals. Nest is a good example of a product experience that goes that extra mile—from just informing users with its data, to using that data behind the scenes to fuel the product behavior in an adaptive, contextual manner.

AUGMENTING THE SMARTPHONE: BIKN

BiKN (Figure 6-5) is a product ecosystem aimed at helping people find their stuff using the iPhone, and vice versa. It includes an iPhone smartcase that pairs wirelessly with a set of keyring-size tags that can be attached to things people lose frequently (or are just terrified of losing). All of that is wrapped in a mobile app that interfaces among all the devices.

FIGURE 6-5

The BiKN ecosystem of devices, comprising a smartphone (with the BiKN app), a smartcase, and a set of connected tags.

The most obvious use case for this product is finding lost keys or a purse, where the app can lead the user directly to the location of the tagged objects. Another scenario might be getting an alert if a tagged dog or cat wanders beyond a certain distance limit the user has set—a helpful way to make sure a pet doesn't leave the back yard, for example. BiKN can also work the other way around, helping users track down their phones using the tags. If she misplaces her phone, a user can simply page its case using any of the tags, and it will respond, even if the phone is off or out of battery.

The ecosystem experience

THINGS	Smartphone, accessory (smartcase), electronic tags
DEVICE COMMUNICATION	Digital, physical
DEVICE RELATIONSHIPS	Complementary

The ecosystem BiKN has established demonstrates a complementary experience, which involves several new aspects we haven't seen so far:

Bidirectional control

> The control flow between the devices is *bidirectional*: the phone can page the tags and lead people to their locations, and each tag can also page the phone and help locate it.

> If you revisit all the control-based ecosystems we've discussed so far, you'll notice that there was a very clear, one-directional power relation between the device that controls (a mobile device—smartphone or tablet) and the device being controlled (a stationary device—TV, thermostat).

> BiKN chose to approach things differently—a design decision that reflects careful use case analysis, with a dose of creativity. Think about it: many of the reasons that make the smartphone so suitable as an ecosystem locator (e.g., being always on, its small size and mobility) also make it one of the things we are most terrified of losing—but it's easily done. Furthermore, it follows Murphy's law: when someone does lose his phone, it's going to be when the device is on silent or shut down, and it's that much harder to find. BiKN's approach introduces a new application of complementary design, emphasizing the importance of using the framework approaches

as building blocks. The way you put them together depends on the use cases at hand and the way devices relate to one another in your product context.

Physical and digital communication

Until now, the complementary relationships discussed were established through wireless connection (usually WiFi). However, a multi-device experience doesn't have to be bound to that. BiKN shows how an ecosystem can combine physical connections between devices (smartphone and smartcase) and wireless communication (smartcase and tags). Both types of connections are essential for the overall experience.

Design lesson: Augmenting device capabilities with hardware accessories

BiKN is the first example we've examined so far that involves augmenting the smartphone with hardware accessories (in this case, a smartcase), enhancing its capabilities as a smart device. So far we've seen only examples that relied on software to do that (like turning the smartphone into a remote control through an app). Introducing hardware accessories to the ecosystem significantly expands what we can do with the existing devices in play, giving them new "powers" that serve people in new contexts. In some cases, we can practically converge multiple separate devices (as we know them today) into a single device that provides all the required functionality in a modular way. (Our next example, Square, will demonstrate that configuration by turning a smartphone or tablet into a cash register.)

In that respect, what is especially clever in the way BiKN designed its ecosystem is how it integrated its technology into a phone case—an accessory that most (if not all) iPhone users already put on their phones. This smartcase provides the basic device protection all cases do, but at the same time it augments the phone's capabilities by turning it into a "lost items detector." BiKN therefore taps into an already established habit among users, significantly reducing the learning curve involved in the assembly process, as well as omitting the need for users to carry around yet another piece of hardware.

RETHINKING USER BEHAVIORS: SQUARE

Square (Figure 6-6) is another great example of how product designers can augment the phone, giving it new capabilities that build upon its existing strength as an always-on smart device. The product ecosystem is based on a little plastic square device—a credit card reader—that can easily plug into phones or tablets and turn them into cash registers on the fly. This enables small businesses to utilize their existing devices for credit card payments (and it has much lower transaction fees compared to credit card companies).

This modularity in ecosystem composition saves a lot of the resources, complexity, and electronic waste involved in building and maintaining more and more proprietary systems that are made up of dedicated sets of devices—all of which involve separate infrastructures and work processes.

FIGURE 6-6

Square demonstrated on the iPhone—the device is plugged into the headphone jack, turning the smartphone into a cashier on the fly.

The ecosystem experience

THINGS	Accessory (reader), electronic devices (smartphone, tablet)
DEVICE COMMUNICATION	Digital, physical
DEVICE RELATIONSHIPS	Complementary, continuous, consistent

As with BiKN, the core ecosystem experience is a complementary one—the Square accessory complements the smartphone or tablet by augmenting it with credit card processing capabilities. Consistency comes into play with the smartphone and tablet serving as alternative devices; either can have the Square plug into them, and the app design is the same for both.

But Square goes much further than just addressing business owners' needs. It also streamlines the payment process for consumers. A year after launching the Square ecosystem for small businesses, Square extended its product narrative to the consumer experience, offering a fluent continuous experience for purchases. Square's iPhone app, Card Case, completely streamlines the sequence of activities involved in paying at the cashier (Figure 6-7).

FIGURE 6-7
Square's Card Case iPhone app, handling the consumer side of the payment process.

Traditionally, when people want to buy something, they go into a store, choose what they want, and proceed to the cashier. At that point, they need to open their bag and/or reach for their wallet, take it out, decide how they want to pay, and possibly sign, swipe, or wait for change.

Square changes all of that. With the Card Case app, as long as users have their smartphones nearby, they only need to tell the cashiers their names. They don't need to pull out their phones, or even open the app, because Card Case works in the background to authorize the payment (leveraging Apple's geofencing technology) and then sends a receipt to the phone. That's it! All paid and done.

Design lesson: The power of technology in enforcing naïvete

We saw in Chapter 3 how we can reinvent cooking by adapting the multi-device experience as users step through their activity flows. Square now further demonstrates that even the payment process can be disrupted, changing completely the user flows that have dominated for years—for both sellers and buyers.

One of the most powerful aspects I see in all the new technology and connected devices we have available is the way they enforce naïveté. The ability to step back, look at the world around us with fresh eyes, and challenge existing premises in a naïve way—like kids who keep asking "but why?"—is key to identifying opportunities for change. Especially with technology enabling us today, much more than before, to follow them through—disrupt the current state of things, reinvent user experiences, simply flows, clear out friction points, and make people's lives better, easier, and more productive.

Discussion: The Quantified Self Movement

An increasingly popular IoT realm today is the *Quantified Self movement.*

This term was first coined in 2007 by *Wired Magazine* editors Gary Wolf and Kevin Kelly, and refers to building self-knowledge (as a basis for self-change) through tracking and analyzing data about one's daily life. The growing availability of consumer wearable technologies (like watches, body sensors, activity trackers, and other data-emitting tools), which seamlessly collect people's data and make it accessible to them, plays an important role in promoting this movement. The most popular application of Quantified Self today is in the realm of health and fitness (Figure 6-8), which includes a plethora of product ecosystems, such as Fitbit, Jawbone, Nike+, BodyMedia, and LUMOback.

These devices collect data about people's bodies and physical activities, such as exercise time, distance and pace, sleep patterns, posture and movement, body temperature, pulse, and blood pressure and other physiological signals. Then, through a corresponding app or website, the data is synced, analyzed, and presented in a dashboard for them to use.

FIGURE 6-8

A selection of popular fitness trackers (from left to right): UP (by Jawbone), NikeFuel (by Nike), and Flex (by Fitbit).

The question that often arises, though, is *what now*?

How can we make this data actionable for people, encouraging them to make the leap from *self-measurement* to *self-change*?

Right now, people are getting continuous data flows about themselves (which can quickly become quite massive, depending on the extent to which they're quantifying themselves), yet it's not always clear how to make sense out of that data, let alone act on it. Walking 4,738 steps today versus 4,512 yesterday versus 5,038 the day before—is that good? Should they do better? Does it affect anything? And how long can people keep it up? This problem intensifies when the self-data collection is done from different products, each providing its own data set, sometimes using proprietary measurement units that are incompatible.

Don't get me wrong: collecting more self-data increases self-awareness, which is a first important step to self-change. Self-awareness empowers people to make better, more informed decisions about their choices and daily activities. However, the distance from *having the information* to *taking actions*, consistently, is pretty damn long. To help people make that leap, we need to design our products in a way that extracts meaningful knowledge and insights from the raw data, and uses that intelligently to encourage people to make (even) small behavior changes. Over time, these small changes add up to big improvements in overall health. Furthermore, when done right, these little changes progressively shift from a sequence of ad hoc, conscious decisions to continuous, stable life habits.

To help you get started, there are three key design guidelines that promote turning data into actions: good metrics, right-on-time notifications, and social motivators. Remember, though, that this is only one aspect of designing for behavioral change.[4] There's a broad range of affective, cognitive, behavioral, and social factors that are involved in this process, and should be researched and incorporated into the product design.

USE GOOD METRICS

In their excellent book *Lean Analytics*,[5] Alistair Croll and Benjamin Yoskovitz define the key characteristics of a good metric, a definition that applies to self-analysis just as well as to product performance analysis:

Comparative

> Comparing a metric to other time periods (i.e., personal progress over time) or other people (i.e., a comparable reference group—an important social motivator) helps put results in perspective, and gives users better insights into which way they're moving. "You increased your calorie burn by 540 calories, or 15%," for example, is more meaningful than "You burned 1,730 calories."

Understandable

> A good metric needs to be clear and easy to understand; otherwise, it will be much harder for people to map a change in the metric into a change in behavior. Looking at NikeFuel points, for example, knowing that the user earned 438 points provides some information, but still leaves her in the dark about the exact meaning and impact. These points are also harder to remember and discuss with friends (as opposed to running 7.5 miles, for instance), especially if her friends are not part of the Nike+ ecosystem.

Ratio-based

Ratios are easier to act on, and they are inherently comparative. For example, a person knowing he ran 7.5 miles is a good piece of information. However, a better one would be that he ran it in 45 minutes, and thus had a speed of six miles per hour. This gives him a stronger reference point upon which he can act.

In addition, ratios allow people to draw connections between a flexible set of meaningful factors (even if they don't seem to be directly linked). Let's say, for example, that a user tracks her food intake, exercise, and mood. By looking at ratios, she can learn, for example, that starting the day with pastries makes her feel good for an hour, but then leads to grumpiness throughout the day, or that when she exercises in the afternoon she feels much more refreshed and energetic than when she works out in the morning. Such ratios can help people understand how their overall health, happiness, and well-being are affected by their daily life choices. These tangible connections between their actions and their emotional and cognitive states serve as stronger drivers for behavior change, as they shift the motivation from *have to* change behavior (which is often perceived as a punishment that people look for ways to avoid) to *want to* make different choices, as these changes lead directly to a much better feeling.

Drives behavior change

The most important criterion for a good metric is whether people can easily answer the question: *what will I do differently based on changes in the metric?* (Preferably, having the answer drive the *desired* behavior change.) One example is the ratio indicated previously that correlates "dry" metrics with mood and feelings. It's clear that if someone sees that pastries make her grumpy all day, she should change her breakfast to something that doesn't carry that emotional effect. Another way to go about it is to have the user set her main goal (lose five pounds in two months, for instance) and derive a good metric or metrics from that, in a way that clearly associates improvement in the metric to getting her closer to her goal (correlating food intake, calories burned, exercise schedule, etc.). Note that goals can and should change over time, as the user progressively improves or reaches the initial goal set.

SET UP EFFECTIVE ALERTS AND NOTIFICATIONS

You've built an effective dashboard with good metrics—great! You have the basis set up. However, the main drawback of the dashboard is that it requires user action to get to it. Users need to actively look for the app or browse to the website, sign in, and use it.

With the app overload problem people already face (a topic I discuss in Chapter 8), they can easily forget or lose sight of your app (especially if it's not placed in the default home screen) and miss out on all those good metrics. That's where a smart ecosystem notification mechanism can come in handy:

Notifications in the activity tracker/sensor
> Triggering important activity alerts or notifications on the tracker can be very effective as an ongoing feedback mechanism. The main advantage is the real-time trigger initiation, taking place when the relevant event occurs and allowing for an immediate action in response. Events can be, for example, slipping on desired behavior, reaching the daily goal, running out of battery power, or triggering manual alerts set by the user. LUMOback's posture sensor provides, for example, a gentle vibration when the user slouches to remind him to sit or stand straight. The Jawbone UP allows people to set the band to vibrate when they haven't moved for a certain amount of time.

> Aside from vibration feedback, most trackers also incorporate a small display area, which communicates visually (possibly aurally as well) the activity status and other alerts. The Nike+ FuelBand, for instance, displays the current and goal fuel points on the device, along with a visual progress bar. Similarly, the Fitbit uses a thin bar of lights to convey how people stack up against their personal goals. Both light up excitedly when the daily goal is reached.

Notifications in the complementary devices (smartphone, tablet, PC)
> Notifications can be sent to complementary devices as well, as a teaser to encourage users to log into the app and access the dashboard and other features it offers. The types of notifications that usually fit these devices are:

> • Secondary alerts about app activity, like friends joining the app, messages received, new feature announcements, etc.

- Special accomplishment notifications. While the wearable tracker is real-time-focused, the complementary device can promote accumulated milestones over time, adding a different flavor to the experience. This way, notifications like "Congrats, you've just reached 450 miles—the walking distance from San Francisco to Los Angeles!" can be a fun encouragement from time to time.

- Recurring activity summaries. Notifications can also be sent in a predictable schedule, such as a "weekly summary" every Friday morning, with aggregated metrics from the past week. These summaries can be integrated as a system notification or sent via email.

In any case, whichever notification strategy you assemble, make sure you keep in mind two important principles:

- **Don't overload.** It's important to be mindful about the number and frequency of notifications you send people, so that you don't overload them. When people get overwhelmed with too many notifications and alerts, or too much information in general, they struggle to digest it all and make a decision, and often simply start ignoring the feedback. Remember that every beep, every vibration, every red circle, every update in the notification bar is an interruption. Also, you're not the only product sending alerts to users, so try to play responsibly with their attention span and, well, sanity.

- **Think holistically.** Plan your notification strategy from an ecosystem perspective, considering the cross-device flow. This means that alerts sent to the activity tracker shouldn't be broadcasted to all the other devices, unless you identify a very specific event that justifies it—for example, an exceptional goal achievement that deserves an ecosystem celebration. Or, if the sensor is worn on the body in an area that is not easily visible (like the ankle or the back), it might make sense to send a low-battery alert to the smartphone as well (at least at the beginning, until users learn the tracker feedback model).

As a general rule of thumb, notifications that have been accessed on one of the complementary devices (like the smartphone) should be marked as viewed across the other devices as well (tablet, PC), preserving a continuous, seamless flow across devices. There are a few exceptions to this rule, but they apply to different types of ecosystems that I discuss later in the book.

BUILD SOCIAL PILLARS

When it comes to people changing daily life habits, such as health and fitness, social connections can facilitate the change and supply important motivation that enhances ongoing activity. Beyond simple integrations into popular social networks, building an active community of people around the product core, who are committed to the same goals, helps form a culture of active participation.[6] Community members also serve as a source of knowledge, advice, inspiration, support, encouragement, praise, social acceptance, and recognition. On the data side, collecting information on community members and their activity, as well as the ongoing social engagements between them, feeds the system with an important flow of data. This data can continuously improve the system learning, analysis, recommendations, adaptive behavior, and personalization, leading to a better experience overall.

Nike+, Fitbit, RunKeeper, and Fitocracy are some fitness ecosystems that are doing a really good job of keeping the community alive and running. It is worth checking them out, and experiencing firsthand their multi-layered social design and gamification mechanisms. Specifically, Nike+ leads a lot of the innovation in this area, investing a lot of thought and creativity in weaving social motivators along the entire user journey—before, during, and after runs. One clever example is the "Cheer me" feature: during a run, the Nike+ Running app automatically posts a status update on the user's behalf on Facebook (or Path). Each time a friend likes or comments on this status update, the runner hears a stadium crowd cheering as part of the in-run feedback. If you think back to Chapter 3, this design follows one of the key processes of the 3Cs approach: (1) break down the use case to its atomic particles, (2) analyze each different step along the flow, (3) find the relevant contexts where the experience can be optimized, and (4) Just Do It!

INTEGRATED MULTI-DEVICE EXPERIENCES: NIKE+

I've mentioned Nike+ occasionally in this book, but would like to take the time now to take a deeper look at this ecosystem. Why?

First, Nike is one of the strongest pioneers in leveraging this era of connectivity. It's established an innovative ecosystem around promoting a more active athletic lifestyle, which offers a rich, personalized experience distributed across a variety of devices. Its work in the field is groundbreaking and serves as a powerful reference from which we can learn.

Second, it integrates several multi-device experiences that are intertwined. As a result, its overall ecosystem is quite complex—made up of many flows, devices, and contexts. This not only makes it interesting to analyze, but also highlights well the benefit of approaching it through the 3Cs framework.

Finally, this ecosystem expands beyond just Nike+, offering integrations with other ecosystems and together creating an even stronger value offering. Exploring these partnerships exposes new growth opportunities for products as a way to scale and gain more traction in this connected world.

The ecosystem experience

THINGS	Wearable devices (watch, band, shoes), accessories (sensors), electronic devices (smartphone, tablet, PC, media player, game console)
DEVICE COMMUNICATION	Digital, physical
DEVICE RELATIONSHIPS	Complementary, continuous, consistent

Central to the Nike+ ecosystem are a few underlying elements:

NikeFuel

> This is a newly created fitness metric by Nike, based on the rate of oxygen consumption and motion. It counts all the activities of a user's athletic life and is calculated the same way for everyone, designed to be comparable across the Nike+ community.

NikePlus.com

> The online hub for all Nike+ activity. All the user's workout data is synced with her account on the site, so she can track all her activities and compare her results over time, set personal goals, share results with friends, and more. Because it is such a rich online hub (providing activity tracking reports, maps, and other types of analysis), it is mostly suited for bigger-screen displays like the PC or tablet.

Nike+ community

> Nike puts a lot of effort into establishing an active, dynamic community of athletes who can provide support, incentives, and guidance to help users keep up an active lifestyle. Nike does this mainly through NikePlus.com, which doesn't just serve as a personal platform to track all user activities, but also encourages people to feel

part of a bigger collective—sharing achievements with friends, comparing results with them, challenging them, getting recommendations, and more.

These notions rely on and are continuously fueled by the large set of devices and things Nike offers, which constantly grows (see Figure 6-9).

FIGURE 6-9
Nike+ ecosystem of devices, sensors, and apps.

While this richness is compelling and addresses many different needs and use cases, as someone interested in engaging with this Nike+ ecosystem, I found myself trying to figure out how these components work together as a system, and—more importantly—which one(s) fit my needs. I kept asking myself, what is the relationship between all these devices? Do I need all of them? Some of them? How do I choose? Where do I start?

In trying to figure that out, I found that Nike provides on its website the comparison table shown in Figure 6-10.

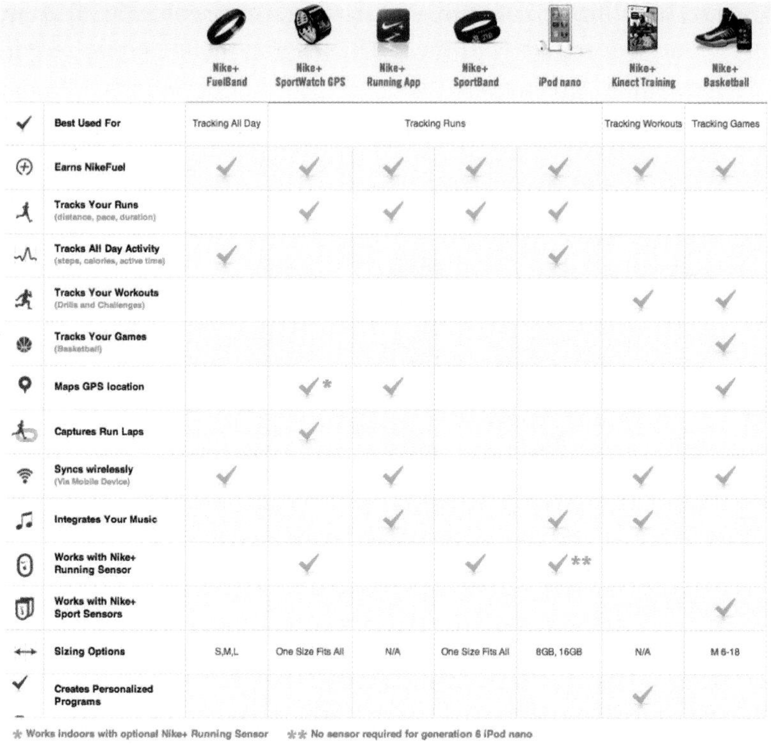

		Nike+ FuelBand	Nike+ SportWatch GPS	Nike+ Running App	Nike+ SportBand	iPod nano	Nike+ Kinect Training	Nike+ Basketball
✓	Best Used For	Tracking All Day	Tracking Runs				Tracking Workouts	Tracking Games
⊕	Earns NikeFuel	✓	✓	✓	✓	✓	✓	✓
🏃	Tracks Your Runs (distance, pace, duration)		✓	✓	✓	✓		
∿	Tracks All Day Activity (steps, calories, active time)	✓				✓		
🏃	Tracks Your Workouts (Drills and Challenges)						✓	✓
⦾	Tracks Your Games (Basketball)							✓
◉	Maps GPS location		✓ *	✓				✓
⚑	Captures Run Laps		✓					
📶	Syncs wirelessly (Via Mobile Device)	✓		✓			✓	✓
♫	Integrates Your Music			✓		✓	✓	
⊙	Works with Nike+ Running Sensor		✓		✓	✓ **		
⊡	Works with Nike+ Sport Sensors							✓
↔	Sizing Options	S,M,L	One Size Fits All	N/A	One Size Fits All	8GB, 16GB	N/A	M 6-18
✓	Creates Personalized Programs						✓	
—								

✻ Works indoors with optional Nike+ Running Sensor   ✻✻ No sensor required for generation 6 iPod nano

FIGURE 6-10

Comparison of Nike+ products (source: *http://nikeplus.nike.com/plus/products/*).

While this table provides a good, comprehensive overview of the different features Nike+ offers, I felt it still didn't give me a clear answer as to what would best fit my needs, and which devices I should get as a result, for these reasons:

- The overall amount of information is difficult to absorb, and the tabular organization makes it hard to synthesize the different factors.

- Some of the factors are very important to the initial decision-making step (screening what could be relevant for me, like what the device is best used for and what it tracks), while others seem secondary (too granular for this stage, or just no deal breakers that can come later in the process, like sizing options and personalized programs).

- I wasn't sure why some of the devices were at the top, while others were on the left with the software features. This split also made me wonder whether the sensors on the left are required with the other devices at the top, or are merely optional.

Using a flow diagram for mapping the multi-device ecosystem

This is where I put my UX hat on and looked at the 3Cs framework to see if I could use it to help clarify the relationships between devices and the different options in front of me. To do that, I drew a flow diagram. I find these useful in my work to look at ecosystems (especially complex ones) from a bird's-eye view, in order to map the main flows and connections, as shown in Figure 6-11.

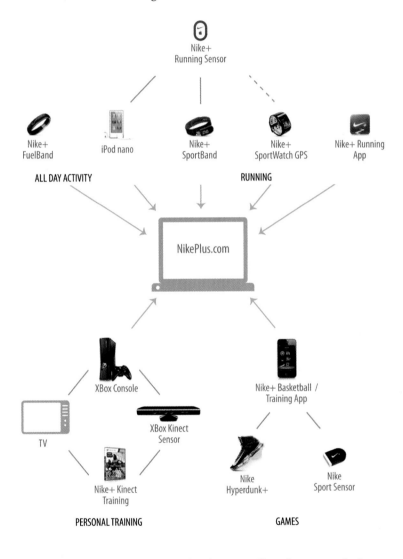

FIGURE 6-11

Flow diagram of Nike+ ecosystem, based on the 3Cs framework.

What do we see in this flow diagram?

- All the ecosystem components are included in the diagram.

- Orange lines indicate a complementary relationship between devices. Must-have and nice-to-have options are signified by solid lines and dashed lines, respectively.

- Green lines represent a continuous flow between devices. In this case, a directional arrow is added to indicate the transition flow between devices.

- Devices offering a consistent experience are not connected with lines, as they are separated from each other, serving as substitutes in a given context.

- When there's a clear context of use for a certain flow, it is conveyed through the grey strip, which frames the flow area.

Now, just like with the classic game *Chutes and Ladders*, any path you can navigate through—starting from the surrounding devices and progressing toward NikePlus.com—is an option to pursue. For example, if I'm into running (which I am), I can get the Nike+ Running Sensor, complemented by an iPod Nano. Alternatively, I can just download the Nike+ Running app (which doesn't require any additional devices—other than the smartphone, of course). A third option would be to buy the Nike+ Running Sensor, complemented by a Nike+ SportBand.

Through this diagram, you can clearly see the bigger-picture view of the ecosystem flow, as well as the universe of options in terms of the set of devices (and apps) that make up each ecosystem use case. Note that you also get useful insight into devices that are instrumental across multiple experience paths, which could indicate their role and overall weight in the ecosystem.

Joining forces

If you look at the bottom of the Nike+ flow diagram, you'll notice that there's an integration between two product ecosystems there: Nike+ and Kinect for Xbox 360.

These two players partnered together, creating an integrated complementary *Nike+ Kinect Training* experience that offers a new way to train indoors: Nike+ brings the training knowledge and fitness community,

while Kinect brings the motion analysis technology that allows personalized attention to users' form and movements while they're working
out in front of the TV (see Figure 6-12).

FIGURE 6-12

Nike+ Kinect Training, demonstrating how ecosystems can be integrated to
offer a larger pie rather than competing for the slices.

Such integration benefits all sides:

Nike+

> With Xbox integration the Nike+ ecosystem expands to include the
> TV and game console, attracting new audiences and creating more
> contextual touchpoints for existing users that can further foster
> use habits. The more people engage with Nike+ activities, and the
> more frequently, the more data flows into the Nike+ community,
> which can then be used to improve the experience and increase
> traction through a positive feedback loop.

Xbox

> Nike+ enriches the Xbox experience by extending the product's
> reach and offering beyond video games into sports and fitness.
> This could resonate with additional user groups, contexts, and
> scenarios—resulting in increased Xbox ecosystem activity and
> engagement. Furthermore, as with Nike+, additional use cases for

the Xbox mean more ways to connect to the product and more frequent use—all contributors to forming stronger habits around the Xbox product.

Consumers

The more integrated related experiences are, the more streamlined and frictionless people's daily flows are. Many barriers for adoption and ongoing use brought on by costs, complexity, setup, learning curve, and device or app overload are significantly reduced. Furthermore, such integrations that bring in new content and features to the product promote discoverability and serendipity among consumers—two aspects that are important to maintain people's interest and active participation.

Building a powerful ecosystem doesn't have to be something you do on your own. We saw the Amazon Kindle/Audible.com partnership in Chapter 2. This example of Nike+/Xbox further enhances the idea that ecosystem collaboration enables the parties involved to develop a product offering beyond what each could potentially do on its own (at least in terms of time and resources). In addition, consumers don't need to set up separate ecosystems for every need, or find themselves trapped by the manufacturer/platform constraint. They can progressively extend their existing multi-device systems to meet more needs and use cases.

This last point touches upon the challenge of *walled gardens* in a connected world—a topic discussed in more depth in Chapter 8.

WEARABLE-BASED EXPERIENCE: PEBBLE WATCH

The Pebble Watch is a smartwatch that was developed by Pebble Technology (Figure 6-13). The product was Kickstarter-funded and, remarkably, raised over $10.2 million through nearly 69,000 individual backers, officially breaking Kickstarter's records and the startup's own goals ($100,000, which was achieved within the first two hours)!

The Pebble Watch is based on epaper technology and uses Bluetooth to connect wirelessly to an iPhone or Android phone, alerting wearers about incoming calls, emails, and messages with a silent vibration. Additionally, the watch can be customized with downloadable watchfaces (changing the look and feel of the main screen), and simple Internet-connected apps for activities like cycling, running, and golf, which surface key activity data like speed, distance, and pace.

FIGURE 6-13

The Pebble epaper watch for iPhone and Android, alerting users about events like incoming calls, emails, and messages as they occur. The rest of the time, it functions like a regular wristwatch.

The ecosystem experience

THINGS	Wearable watch, smartphone
DEVICE COMMUNICATION	Digital
DEVICE RELATIONSHIPS	Consistent, continuous

From an experience design perspective, the Pebble Watch has a unique offering: it mainly relies on the content of the smartphone and selectively pulls in contextually relevant data, displaying the most important pieces on the watch face, with the rest in the phone.

This design approach supports both consistent and continuous flows. The watch replicates some of the smartphone functionality, serving as a substitute for it. For example, it provides the basic clock functionality (displaying time and date) and allows users to set an alarm. In this respect, it provides consistency.

In most cases, however, the watch doesn't really *replace* the smartphone, but rather acts as the starting point for a flow that *continues* onto the smartphone. By focusing on providing a simple, at-a-glance display for important data on the go, the Pebble Watch does triage for users, helping them decide whether they should take out the smartphone and continue the flow there (replying to the message, answering a phone call), or whether their response can wait for later (where the entire flow will be handled on the smartphone as well).

Design lesson: Focus, simplicity, context

Pebble demonstrates clear focus on the use cases where a smartwatch can really offer added value compared to the smartphone. The design is simple; it's not an effort to replace the smartphone, cramming loads of sophisticated functionality into a 144 × 168–pixel display. Rather, it works with the smartphone in a context-driven way to leverage each of the devices' strengths and build an overall better experience.

Having been a Pebble user for a long time, I find it very useful, and along the way I have experienced a few interesting behavior changes:

No more phone pecking (and much more peace of mind!)
> As I have many meetings during a typical workday, and I work in an open space environment, my phone is always on silent.

> Before I had a Pebble, I used to take out my phone and check it every few minutes, wondering if I'd missed any phone calls or text messages. This added up to probably hundreds of times a day pecking at the phone.

> With my Pebble, I now rely completely on the watch to notify me of an incoming call or text message. Thus, I don't take out my phone unless I want to take a specific action like checking updates on social networks, sending a message, searching on Google, taking a picture, and so on. This has reduced my microinteractions with the smartphone considerably, establishing a focused interaction pattern that is event- and action-triggered.

Connecting Pebble to emails didn't prove effective for me
> I connected my Pebble to my email account, thinking it would prove to be as beautifully useful as it is for calls and text messages. I was wrong.

> Why? Because once I connected the watch to my emails, it didn't stop buzzing on my wrist. With emails coming in every few minutes, the alerts' effectiveness turned from super-useful to almost useless for me. I was overloaded with notifications and could no longer distinguish between important and insignificant. Also, the

vibration effect itself is strong—which works well when it's triggered every couple of hours or so, but when it's nonstop, it becomes
unsustainable.

If I could set in Pebble specific email senders for whom I would
like to get alerts, I would probably turn the email feature back on.
Until then, I prefer it to be selective, focusing on calls and text
messages only (for me, these signify important events that usually
require immediate action).

Changing perception of costly actions

With Pebble playing triage, I found myself changing my attitude
toward basic smartphone actions I didn't give much thought to
before. Gradually, as I got used to simply looking at my wristwatch
to get the info I need instantly (like who just texted me and the content of the message), it became more demanding to follow the old
sequence of (1) taking out my phone, (2) unlocking it, (3) tapping
the incoming message notification, (4) getting to the app, and (5)
opening the message to read it.

An important advantage the smartwatch offers over smartphones
is privacy. While smartphones do provide the option to display
incoming messages on the lock screen (saving the aforementioned
action sequence), they also pose a privacy concern. Smartphone
screens are easily visible to people around you due to how and
where they are held, as well as their often being placed face up on
tables and desks. This, along with the (publicly) distracting incoming message alert—a sudden sound, the screen getting lit up—
makes your (private) messages readily accessible not only to you,
but also to those around you. With the Pebble Watch, the alert is private (vibrating quietly on your wrist), and together with the small
screen size, the bland display, and the watch position, it ensures
that you're the only one who can effectively read the messages.

If you think about it, this change is similar in many ways to the process we went through with text messaging. Before we had texting,
people contacted their friends and family by calling them. The call
action seemed to be the most natural and easiest way to directly
communicate. Once text messages caught on, a new communication space opened, progressively pushing calling further up in the

"perceived communication effort" scale. Since then, this space has filled up with even more channels, like emails and chats—all of which often precede picking up the phone and calling for users.

Question to the Reader

How would you imagine that other wearable devices (like Misfit Shine, Google Glass, and Plantronics smart headsets) could potentially change behavior?

Try to think about aspects like:

- The body part they're worn on, and what this means in terms of inter-action opportunities (and challenges)

- Functionalities and flows that are currently handled by other smart devices, but would benefit more from being integrated into a wearable

- Contexts of use where the wearable device is optimal for use and/or can better handle existing friction points (versus ones where other devices might be a better fit)

- Wearable with display versus without any, especially in terms of how that may impact relationships with other smart devices

- Relationships between multiple wearable devices used in parallel

TAPPING INTO SERVICE DESIGN: TESCO VIRTUAL SUPERMARKET

In 2011, Tesco built a virtual supermarket experience at a subway station in South Korea, all based on QR codes (Figure 6-14). A large, wall-length billboard installed in the station platform is designed to look like a series of supermarket shelves that display images and prices of a range of common products. Each sign also includes a QR code.

While waiting for the subway, travellers can scan the code of any product, thereby adding it to their online shopping cart. After the transaction is completed, the goods are delivered that day to the address provided.

FIGURE 6-14

Tesco virtual supermarket—on the right is the digital billboard installed in the train station, and on the left is a close-up view of the product scanning done through the mobile app.

The ecosystem experience

THINGS	QR code–based billboards, electronic devices (smartphone, tablet)
DEVICE COMMUNICATION	Digital, physical
DEVICE RELATIONSHIPS	Continuous

This ecosystem offers a new type of continuous experience that bridges the physical and digital spaces. The sequence of activities starts with the digital wall, which hosts all the products. Through QR code scanning, the user can select the desired items, which essentially passes along the experience into the smartphone, where the transaction itself is performed. Then, when the transaction is completed, the experience transitions back to the physical world through the delivery of groceries to the customer's home.

Design lesson: Identifying new contexts of use

This ecosystem design shows careful attention to an important context (waiting at the train station) that most of us don't even think about. We're so used to the given state of things (waiting for the train while doing nothing, playing with a smartphone, or reading a book) that when we do think about this context, we focus on which new smartphone game to build.

Tesco not only addressed the potential of this context in a new way, but also identified a real need that provided practical value to people: they could use their waiting time at the subway station to do their grocery shopping. By doing so, people save even more time by not having to make an extra stop at a grocery store on the way home.

This example joins a few others we've seen so far (like Allrecipes and Square) that highlight the importance of constantly observing existing user behaviors and pains, and rethinking the ways we can approach and solve them through design.

Design lesson: Stepping into service design

The multi-device experience Tesco designed not only connects walls with smartphones and physical with digital, but also makes the experience part of a bigger service design that includes the delivery and packaging processes.

As more and more things around us get connected—offering more touchpoints between companies and consumers, as well as enabling broader activities, processes, and data transfer—the need to adopt service design thinking will increase. Approaching the design problem from a service perspective—considering the time, place, people, technology, and processes that form the full experience along all touchpoints—will open up more opportunities for innovation and greater impact on people's lives.

Getting Creative with QR Codes

I have a confession to make: I don't like QR codes.

I absolutely love the idea of connecting the physical and the digital with a click, but I find the QR code way of doing it technical and disengaging.

It starts from the name itself—QR code—which is quite deterring, and continues right to the black-and-white-matrix barcode design. It's not very inviting to use, nor especially delightful to the eye, and it carries no indication whatsoever about its value proposition.

Then we get to the usability challenges.

First, users must download a dedicated QR scanning app—a significant barrier for adoption. What makes QR scanners even more confusing is that the user experience is very similar to taking a regular camera shot—an action people are used to doing many times a day, *through the camera app* (which is typically conveniently accessible in the main home screen of the phone). However, simply using the camera doesn't work in the case of QR codes. There are obviously technological issues involved, but it doesn't change the experience of the people using it.

Second, the app usage itself can get cumbersome at times. Users need to make sure the code is scanned from an appropriate distance and gets captured properly in the scanner frame—a process that often requires quite a few adjustments—making the overall experience somewhat clunky.

Finally, QR codes are limited in the actions they can trigger, and are usually used to send the user to a dedicated web page or to display more information about a person or business.

With that said, QR codes are very easy to make, print, and distribute, and thus you can find a lot of them out there—mostly in newspapers, magazines, brochures, and billboard advertisements. Their primary users are campaign managers aiming to accelerate conversion by minimizing the gap between seeing an ad offline and acting upon it. Other than that, QR codes replace traditional barcode systems for commercial tracking, entertainment and transport ticketing, and in-store product labeling.

In the current state of things, where there's no immediate substitute for the benefit QR codes provide in terms of connecting the offline and online, you might want to use them as another channel for interacting with your users. Still, this doesn't mean that you need to take them as is. With the right creative juice, even a heavily technology-driven implementation can become more colorful and fun. One exceptionally enticing use of QR codes that demonstrates this is Pizza Digitale, by Scholz & Friends Hamburg Recruiting (Figure 6-15).[7]

FIGURE 6-15

A special pizza, imprinted like a QR code, which directly links to a mobile landing page focused on hiring digital creatives for Scholz & Friends.

Pizza Digitale was a campaign run by Scholz & Friends with the goal of finding digital creatives for the agency. To achieve that, for a period of four weeks, the company sent a special QR code–imprinted pizza to every order from other major agencies' employees. Scanning this QR code led to a tailored mobile landing page with a clear message about the Scholz & Friends search for digital creatives (along with a prominent "Apply now" call-to-action button).

The outcome was encouraging: according to Scholz & Friends, many job interviews were conducted as a result, which led to some new teams being hired for its digital department.

SURPRISE AS DESIGN STRATEGY

The main reason Pizza Digitale was so engaging was how it took QR codes completely out of their usual context (printed black-and-white labels) and applied them in a different, unexpected, amusing way (as a pizza embellishment!).

The element of surprise can be an effective (and affective) tool to delight people, capture their attention, and make your product more memorable and viral. It "elevates a piece beyond the banal."[8] Thinking about ways you can effectively surprise your users—within or between devices—can add an extra edge to the overall product experience that helps separate it from others.

AUGMENTED REALITY: IKEA'S 2013 CATALOG

IKEA's 2013 catalog (Figure 6-16) introduces an enriched browsing experience when paired with a smartphone or tablet. It leverages the camera as a communication channel between the physical and the digital (similarly to QR codes), but it uses *augmented reality* (AR) to "bring the catalog to life." Using the IKEA catalog app while browsing the printed catalog lets people unlock extra content in it. When they scan selected pages in the catalog (marked with a special icon) using their smartphones, additional images, films, and 3D models magically appear on the screen, adding a new layer of information and interactivity to the paper-based experience.

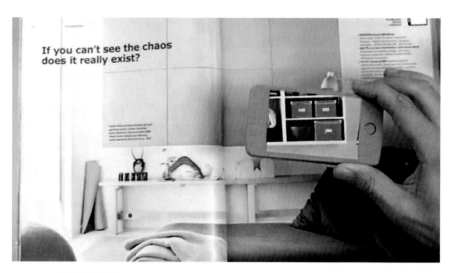

FIGURE 6-16

IKEA 2013 catalog, introducing an augmented experience in collaboration with the smartphone.

The ecosystem experience

THINGS	Printed catalog, electronic device (smartphone, tablet)
DEVICE COMMUNICATION	Digital, physical
DEVICE RELATIONSHIPS	Complementary

The IKEA catalog demonstrates a new type of complementary experience where the mobile device (smartphone or tablet) serves as a companion to a physical object (printed catalog) rather than another electronic device.

In Chapter 4, we saw through a set of examples how complementary design can extend the experience beyond place and time constraints. Now we see that it doesn't end there—we can expand it also beyond just digital devices, connecting together the physical and the digital to provide an overall enhanced experience.

Design lesson: QR supports continuity; AR provides a complementary experience

Both QR codes and AR technology rely on the camera as the connecting link between the physical and the digital. However, they provide very different experiences.

While QR codes serve as a springboard from offline to online, supporting the *continuity* of task flows between these two spaces, AR provides a very different experience. It *complements* the experience with a special lens that accompanies users along their journey while interacting with physical objects.

This complementary experience is similar in many ways to the second-screen experience discussed in Chapter 4. There is a main viewing activity taking place on a certain device or thing (TV or catalog, respectively), and the mobile device adds an extra screen to the experience, offering supplementary content and interactivity during the viewing experience. This conceptual resemblance fosters the idea that the 3Cs are not confined to a specific *set* of devices, but rather are used to address task flows and different use cases. Focusing on that allows us to interpret these approaches into design decisions in a variety of ways, depending on the context at hand.

There is one important difference, though, between the TV-based second-screen experience and the IKEA catalog experience. In the former case, the companion device complements the TV while the show is running, but the experiences are essentially separate, and the user's attention is split between the devices—ping-ponging between them. At any given moment, either people's eyes are on the TV watching the show, or they're engaging with complementary content and activities offered on the companion device. The second-screen app is in many ways independent from the TV, and can be consumed on its own.

With the IKEA catalog, however, the interaction is very different. The companion device serves as a special lens through which people can consume content in the physical world (in this case, the catalog) in an enhanced way. The two players are inextricably tied to each other and have to be used in conjunction in order to "unlock" the second-screen experience—the latter cannot be used on its own. This disparity is illustrated in Figure 6-17.

FIGURE 6-17

The difference between using the smartphone as a second-screen companion for the TV (left), splitting the user's attention between the two devices, and using it as a lens companion to browse through the catalog (right), keeping the user's attention focused on the same spot.

Taking it one step further, if you think about this IKEA catalog AR experience in practice, the use of smartphones or tablets for augmenting the print magazine is not optimal in terms of interaction. The mobile devices actually get in the way of browsing the magazine comfortably. Put yourself in the user's shoes and try imagining yourself lying on the couch in a relaxed, laid-back mode, engaged with a magazine. Now, having to both work through the pages comfortably (using your hands) and operate the smartphone (also using your hands)—holding, aiming, tapping—is not a very smooth experience. In this case, a hands-free mobile device, like glasses, would provide a much more natural, convenient engagement with the magazine. With that said, until smartglasses become a commodity, using the smartphone or tablet serves as the next best thing you can offer your users. They still provide a good-enough experience and have an important educational benefit in terms of multi-device experiences and the value they entail.

A MULTI-DEVICE (OPEN) PLATFORM: SMARTTHINGS

As the last example for this chapter, we'll discuss SmartThings—a highly ambitious multi-device platform that represents a grander vision of a connected world (Figure 6-18). This Minnesota-based startup, founded in 2012, aims to bring home automation into the smartphone age in a cheap and easy-to-use way.

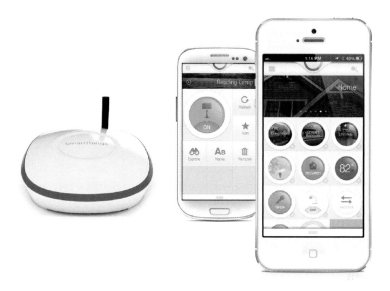

The SmartThings ecosystem: hub and smartphone.

The SmartThings platform is based on the following set of things:

- A hub that connects to the cloud via a router (a cellular version is also in the works)
- A range of smartphone-controlled sensors that monitor things like motion, moisture, and temperature
- Smart plugs that can regulate power to lamps, blenders, and other appliances
- SmartApps for controlling all the connected devices remotely

SmartThings is an open platform that encourages developers to continue expanding it by providing their own connected devices, along with SmartApps for controlling them. These sets will be offered in a marketplace as ready-to-go apps that can be used by many others. This market is essentially an application store, just like the ones we have for mobile phones and tablets, but these apps will interact with a variety of other devices in the surrounding environment via SmartThings sensors.

The ecosystem experience

THINGS	Hub, smartphone-controlled sensors, smart plugs, electronic devices (smartphone, tablet, PC)
DEVICE COMMUNICATION	Digital, physical
DEVICE RELATIONSHIPS	Complementary, continuous

As opposed to the previous examples, which were specific product eco-systems with a set of predefined use cases and flows, SmartThings is a platform that offers a set of smart devices with ways to connect them in various forms. From there, it's up to the users (especially the developer community) to piece them together into personalized, cross-device experiences that fit their daily lives.

To get a better sense of what these might be, let's take a look at some SmartThings potential use cases:[9]

Continuous experiences

SmartThings focuses on the user's *personal* sequences of activities through the day, and how these can be optimized via smart inter-actions between an ecosystem of devices and sensors. For example, if a person outfits her bed with a SmartThings accelerometer, it can recognize when she's up for the morning and tell the smart plug on the coffee maker to turn on. By the time she gets to the kitchen, the coffee is ready.

Complementary experiences

SmartThings also offers a set of complementary use cases, where a collection of devices and sensors work together collaboratively, complementing one another to assist with various needs. For example, fixing a location tag on a pet's collar can send an alert to the smartphone when he leaves the yard. By attaching a moisture sensor to the pet's water bowl, pet owners can be notified when it's empty.

These are just a few examples of how SmartThings can be used to help manage daily activities by adding intelligence to everyday things. The possibilities are practically infinite—especially given the open plat-form, which enables developers to add more things and apps to the ecosystem.

Design lesson: The complexity and trade-offs behind the freedom "to do anything"

Having such complete freedom to do anything might sound appealing at first. However, it can pretty quickly become overwhelming and paralyzing. As you think about the design challenges incorporated in building such a platform, you might realize how huge they are, and how many trade-offs are involved and require attention:

- Functionality versus simplicity

- Full customization versus predefined settings

- Sticking to familiar versus disrupting or promoting novelty

- Designing for existing devices versus planning for future devices

- A platform for everything versus an initial focus on a defined subset

- Open, flexible platform versus structured principles and guidelines

- Beginners versus advanced

- Platform building block focus versus use case focus

- Touch-based versus touch-free (voice, body gestures)

- Private versus public

Given that it all takes place in a completely new territory that is just emerging makes it that much more complex. There are no clear answers to any of these questions at this point; it's going to take time and experimentation to find the right balance along all these dimensions.

Design lesson: Keep focusing on the people

One thing that is important to keep in mind as we enter this all-connected wonderland is that the best multi-device experiences are still, and always will be, those that first look at people and what *they need* rather than focusing on technology and what *it can do*. And when it comes to people, there are a few core design guidelines I always follow:

- People connect better to stories or use cases than they do to software or hardware features.

- People always benefit from anchors to start from, get inspired by, and build upon. Telling people "do whatever you want" without any guidance or direction (especially at the beginning) often leads to them not knowing what to do. Thus, they do nothing.

- People need to see (and preferably feel) the core value they're getting *now*. Relying on future promise is not enough. And the faster they actually get the value, the better.

- Everyone starts as a beginner (even the tech-savvy). Knowing how to use a product entails much more than having the technical skills to use the device.

- Other people matter. They help us make decisions (and then feel good about them), they give reassurance, and they serve as yet another type of anchor to hold on to. The more people are included in the reference social group and the closer they are to the individual, the stronger their impact.

- Emotions are the strongest drivers to action.

In his great book *Designing for Emotion*, Aaron Walter describes the profound impact of creating as:

> An experience for users that makes them feel like there's a person, not a machine, at the other end of the connection.

Furthermore, he shows the key role that emotional connections play in building trust among people. Emotional connections establish a conversational space where people feel encouraged to connect and provide feedback, and are motivated to stick around even when disappointments happen:

> People will forgive shortcomings, follow your lead, and sing your praises if you reward them with positive emotion... Emotional design turns casual users into fanatics ready to tell others about their positive experience. It also offers a trust safety net that encourages your audience to stay when things go awry.[10]

In our context of designing multi-device experiences, establishing such a trusted space to operate in is critical. This connected world is just emerging, and while we can see pretty clearly the promising vision it holds, when we get down to the design details it gets much blurrier. There are a lot of questions and uncertainties, so we need to create a conversation with our users. We need our users to stay with us and give us feedback so we get better and grow together.

And it all comes back to focusing on them and providing them with a meaningful value offering that combines functional and emotional reward.

Case Study: Neura—A User-Centric Approach to the Internet of Things

ORI SHAASHUA, HEAD OF PRODUCT AND INNOVATION, NEURA

Ori Shaashua is in charge of Product and Innovation at Neura. He is an avid creative, fascinated by the hardware-software-data triangle. Ori enjoys designing physical and digital experiences. He has 12 years of experience in product development management and design, encompassing the entire chain of development from inception to market. When he's not designing the next great product, he spends time in his workshop inventing odd stuff and disassembling odd pieces of equipment.

Neura[11] takes a user-centric approach to the Internet of Things, making the devices around us cognizant of the users they serve, making them "intelligent" rather than "programmable." By recognizing habits and behavioral patterns (having adaptive machine learning at its core), Neura empowers devices with predictive and adaptive abilities, making our digital experiences more human.

Unlike machine-to-machine ecosystems that focus on processes and interaction in a "purely" machine-oriented setting, the Internet of Things is consumer-facing. Placing humans at the center of attention significantly changes the mechanics of the ecosystem from the ever-so-predictable machines to the completely unpredictable (not to say improbable) humans.

Moreover, contextual components take a center role, as the consumer-facing IoT is not about things but rather about people and their interaction with devices, locations, other people, and the Web.

This case study will revolve around a Neura-enabled application: Weave. Weave focuses on wellness and improving lifestyle by enabling interoperability between various wearable devices and contextual elements. Weave helps users better understand how their activities (context) and different metrics interact, driving better habits and change.

RECOGNITION AND VISUALIZATION OF REAL-WORLD EVENTS AND USER BEHAVIORS

Weave lifeline, handling multiple data feeds from devices and sensors

The amounts of data streams in the IoT are enormous. As users are expected to own or co-own dozens of connected devices within the next decade, the expected amount of data that will be generated is something the world has yet to face. In fact, sensors and devices will account for an increasing piece of the global data pie.

Not only that, but user data can come from multiple sources that are based on different and inconsistent measurements, units, and scales.

Beyond enabling users to "own" the data generated by the sensors they wear and the devices they use, Weave's main goal is to make sense of it all.

Often, the lacking component in apps today is context—questions like *where did I earn these fuel points?*, *which activity should I promote?*, and *how is my weight affected by my sleep?* don't receive an answer in a purely sensory, data visualizing interface. Seeing one metric at a time with no connection to place, event, or other metrics has very little value. Seeing multiple segmented metrics from multiple vendors makes it even harder to extract actionable value (see Figure 6-19).

Advanced analysis and data correlation has enabled us at Neura to filter what matters and provide users with relevant, context-aware insights and actions rather than raw metrics.

Visualizing segmented, individual feeds from different devices is not necessarily the only method of approaching this experience. It was clear to us that the favorable way to serve users with what they need, when they need it, is to understand their needs and intentions. Moreover, the experience must be forward-looking. In other words, showing the past and expecting the user to put in the mental exercise to then figure out what needs to be changed in the future to achieve better results will, eventually, result in a partially successful experience. On the other hand, through the analysis of users' behavior and the recognition of patterns, Weave sheds light on possible activity changes and visualizes it in a live, actionable storyline.

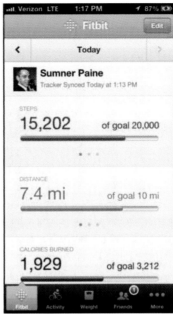

FIGURE 6-19

Different metric data visualizations from two device vendors (Nike+ and Fitbit) that need to be integrated into a single user-centric, context-aware experience.

We have decided to "normalize" branding elements in favor of the essence a device provides (e.g., fuel, steps, calorie burn all indicate the intensity of an activity). Therefore, Weave uses a contextually aware, time-based view of event-driven data from devices and actionable controls presented via a user timeline, shown in Figure 6-20.

FIGURE 6-20

Neura's timeline, providing an actionable time-based view of event-driven user data.

Weave Insights, an adaptive intervention in daily life

Weave Insights (Figure 6-21) help users drive change in their wellness lifestyle. Insights are personalized for every user, as they are derived from the user's own wellness metrics and routine habits and not general crowd statistics.

FIGURE 6-21

Weave Insights,
personalized to the
user.

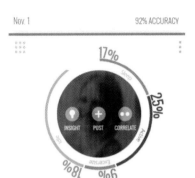

Some insights need to reach users in real time, as they may affect the user's next steps or impact his daily schedule. When approaching the Insights UX, we were faced with three questions:

- How do we make insights dominant and visible as they arrive in real time and also allow users to access them later on?

- How do we emphasize the fact they are personally tailored for the users and based on adaptive learning of current data?

- How do we keep it concise, simple, and clear, so that it can be understood at a glance, even on the go?

The final Insights UI is a responsive area that expands above the home screen when a relevant insight is generated. Less time sensitive insights wait for the user to proactively expand this area in order to be nonintrusive and accessed when needed.

The UI contains three components:

- **The insight itself,** in a clear and readable font. The wording is designed to feel personal and specific: "Go to sleep now and be more active by 450 steps tomorrow," or "Your average business meeting is worth 378 calories."

- **The insight time,** which shows relevancy and also serves as a timeline, enabling users to browse.

- **The insight accuracy,** which provides users with a transparent view into one aspect of our machine learning process and raises the perceived reliability of the insight mechanism.

Weave Correlations, a micro infographic with a "bottom line"

Weave Correlations (Figure 6-22) aim to show users how different habits and behaviors affect one another and visualize trends and changes in wellness metrics over time. Correlations enable users to know themselves better, understand the cause and effect between different indicators, and, very importantly, validate positive changes in their lifestyles.

Correlations are based on analysis of users' past data. Weave aims to make users aware of long-term changes they have gone through. Yet, the final goal is to enable users to derive conclusions and drive change. Therefore, we have decided that this feature should not only provide a bird's-eye view of the past, but also emphasize the bottom line (e.g., "An average burn of 1,500 fuel points/day results in 2 pounds' weight gain a month"). When approaching the Correlations UX, we were confronted with three challenges:

- How do we wrap up data from a whole month into the small real estate made available by a portrait smartphone?

- How do we enable users to see specific data points while providing a "zoomed-out" view visualizing long-term trends and changes?

- How do we enable navigating over time and across different correlations (e.g., weight/activity, sleep/activity)?

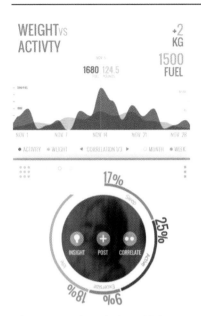

FIGURE 6-22

Weave Correlations, providing ratios between different metrics over time for promoting long-term changes.

The Weave Correlations UI is a responsive area that expands above the home screen. We chose to preserve portrait orientation even though it allows less real estate for high-resolution data. The bottom line receives higher priority, and trends can be visualized even with a small graph. Here are some key points:

- **The draggable line** enables users to see the data behind every specific point on the graph, eliminating the overload of unrequested points or numbers.

- **The "bottom line"** is clearly presented on the top right next to the metrics displayed in the correlation.

- **Three-dimensional navigation** was solved intuitively:
    - Dragging the graph navigates the time range dimension.
    - Dragging the line navigates inside the visible time range.
    - Navigating across correlations was separated from the preceding two, as it is not time related.

The resulting screen enables users to better understand themselves by taking a quick look at changes their bodies are going through while saving them the related computational and mental exercise.

Summary

- The 3Cs framework continutes to offer guidance as we evolve past the core devices, because in essence users' core needs, goals, and task models do not change as a function of the number of available devices. At the same time, given the plethora of things joining the ecosystem, we need to consider these new additions and the types of communications they introduce.

- Through a diverse set of examples, you learned some of the core design principles behind multi-device experiences in the Internet of Things (IoT) era. These include:

  - The key role of adaptive design (through Nest) in making the critical leap from mere data collection to extracting useful information—and, most importantly, acting upon it in a context-driven way, seamlessly, and thereby empowering people to better perform on life's stage.

  - The importance of naïveté in identifying opportunities for change and innovation. Square and Tesco both demonstrated how rethinking user flows, behaviors, and habits that most of us take for granted can disrupt industries and offer significantly better user experiences.

  - The power of going beyond wireless communication to hardware augmentation. BiKN and Square demonstrated how we can further empower smartphones (and tablets) to take on new roles.

  - We looked at new ways complementary and continuous approaches can be used when more things are available—from taking complementary experiences beyond the digital sphere and incorporating physical items (like the AR-enhanced IKEA catalog), to supporting personalized continuous experiences comprising any sequence of activities people perform (through SmartThings).

NOTES

1. Dave Evans, "The Internet of Everything: How More Relevant and Valuable Connections Will Change the World," Cisco IBSG, *http://bit.ly/18XgY7r*.

2. Kevin Ashton, "That 'Internet of Things' Thing," *RFID Journal*, July 22, 2009, *http://bit.ly/18XhbHO*.

3. "Embracing the Internet of Everything To Capture Your Share of $14.4 Trillion," Cisco ISBG, 2013, *http://bit.ly/1hAdA81*.

4. Stephen Wendel, *Designing for Behavior Change* (Sebastopol, CA: O'Reilly Media, Inc., 2014), *http://oreil.ly/1bWj3Ol*.

5. Alistair Croll and Benjamin Yoskovitz, *Lean Analytics: Use Data to Build a Better Startup* (Sebastopol, CA: O'Reilly Media, Inc., 2013), *http://oreil.ly/lean_analytics*.

6. Juho Hamari and Jonna Koivisto, "Social Motivations To Use Gamification: An Empirical Study Of Gamifying Exercise," AIS Electronic Library (AISeL), 2013, *http://bit.ly/1bQaap3*.

7. *http://bit.ly/1d4r0pl*

8. Tom Dixon and Jennifer Hudson, *The International Design Yearbook 19* (London: Laurence King, 2004).

9. These examples were taken from SmartThings marketing materials (*https://shop.smartthings.com/*; *http://kck.st/Oy3Wlx*).

10. Aaron Walter, *Designing for Emotion* (New York: A Book Apart, 2012), *http://amzn.to/1cbZO95*.

11. Author note: in the interest of full disclosure, Neura was one of the startups I worked with as part of my activity as the UX mentor at UpWest Labs accelerator.

[7]

Multi-Device Analytics

In this new space of multi-device experiences, it's more important than ever to track and analyze user data. This is our way of seeing how people use multiple devices—and glimpsing how we can design better experiences. This chapter discusses new analytics questions and needs that should be addressed so that we can glean the insights that will help us build future-friendly ecosystem experiences.

User Data Is User Feedback

We all design products we believe people will need, love, and use, and we rely on different methods and information sources for our designs: market data analysis, UX research, best practices, industry standards, our own knowledge, pain points we identify, and our (informed) intuitive grasp of the product's value. These are all important tools to get us going.

In order to build a sustainably engaging experience, make informed product decisions in the process, and assess our product's success in a reliable way, we need *data*.

Data, data, and more data.

By *data*, I really mean feedback from our users to let us know what they do with the product and how it serves them. We need to know what makes them happy and what frustrates them, where they get engaged and where they lose interest, where they sail smoothly through the product flow and where they get stuck.

This feedback can come in two forms:

Words

> What people *tell us* they did, do, or will do (and why). This feedback is typically qualitative in nature, providing us with a rich, in-depth understanding of underlying reasons, motivations, settings, and perceptions behind an observed behavior or pattern. We can gather this kind of feedback through UX research methods (such as interviews, diary studies, or focus groups), or by using built-in feedback tools within the product itself (like a "Send feedback" link that gathers data using a form).

Actions

> What people *actually* do. This feedback is quantitative in nature, collected through tracking user behaviors and interactions with the product in real time. It is statistically reliable and generalizable (assuming a sufficient sample size), relying on numbers to discover and describe usage patterns. This feedback is often gathered through online analytics tools, which measure and analyze user engagement across a rich set of metrics and dimensions that define behavior patterns.

These two types of feedback complement each other in the data they provide: actions tell us the *what*, while words shed light on the *why*. Having a continuous stream of both types of feedback is an ideal way for us to gather all the feedback we need. If you can allocate the required resources, conducting ongoing qualitative and quantitative research will generate the best, most comprehensive insights about your users.

However, time and resources for gathering exhaustive feedback are not always available. And in these cases, we are faced with the task of prioritizing feedback gathering alongside other product development needs. We need to make a choice: which of the two feedback types should we prioritize?

ACTIONS SPEAK LOUDER THAN WORDS

The old saying "actions speak louder than words" is probably as relevant today—if not moreso—as ever, particularly when it comes to multi-device experiences.

In an increasingly connected world—which is getting more crowded, social, context-sensitive, and device-rich—focusing on what people *actually do* as a way to understand their intents, behavior patterns, and engagement models is a necessity.

More user diversity

In the five-year period from 2007–2012 alone, the world's Internet population doubled (!) to 2.27 billion (see Figure 7-1).[1] Mobile phones have rapidly disseminated over the past two decades, with the number of global subscribers reaching 6 billion in 2012 (87% of the world's population).[2]

Internet population from 2007 to 2012 (a 2x increase in 5 years)

FIGURE 7-1

Internet population growth from 2007 to 2012. (Data source: Internet World Stats. Map source: Pingdom.)

The more people there are connected to the Internet and actively using digital products, the harder it becomes to gain a comprehensive understanding across all the target groups without actually collecting usage data. The increasing diversity of demographics, culture, mental models, use cases, habits, and literacy makes it much harder to reach a representative sample through traditional qualitative research methods.

More use contexts—especially on the go

People no longer just sit in their quiet homes in front of their stationary PCs, absorbed in the websites they're browsing. The Internet, along with other technological developments, brought in the always-on era; everywhere people go, they engage with their devices. They check their mobile phones 150 times a day, are constantly interrupted (new emails, new SMSs, new app updates, incoming calls), and hop from one app to another, multi-tasking their way through the day. The increasing number of connected devices only enhances these behaviors.[3]

From a user behavior analysis perspective, the implications are:

- Contexts of use are constantly shifting, especially as mobile usage increases, leading to more actions taking place on the go.

- Any given product is not being used in isolation, but rather as part of a bigger context that involves a set of temporal, spatial, social, and emotional factors.

- A single task flow can extend over a long period of time, along a sequence of activities that take place across varying contexts (continuous experiences).

Reproducing this dynamic set of contexts and associated factors is practically impossible in a laboratory setting. And these have a significant effect on the actual behavior and decision-making process in real life.

More connected devices

The world of many devices adds in two factors to consider:

Unfamiliar territory

Multi-device experiences introduce new UX paradigms, interaction patterns, and ways to approach use cases. This requires us to:

- Help establish new mental models and habits among people centered on the benefits multi-device experiences provide.

- Stay closely tuned to our users, learn how they actually use the product, and adapt to their developing needs.

Interaction effect

As mentioned in Chapter 1, once new devices join the family, they not only introduce new behavior patterns around them, but also affect how and how often people use their existing devices. These changes can manifest in three ways: a decreased use of existing devices, an increase in usage, or a different kind of usage. Either way, we need to detect and analyze these dynamic changes and trends to get a holistic understanding of the ecosystem.

To capture these dynamic changes and extract meaningful patterns and behaviors, we have to analyze a large quantity of user data, building a knowledge base around people's engagements with multiple devices over time.

Asking people how they would use multiple devices might not be very useful at this point in time, and it might actually be quite limiting. Most people aren't aware of the opportunities, or don't imagine how far they can go (especially as we broaden our ecosystem lens to the world of the Internet of Things).

Social influence

Social interactions on the Web have picked up at a fierce pace with the emergence of YouTube, Facebook, Twitter, and other social media. The social layer is becoming an integral part of digital experiences, influencing the way people behave and interact.

In the context of this discussion, the way social connections influence people's online behavior needs to be captured. For example, what (and who) triggers them to action, what keeps them engaged, who influences them the most, and what motivates them to share and actively contribute to the online conversation? These are just some of the questions we need to ask in the social arena, and even within this narrow set, multiple factors come into play—conscious and unconscious, rational and emotional.

Another consideration is that, testing a demo version of your product when it's not yet connected to users' real data (e.g., their friends, their generated content, their social environment) detaches them emotionally from the experience, and you lose the contextual and social factors that impact their decisions and behavior patterns in real life.

For these reasons, assessing people's *actual* engagement in real time is a more reliable way to capture the set of social factors involved, rather than relying on self-reporting.

HOW DO WE GATHER DATA?

In the past, getting usage data from thousands of people at once was impossible, and getting real-time data was a pipe dream. The best you could do was spend a lot of money on focus groups or surveys to conduct your market research. Technology (and especially the Internet) facilitated a sea change in data analytics: not only could data be collected, stored, analyzed, and disseminated more easily than in the past, but there was also a lot more of it. A large set of web analytics tools became available to help with this research. Some examples include Google Analytics, Omniture, SiteCatalyst, WebTrends, Crazy Egg, Optimizely, and ClickTale.

Out of all these tools, Google Analytics is by far the most widely used. It's one of the most powerful tools for monitoring and analyzing traffic on your website, offering a wide range of reporting and analysis capabilities.[4] In addition, this is the only tool I know of that has started approaching the challenge of multi-device experiences (with Universal Analytics, announced in October 2012),[5] and it is therefore becoming a benchmark for this realm. For that reason, we'll look at the Google Analytics conceptual framework—terminology, data structure, metrics, and dimensions—as a reference for our discussion on multi-device analytics.

Discussion: Multi-Device Measurement Using Google Analytics

DANIEL WAISBERG, ANALYTICS ADVOCATE, GOOGLE

Daniel Waisberg is an analytics advocate at Google, where he is responsible for fostering Google Analytics by educating and inspiring online marketing professionals. Both at Google and in his previous positions, Daniel has worked with some of the biggest Internet brands to measure and optimize online behavior. He is also the founder of online-behavior.com.

As you are learning in this book, people's behavior is no longer limited to a single device, and very often they jump between devices, expecting a smooth transition. There is a myriad of techniques to create rich experiences that can satisfy (and hopefully amaze) users. But how can we deeply understand if and how those techniques are working? One word: analytics. Using a good analytics tool, we can "see" how people behave, what they like, and what they don't.

While there are a multitude of tools out there, Google Analytics is still the one that can provide the best analysis when it comes to understanding multi-device behavior. But more important than the tool is how we design the measurement strategy and metrics. In this short sidebar, I will provide insights into how we would approach the implementation of a multi-device measurement strategy on Google Analytics.

WHAT TO MEASURE?

The first, most important, step when it comes to analytics is to be able to envision the end result of the measurement; if we are able to dream about the perfect report and analysis, we will almost certainly be able to collect the data in order to build it. Our goal is to know which information will help us make better decisions before we start collecting data.

Multi-device behavior presents a challenge in that the goals might not always be clear for all devices, and they certainly come in larger quantities; companies will usually have different objectives for the Web, tablets, and smartphones.

To exemplify some of the measurement concepts I describe in this sidebar, I will use a service that I find interesting: BigOven.com. The company provides an end-to-end service for people who enjoy cooking or simply want to have a centralized place to organize their meals and day-to-day menus. BigOven has a website, an Android app (different UX for tablets and smartphones), and an iOS app (different UX for iPhone and iPad). While the web interface provides all features in an equally distributed way, the apps focus on different aspects of the product (even though most features are also available).

Table 7-1 shows how I would define some of the goals for each device.

TABLE 7-1. Macro and micro conversion goals for BigOven.com, divided by device*

GOALS	WEBSITE	TABLET	PHONE
Macros			
Registration	✓	✓	✓
Purchase	✓	✓	✓
Recruiting	✓		
Sponsorship	✓		
Micro			
Click Advertisement	✓	✓	✓
Invite FB Friend	✓		
Share Recipe	✓	✓	✓
Grocery List Ended			✓
Read Recipe	✓	✓	✓

*Please note that this table is an example drawn from my own imagination. Once we have the table, we can proceed to visualize the types of metrics we will use and the data we will need to collect.v

HOW TO APPROACH GOOGLE ANALYTICS

After we've decided on the goals and metrics to be used for each of the devices, we should start building a design for Google Analytics in order to collect the necessary data. The design is an important step, because if the data is not clear and easily accessible, it won't be used.

Our first challenge is to make sure we can measure the behavior of visitors across devices (i.e., to make sure we count a person only once if he or she uses both the website and a tablet). The most important point here is that we can analyze multi-device behavior *only if* customers log in to the website or app. (Learn more about Google's Universal Analytics, the technology that enables multi-device measurement, at *http://goo.gl/pCQYxG*.)

Once we have this important piece of the puzzle in place, we can start building the model with which we will collect the data. Here are some of the decisions we will need to make along the way:

- What type of information should I save on a per-customer level?

  In order to understand and segment our customers into relevant groups, we should save, for example, the type of customer (paid or free), the registration date, whether the person has signed up to the newsletter, and other information. For five questions you should ask before implementing custom dimensions, see *http://goo.gl/hRs9Gs*. Read more about how to implement custom dimensions and metrics at *http://goo.gl/XxwhC* (for websites) or *http://goo.gl/H2jRd* (for apps).

- What level of detail do I need?

  For example, is it important to know about every click on every button, or is it sufficient to track pages, screens, and major buttons? For example, I would not use BigOven to send an event to Google Analytics every time a person checks an item off a grocery list, but rather only when a list is completed.

- Can I measure ecommerce transactions on my site or app?

  This is an excellent feature on Google Analytics, to understand who is purchasing and how he or she discovered the site. But it might be tricky if the site or app uses a third-party cart. Read more about measuring ecommerce for a website at *http://goo.gl/AmDf3*, or for an app at *http://goo.gl/1JU0i*.

- How can I integrate my Google Analytics account with other sources of data?

  If, for example, you use Google AdWords, AdSense, or other tools, you might want to import their data into Google Analytics in order to enrich it. This ebook describes how to do it: *http://goo.gl/Xo12W*.

There will be other questions you will need to answer, so I recommend browsing through *https://developers.google.com/analytics/* or using one of the resources provided at *https://support.google.com/analytics/* to learn more about how to approach a Google Analytics implementation.

WHAT'S NEXT?

The tools to collect the data are advanced and flexible. However, there are challenges you must overcome in order to build an insightful multi-device analytics culture.

The first challenge is *people*: where can we find the professionals with the necessary skills to build and use Google Analytics for multi-device environments? What should those professionals know, and how can we teach them?

The second challenge is *visualization*: how can we take the aforementioned data and organize it in such a way that it will be easy to understand and provide the insight needed by the company?

The third challenge is *mindset*: how do we convince business owners that Google Analytics is an investment that should be among their top priorities? Companies already recognize the importance of being data-driven, but this knowledge does not always translate into budget.

The challenges are not easy to solve, but the field is growing in giant steps, and some of the brightest minds in the industry are working to find new ways to measure behavior across devices. So keep your ears open, and happy analyzing!

Multi-Device Analytics

What does it mean to have a multi-device analytics platform? Which kinds of questions would it need to address? Does it require any paradigm shifts in the way we approach web analytics today?

These are some of the questions I kept asking myself when trying to conceptualize a multi-device analytics platform. I found that approaching it from the 3Cs perspective—analyzing the data needs separately for the consistent, complementary, and continuous approaches, along with looking for common themes—was instrumental in defining the analytics paradigm for multi-device experiences. The set of product examples associated with each approach turned out to be very helpful in concept-testing these themes, making sure that they covered the analytics essentials across a variety of use cases.

As a starting point, when considering multi-device experiences, you'll encounter two fundamental analysis needs:

Cross-device analysis

In a multi-device world, websites are just one piece of the puzzle. Mobile products play an important role via native apps, web apps, and hybrid structures. Then there's the TV, game consoles, wearables, and many other connected devices that are on their way. Getting an in-depth usage analysis across all these devices (not just for each one separately, but also of the relationships and dynamics between them as a group) is key to understanding the ecosystem performance as a whole. This is especially important when you are looking at contextual experiences (complementary or continuous), where the different devices create together the experience ensemble.

User-based analysis

When it comes to multi-device experiences, a single task flow can span multiple devices in different contexts. This makes the ability to understand how *people* navigate their way through the product flow increasingly important. While visit-based analysis provides valuable granular information about every engagement with any page, in a multi-device world, the contextual connections and flows between devices are inherent to the experience design; thus, analyzing people's journeys across multiple visits (and devices) is essential.

Let's take a closer look at how these needs come into play through the lens of the 3Cs framework. As you probably recall, when it comes to the consistent approach, the entire experience can be consumed on any device separately. As a result, the experience is essentially device-independent, with each device acting as a solo player. This device relationship is very different from both the complementary and continuous experiences, where devices work together as a group in order to support the end-to-end user flow.

We saw in previous chapters how this fundamental difference leads to very different multi-device user experiences. Now we will see that it affects the analytics approach as well. This shouldn't come as a surprise, really, as this *data* is merely a quantitative expression of users' actions and interactions. Accordingly, how these interactions play out in the experience itself also affects the analysis model needs.

CONSISTENCY: APPLYING THE CURRENT ANALYTICS PARADIGM ACROSS DEVICES

In consistent ecosystems, where the entire product experience is available on any device, the existing analytics paradigm holds. All we really need is to be able to apply the rich, powerful collection of web analytics tools we already have to other devices as well. That would provide a robust basis from which to start.

The next step would be to compare, correlate, and segment sets of device-focused data in order to identify any possible ecosystem trends. Important use patterns might emerge around certain devices versus others. For example, even though people *can* consume everything, everywhere, anytime, it doesn't necessarily mean that they *do*. You might find out that certain content types are consumed only on specific devices, while other devices are used for different actions. This is invaluable data that can potentially indicate that you should transform the consistent experience into a complementary and/or continuous one—at least in certain areas of your product—to better suit your users' needs and simplify the experience overall. In other words, through the data you collect, you might find use patterns across devices that should inform the product design, and that better articulate the ecosystem narrative. Remember, though, as discussed in Chapter 5, if you *can* define that narrative early on, distributing the experience across devices in a contextual way (instead of shipping all the features across all devices), you should take that route. Pulling out features after the product is launched is always harder than making those hard decisions (i.e., saying no) early on during the product's inception. Still, both are doable, and both are better strategies than just leaving heaps of unnecessary features, configurations, and content in the interface.

Table 7-1 details some of the basic questions we need to answer as part of consistent experience analysis. In this table, we are looking at four main dimensions of analysis:

Single-device versus multi-device
> Focuses on understanding how users' behaviors change when they move from a single-device product to a multi-device ecosystem— assuming you already have an existing product running on (at least) one device, and that you're collecting analytics data on its usage.

Usage patterns per device
> Goes in depth into the usage patterns for each device independently.

Usage patterns across devices
> Looks for potential relationships between devices, in terms of adoption as well as ongoing usage.

Technology
> Explores patterns and trends around specific platforms and technological implementations.

TABLE 7-1. Questions to answer when analyzing the consistent experience

Single-device vs. multi-device	• What share of people use the product across several devices? How do they compare to those using only a single device (in terms of behavior, engagement, and conversions)? • Overall, how have users' activity and engagement with the product changed compared to when it was available only on a single device? • How does this translate to goal conversions?
Usage patterns per device	• Which devices do people use the product on? • Are there significant usage differences between devices (product-wise, context-wise, or audience-wise)?
Usage patterns across devices	• Are there any potential dependencies or other relationships that arise from the data? (This could imply users trying to manually build complementary experiences or continuous ones.) • Are there any themes in terms of multiple-device adoption (e.g., order of device use, frequency, ecosystem setup)?
Technology	• How do performance and usage patterns differ between native apps and web apps? • How do usage patterns compare between platforms (e.g., iOS and Android)? Across platforms?

COMPLEMENTARY AND CONTINUOUS: EXPANDING THE ANALYTICS PARADIGM TO NEW DOMAINS

As we step into the world of contextual experiences, we enter a whole new analytics ballgame that involves use patterns across connected devices (complementary or continuous).

In fact, these approaches encourage us to rethink some of the basic assumptions behind data analysis in light of the new ecosystem patterns (just like we did with users' task flows). Let's see what that could mean in terms of multi-device analytics.

"Visit" redefined

I've talked previously about the importance of people-based analytics in a multi-device world. However, that doesn't mean we should throw away visit-based analysis. This level of analysis is still valuable as well, since it offers more granular insights into the user interactions within a specific context.

If we take Google Analytics as a reference, a visit (also referred to as a *session*) is defined as ending when more than 30 minutes have elapsed between page views for a single visitor, at the end of a day, or when the traffic source for the user changes.

This definition of a visit unit is very useful as a consistent analytics "currency" through which data is analyzed and interpreted across reports.

However, when we think about multi-device experiences, which are not bound to the desktop and can incorporate usage across several devices, several questions arise:

- Should a session be defined in the same manner across all devices, or should it be adjusted per device? For example, we know that the stationary desktop engagement is very different from on-the-go, interrupt-driven mobile phone usage.

- How might we handle parallel sessions taking place on different devices at the same time?

- Is a device considered a traffic source? In other words, does changing devices automatically end a session? Using a continuous experience as an example, what if I start watching a movie on my tablet and then shift it to the TV? Should these be considered as two separate sessions, or a single one? And if we do treat them as two sessions, how do we convey the strong tie between them?

I don't have the answers to all these questions—they require more thought and experimentation—but they're important for our data analytics tools to address in order to support a multi-device world.

Introducing goal conversion for an ecosystem

In the context of websites, a *goal conversion* is defined as a successful completion of a goal, as defined by the website owner. This could be a sign-up, download, or purchase. Accordingly, the conversion goal is a standalone action within one of the site's pages, and it is attributed to the session in which it occurs.

In a world of ecosystem experiences, where multiple devices and sequences of contexts all contribute to the same user task flow, the notion of goal conversion will need to expand. If you think about continuous experiences, for example, beyond the "local" actions (or conversions) of each device, there's a "global" ecosystem narrative they constitute as a group, which represents the overall task flow.

Adding this global ecosystem conversion notion introduces the following concepts:

Ecosystem objective

We can measure how well the multi-device ecosystem *as a whole* fulfills its target objective. This means that each time a person achieves an ecosystem objective, a *completion* is recorded—either as a binary value (completed or not completed) or through a point system, where an ecosystem objective is scored on different levels of completion "quality" depending on the anticipated device utilization for each major step in the product workflow. For example, one ecosystem objective for Eventbrite might be to have users attend events using the product. This objective could be achieved in several ways:

- Using just the website to register for an event

- Registering through the website, then using the mobile app to check in

- Registering through the website, using the mobile app to check in, and exploring related events on the tablet when the event is over

In all three options, the ecosystem objective was met. However, there's clearly a different level of product engagement among the goals, each of which reflects different levels of engagement with the Eventbrite ecosystem offering.

Goal dimensions

Ecosystem objectives can be broken down into a set of more specific goals along the end-to-end flow across devices. These goals can continue to follow the existing paradigm, where each time a goal is accomplished, a conversion is logged.

Still, there are additional goal dimensions we need to consider in an ecosystem analysis, as shown in Table 7-2.

TABLE 7-2. Goal dimensions to consider when analyzing an ecosystem experience

Device-agnostic vs. device-specific	• Device-agnostic: an action can take place on *any* relevant device. • Device-specific: you want an action to take place on a specific device (might be due to identifying better ecosystem objective completions when a certain conversion takes place on a specific device, for example).
Independent goals vs. dependent goals	• Independent goals: each time a goal conversion takes place, on any device, in any context, a conversion is counted. This is how goals work today. • Dependent goals: you can create conditional or nested goals, where a conversion is recorded only if it takes place in a given context or some other goal conversion happens first. Think, for example, of a goal like signing into the product mobile app. In a second-screen experience, such an action is truly meaningful if done while the user is viewing the relevant show or live event, where it can actually fulfill its complementary role. Because context plays such an important role in multi-device experiences, it can contribute different meanings (and associated monetary values) to goals and conversions.

Expanding goal flows and conversion paths

Google Analytics can provide an important, broader view of goal completions through several tools that track the flows and paths leading up to conversions:

Goal flow report

Visualizes the funnel steps through which visitors traveled in your website toward a goal (see Figure 7-2). You can also set up your own linear path of pages toward a goal in order to see the extent to which visitors follow that path.

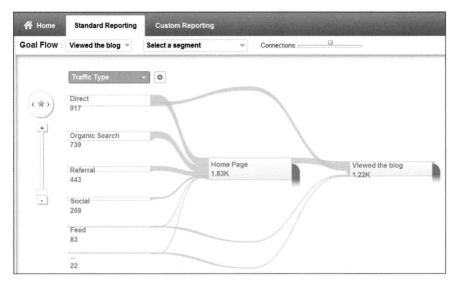

FIGURE 7-2

Google Analytics goal flow report, showing how visitors coming in from different types of traffic (organic, referral, etc.) move through a multi-step funnel.

Multi-channel funnel reports

Show the broader paths that led up to each goal conversion (see Figure 7-3). These reports are generated from the sequences of interactions (clicks or referrals) done during the 30 days prior to the conversion, across all digital channels (search, referral sites, social networks, email newsletters, and more).

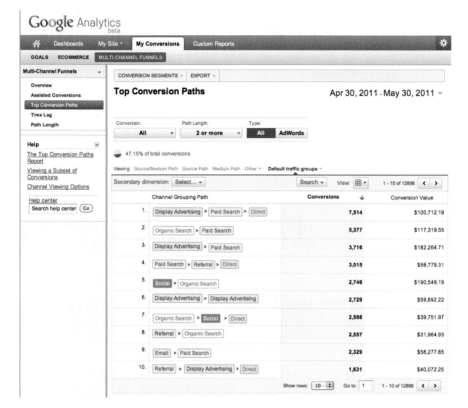

FIGURE 7-3

A Google Analytics multi-channel funnel report—a set of reports that provides insights into the full path to conversion over a 30-day period (rather than just the last click).

In a multi-device world, it's even more important to take this broader perspective on the flows and conditions that lead to the objective. With all the additional devices, contexts, connections, and patterns playing a part in the experience flow, it's going to be very hard to deeply understand, let alone act upon, mere numbers. Data is our primary user feedback channel, through which we try to understand what users are attempting to do (and how we can help them achieve that), what confuses them (and how we can fix that), and what makes them happy (so we keep on doing that). As a result, context continues to be our guiding light—not only for creating multi-device experiences, but also for measuring and analyzing their impact.

What could this mean?

First, it means adding devices to goal measurement so that we understand the device paths people use. This could be translated into two complementary analysis angles:

Device-focused
Viewing the goal flow from a one-device perspective (on some ecosystem timeline), with the ability to drill down to the actions or interactions taken on each device

Scenario-focused
Grouping a sequence of actions or interactions into a single scenario entity, and then seeing how this scenario (or set of scenarios) is pursued across devices

Second, it means addressing concurrent flows and social interactions. Many of the complementary experiences, for example, rely on using several devices at the same time; thus, the goal conversion is a result of parallel flows interacting with each other. We saw in Chapter 4 that many of the complementary experiences are actually social ones, involving multiple actors interacting together at the same time—either in the same physical space or remotely. As this engagement constellation further evolves, it could lead, for example, to different second-screen experiences personalized to different members who are all part of the same social engagement. Analyzing such group behavior is a new type of activity we need to figure out how to measure, so we can better understand how a group of people partake in the same experience and influence one another. This kind of analysis would require collecting the data from all parties involved, knowing that they are all interacting in the same context, integrating the data sets, and analyzing the reciprocal effects on the overall engagement, as well as for each actor.

Examining complementary and continuous flows
On top of addressing the analysis questions just discussed, we also need to deeply understand if, how, and to what extent the ecosystem narrative and design approaches play out in the field. Do people get the ecosystem offering? Do they use it as intended? How do they utilize it across the different contexts?

Contrary to consistent experiences, where the entire experience is simply available everywhere, complementary and continuous experiences are distributed contextually across different touchpoints, and the design is tailored to accommodate user needs dynamically along a flow of events. In these early stages of ecosystem design—where we don't have a robust knowledge base of multi-device behaviors, and a lot of the design is informed by assumptions, intuition, and bits of preliminary research—we need to track a number of multi-device signals:

- What people actually do on *each* device, and when

- Which tasks people choose to engage with on *each* device

- The common use flows between devices

To build a sustainable product, we must discover the potential gaps between our assumptions and actual behavior, and respond to those discoveries. Such data could also help us define the role each device plays in the flow, prompting us to adjust content and features between devices (e.g., adding them, removing them, or changing their prominence in the UI).

As we go even further into the future of the Internet of Things, we will need a way to measure usage of *any device* connected to the ecosystem—even if it doesn't have an interface users engage with. Basically, every connected device should be tracked and added to the integrated data collection and analysis.

Discussion: Paving the Ecosystem Way with A/B Testing

MICHAEL SPIEGELMAN, DIRECTOR OF PRODUCT INNOVATION, NETFLIX

Michael Spiegelman is director of product innovation at Netflix, where he is responsible for the website and tablet products. Previously, he worked at Yahoo!, serving as senior director of entertainment and lifestyle products, general manager of Yahoo! Music, and product manager in the Music group. Before joining Yahoo!, he cofounded a web design, development, and consulting company called Web Paradox, where he handled client relations, business development, and project management. Prior to that, Michael was a consultant at iXL, Arthur Andersen, and PricewaterhouseCoopers.

A/B testing is part art, part science. The basic premise is to objectively determine whether a feature is good for customers or not. To do this, you and your team need to have good alignment on how success will be measured and what metrics are being used to determine success. You can then start to create some hypothesis for what will improve the customers' experience (and in turn, positively affect the metrics you are measuring).

You can then develop features that represent the various hypotheses that you've constructed and test them with a portion of your user base. By looking at standardized metrics and comparing the behavior of users who get the feature to those who don't, you can determine whether the feature you launched is improving the experience.

A/B TESTING IN A MULTI-DEVICE WORLD

Many companies have applied this methodology to improving their websites, but as we've been able to connect many different devices to the Internet, we can test and experiment on these devices too. Here's a framework for applying A/B testing to a multi-device environment:

- Determine which devices you should use in testing.

- Analyze how the context for your users will change based on the device they are using.

- Figure out whether you have different types of customers using each of your devices.

- Assess how your metrics will change based on a multi-device environment.

At Netflix, for example, users can access our service through the website, game consoles (like the PlayStation 3 or Xbox 360), tablets, mobile phones, smart TVs, Rokus, Apple TVs, and other devices—over 800 in all! So how do you decide what devices to test on?

In a perfect world, you could test any of your ideas on all these devices, but rarely is it that simple. Typically, many of those devices use different code bases, so it's additional development work to build the same feature for each platform. Using A/B testing means that you want to be able to launch many experiments, only some of which will work, so it makes sense to build a test on as few devices as possible and then invest in a broad rollout of the successful features. This makes for efficient use of engineering resources and maximizes your ability to test many things to find out what works.

CHOOSING THE RIGHT PLATFORM

One of the first criteria that we use is determining which platform is best suited for a specific feature. People typically use a game console or smart TV in a very laid-back fashion, so a feature that is about rich media playback would be well suited to these devices. Similarly, the touch interface of the tablet is appropriate for features that relate to active management or curation of content.

CONSIDERING DEVICE INTERACTION

Another consideration is thinking through which devices interact with each other, and which are substitutional. For example, if you're building a feature that allows customers to use their phones or tablets as remote controls for their television screens, you could pick one phone or tablet device (iPad, iPhone, Android tablet, or Android phone) plus one connected television device (like a PlayStation, Xbox, Roku, or Apple TV) for the initial test, and then only implement it on the other devices if it works.

If devices are substitutional, this allows you to pick one to develop on and apply the results to others. At Netflix, we found that people started using tablets for the same actions they previously performed on the website. So we could test a feature on the website, iPad, or Android tablet, and apply the results to the others.

FOCUSING ON (MORE) USERS

A further consideration is users: the more users a device has, the easier it is to test on it. This happens because you need a certain number of users to ensure that you can reasonably measure changes in your metrics with a high degree of confidence. The more users, the easier it is to detect small but important movements in the metrics. So if you have several devices that will serve the same purpose, it's generally best to select those with the most users for testing.

Engineering complexity often plays a role. If it's easier for your development team to build on a certain platform, take that into account.

Once you have selected the right devices, you can figure out the test plan for the feature. It's often useful to test multiple variations to figure out the best implementation. The advantage of this approach is that you can distill down your questions into variables to isolate and test. Examples of these variables could include different kinds of ranking algorithms in a search test, different placements of buttons on a website, or variations on a navigation bar on a tablet. Figuring out how many variations to have in a test is more art than science, and there's always a temptation to test everything. Understanding which variants are likely to be material and being willing to bet on those that are most likely (in your judgment) to be successful helps manage scope.

Finally, when you're ready to analyze the results of your tests, understanding how people use the devices may, of course, impact the way you interpret the metrics. People may use their mobile phones to find content that they consume on other platforms, so improving the experience on the phone may impact activity they take on smart TVs; keeping consistent overall metrics will help ensure effective measurement.

Applying A/B testing to a multi-device environment adds complexity to the way you structure the test, do the analysis, and roll it out. But it also allows for a much deeper understanding of your customers and how they use their products, and enables you to create much richer user experiences through iterative design, development, and experimentation.

Additional Analytics Considerations

As part of getting user feedback and measuring ecosystem performance, there are a few more key elements that you need to consider, as they play an important part in the experience.

TV AND SOCIAL ANALYTICS

TV has officially become an integral part of the core ecosystem. Remember: 88% of tablet owners and 86% of smartphone owners use these devices as a second screen while watching TV.[6]

Not only that, but with the wide distribution and broad impact of social media, we see a gradual movement toward bringing the social nature of the TV viewing experience into the digital space. In their book *Social TV: How Marketers Can Reach and Engage Audiences by Connecting Television to the Web, Social Media, and Mobile,* Mike Proulx and Stacey

Shepatin talk about the rapid convergence of the Web, social media, mobile devices, and TV, making it a necessity to look at the larger cross-media, cross-device experiences across all these channels.

Furthermore, they emphasize the critical role social conversations play in these dynamics:

> The core of social TV starts with the backchannel...comprised of the millions of public conversations happening online while television programming airs. Brands who find ways to align themselves with or be part of the backchannel unlock an entire audience with whom they engage.[7]

The social TV domain is also where we currently see the most activity around TV-related analytics. Social TV analytics tracks and measures users' activities in social networks (like posting, commenting, tweeting) in real time, while they're watching their favorite TV shows. From a multi-device perspective, social TV analytics focuses on a specific type of engagement in *second-screen experiences*: social media activities around TV content. Clearly, the focus of the analysis is the content published (rather than the device relationships), but this growing analytics domain still provides deeper insights than we had before about people's behavior and usage patterns as they're engaging with multiple devices.

Most of the TV-related social conversations take place on Twitter, which serves as the main data source for many social TV analytics platforms.[8] In fact, Twitter is trying to leverage this advantage and establish itself as a key player in the analytics domain as well. In 2013 alone, Twitter acquired two social TV analytics companies: Trendrr and Bluefin Labs. In addition, it partnered with Nielsen—the leading TV ratings service in the US and Canada—to create the Nielsen Twitter TV Rating, which aims to form an industry-standard metric that is based entirely on Twitter data.

These market trends further highlight the importance of continuously expanding our data analytics tools to address people's dynamically changing behavior patterns—online and offline.

While social TV analytics is a step in the right direction, there's still a lot we could do to more comprehensively track TV usage, let alone the various ways it interacts with other devices.

Looking at this realm from an ecosystem perspective not only surfaces the need to incorporate TV analytics, but also underscores the critical role of social analytics in a multi-device environment. Both of these are huge topics in terms of analytics that shouldn't be ignored.

MEASURING YOUR ECOSYSTEM ROI

Assessing the ecosystem *return on investment* (ROI) is important for getting buy-in and continued investment in building multi-device experiences, as well as for understanding what produces the highest value for both businesses and users. The next chapter discusses in more depth the challenges involved in developing a product across an ecosystem of devices, especially as we move away from replicating experiences. Some are related to ecosystem adoption (like setting it up, syncing up devices, and dealing with the app avalanche), while others concern the ecosystem design and development (organizational structure, walled gardens, and the additional resources the ecosystem demands).

For these reasons, it is essential to measure the return on ecosystem investment, and learn which ecosystem avenues are most worthwhile, in order to continuously improve the product offering and understand the ecosystem impact.

There are many similarities between the current state of multi-device ROI and social media ROI. There's no doubt anymore whether businesses should have presence there or not: they should. If nothing else, the increased visibility, accessibility, and reach have convinced businesses that it's worth their while. What is still unclear, though, is the best strategy to go about it, how much they should invest in it, and what impact it has on the bottom line. To quote a tweet by Avinash Kaushik, an analytics guru and Google Analytics Evangelist: "Social media is like teen sex. Everyone wants to do it. No one actually knows how. When finally done, there is surpise its [sic] not better."[9]

Multi-device experiences aren't very different at this point.

You can calculate ROI in a variety of ways, such as assigning monetary value to goal conversions, correlating with success metrics that translate into business goals, deriving value from the business model (such as via ads, premium users, or virtual goods), and more. Whichever ROI approach you go with (depending on your business and product offering), you need data to engage in the iterative cycle of track, analyze, improve, and test.

Focusing on design-related aspects of ROI, it's helpful to consider the vast range of new business and marketing opportunities a multi-device world introduces (beyond QR codes on pizzas). Let's look at a few examples.

Ads

In a world of multiple devices, you could potentially distribute different ads on different devices. They could vary in terms of creativity, time, design, interaction, wording, and audience.

You could conditionally surface an ad on a certain device when a specific action occurs on another device. You could explore new gamification approaches like ads getting triggered only when a complementary set of actions takes place across multiple devices ("unlocking" them). You could target ads in flexible ways, such as on certain combinations of devices, in specific contexts, or in a certain order. You could also use the 3Cs framework in the way you approach your ad design—for example, integrating ads as part of a second-screen experience, in a contextual way, so that the ad content fits the content being watched on TV, or offering users a continuous ad flow by allowing them to start watching a trailer on the desktop, for example, and continue where they left off on the smartphone or tablet.

The important takeaway here is to think about the ad design and the ad campaign experience as a whole, like any other multi-device experience discussed so far. One way to go about it is to stick to the consistent approach, and simply replicate the same ad across multiple devices. This will most likely increase your visibility and reach among your target audience. At the same time, it will take you only so far, as a whole set of contexts, needs, and use habits that are often part of the broader user journey are being overlooked.

Alternatively, you could combine consistency with one (or more) of the contextual approaches in the 3Cs framework—complementary and continuous—to tailor your campaign better to users' changing needs. By looking at the holistic ecosystem experience and understanding the device relationships along the user journey across varying contexts, you can establish smart, distributed ad campaigns that can enhance user engagement and introduce new revenue opportunities.

Virtual goods

When you sell virtual goods (a model common in the gaming industry), having a multi-device experience introduces new ways to manage them. One example is to distribute the virtual goods between devices, or focus on making just a few special goods on a specific device, in order to encourage multi-device usage.

Zynga realized this opportunity back in 2010–2011, and applied it to its mobile version of the successful game *Farmville* (see Figure 7-4). The company cleverly leveraged its huge success (84 million monthly active users at its peak in early 2010)[10] by offering certain market items available for purchase only on mobile devices.

FIGURE 7-4

Farmville by Zynga—screenshots of the market design on the Web (top) and mobile platforms (bottom). Certain market items were available only on mobile devices.

For the millions of *Farmville* addicts—some willing to go as far as creating Facebook profiles for their pets just for the sake of earning more points in the game—playing on a mobile device was an easy choice.

For Zynga, that was an effective way—through in-product flows—to get users to try out the mobile experience as an integral part of game play. This, in turn, encouraged users to add the mobile devices into their game routine (on top of the desktop, which was the main device used), introducing new on-the-go opportunities for game play.

Optimizing the multi-device experience

Identifying the delicate optimizations as to what exactly should be offered on each device, at which point in the experience, for how long, to what extent, and at what price (in the case of virtual goods, for example) is not an easy task. It often involves very subtle nuances that are difficult to predict, and requires you to repeatedly collect user data, make improvements based on the insights, and closely follow people's behavior changes as a result. A/B testing is a highly effective way to do that, gaining insights about people's preferences through their actions and optimizing the user experience accordingly.

Zynga has mastered this data-driven approach. The company, described by one of its vice presidents as "an analytics company masquerading as a games company,"[11] conducts hundreds of A/B tests within all its games to learn how people play them, and how the experience can be optimized—especially in revenue-generating channels like virtual goods. If we go back to the *Farmville* example, Zynga optimized its virtual goods design by continuously testing everything, from which virtual goods category sells better to which cow color sells better. Through this data analysis, the *Farmville* team discovered, for instance, that people buy a lot more animals than objects like tractors. This finding led them to more prominently feature animals in the market, and thus increase sales.

Your product's success essentially hinges on one thing: people. More specifically, people who use your product. *Does this product help me achieve my goals? What can I do with it? Do I need it? Do I want it? Is it useful? Is it easy to use?* These are some of the questions that people ask themselves, consciously or unconsciously, as they interact with a product. The answers to these questions shape the way they perceive your product, as well as whether or not they decide to use it.

Summary

- Building a successful, sustainable experience requires data—the *actionable* kind. Data helps us track and gain insights about users and understand how multi-device experiences support and promote their needs, along dynamically changing contexts and via multiple connected devices, en route to their goals.

- The diversity of users is increasing. Measuring how people *actually use* products is a superior strategy for capturing the multiple contextual factors (conscious and unconscious, rational and emotional) that play into users' actions and their engagement patterns.

- It is critical to be able to analyze actual users' actions, engagement flows, and interaction patterns—across multiple devices—not only in order to measure product performance, but also to build long-term success through iterative testing/learning/improving cycles.

This relies on design as much as having an analytics strategy. This also means that some of the analytics paradigms will need to expand or change in order to accommodate multi-device-era needs.

NOTES

1. World Internet Population Has Doubled in the Last 5 Years," Pingdom, April 19, 2012, *http://bit.ly/1km137J.*

2. Measuring the Information Society," International Telecommunication Union (ITU), 2012, *http://bit.ly/1adPND2.*

3. Mary Meeker and Liang Wu, "2013 Internet Trends," KPCB, May 29, 2013, *http://www.kpcb.com/insights/2013-internet-trends.*

4. See *http://bit.ly/1ho31C5, http://bit.ly/IYhSHh, http://bit.ly/1fIarPU,* and *http://bit.ly/19V2emK.*

5. Manav Mishra, "Re-imagining Google Analytics to support the versatile usage patterns of today's users," Google Analytics Blog, October 29, 2012, *http://bit.ly/19WXXFn.*

6. "Double Vision—Global Trends in Tablet and Smartphone Use While Watching TV," Nielsen, April 5, 2012, *http://bit.ly/1cAsIuu.*

7. Mike Proulx and Stacey Shepatin, *Social TV: How Marketers Can Reach and Engage Audiences by Connecting Television to the Web, Social Media, and Mobile* (Hoboken, NJ: John Wiley & Sons, 2012), 4.

8. Jack Marshall, "Social TV War Ends, Twitter Wins," Digiday, September 5, 2013, *http://bit.ly/1kYkGAd;* Ingrid Lunden, "Twitter Confirms Purchase Of Bluefin Labs To Boost TV Analytics And Advertising Services," TechCrunch, February 5, 2013, *http://tcrn.ch/19ArHph.*

9. Avinash Kaushik (avinash), Twitter post, March 2, 2009, 10:39 AM, *http://bit.ly/1aNixm5.*

10. Ben Maxwell, "CityVille Reaches 100 million MAUs," Edge, January 14, 2011, *http://bit.ly/1kmeNzb.*

11. John Rice, "Study: Predicting Player Behavior and How Zynga Profits from Data Analysis," Educational Games Research, September 9, 2011, *http://bit.ly/1eqTL2n.*

[8]

Transforming Challenges

> Along with the huge promise of multi-device experiences, there are, of course, also development and adoption challenges that we must navigate. These obstacles exist both on the consumer side and on the product development side. In this chapter, we'll look at such challenges, explore ways we might transform them, and consider examples of how the future might take shape in the midst of this new, connected world.

New (and disruptive) technologies bring not only new opportunities but also new challenges. Up until now we've discussed the opportunities multi-device experiences introduce in this newly connected world. Yet if we want people to jump on the ecosystem bandwagon and get it moving (let alone steer it), we need to first properly examine the obstructions.

Multi-device experiences, especially those that expand into the Internet of Things (IoT) realm, present a large set of technological, societal, ethical, legal, business, policy, and standardization challenges. Going into each and every one would require a separate book. However, within the scope of this book, we'll look at several key challenges that we already struggle with (even when the experience is focused on the four core devices) and that are more closely tied to—and thus more significantly impact—our daily lives as product designers and developers. These challenges can be grouped into two types:

Ecosystem design and development challenges
Organizational structure, walled gardens, and resources and time to market

Ecosystem adoption challenges
Getting the ecosystem up and running, app overload

Let's start by exploring what these challenges mean and how they block our road. Then, I'll follow with some suggestions about approaches we might take to work past these obstacles.

Ecosystem Design and Development Challenges

The first three challenges touch on the development side of the ecosystem equation. I will focus on the following roadblocks that complicate the building of multi-device experiences: cross-organizational collaboration, walled gardens, and time and resource constraints.

ORGANIZATIONAL COLLABORATION CHALLENGES

In the long history of humankind (and animal kind, too) those who learned to collaborate and improved most effectively have prevailed.

CHARLES DARWIN

This famous quote by Charles Darwin, applied to design, expresses perfectly the need for organizations to implement tight, ongoing, cross-disciplinary collaboration in order to design a successful product ecosystem.

Most organizations today (especially large enterprises) are still very much dominated by a device-focused approach (across UX, product, and engineering), and this stands in the way of establishing an effective multi-device design process. In "The Rise of Cross-Channel UX Design,"[1] Tyler Tate describes multi-channel customer experience research conducted by Econsultancy and Foviance with 650 organizations and agencies. The study identified five key areas as crucial for delivering a well-integrated, compelling, multichannel customer experience:

- Systems and processes
- Leadership and culture
- Alignment with brand
- Customer touchpoints
- Use of insight

I will focus on the first two areas, which are of most relevance to the organizational structure and collaborative culture. According to the research report, most organizations described operational systems and processes as lacking cross-channel integration, and in many cases they were described as strictly tactical, driven by just a single channel (see Figure 8-1).

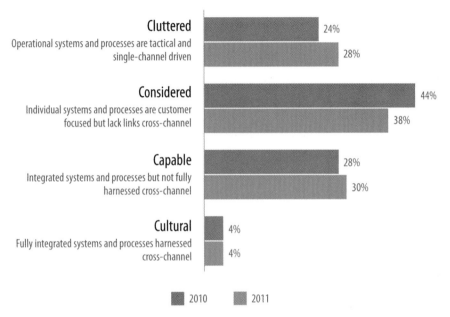

FIGURE 8-1

Comparison view between 2010 and 2011: companies' answers to the question, "Thinking about systems and processes, which of the following statements best describes your organization?" (Source: UX Matters, survey conducted by Econsultancy and Foviance.)

While 90% of companies considered the multi-channel experience to be important, this research revealed that the most significant barrier to success was organizational structure. Specifically, leadership and culture were mentioned as the most important attributes for delivering a positive customer experience (see Figure 8-2).

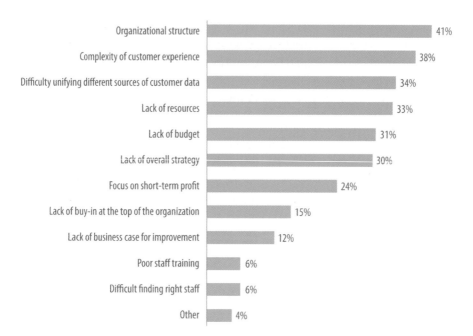

Organizational structure	41%
Complexity of customer experience	38%
Difficulty unifying different sources of customer data	34%
Lack of resources	33%
Lack of budget	31%
Lack of overall strategy	30%
Focus on short-term profit	24%
Lack of buy-in at the top of the organization	15%
Lack of business case for improvement	12%
Poor staff training	6%
Difficult finding right staff	6%
Other	4%

FIGURE 8-2

Responses to the question, "What are the three greatest barriers preventing your organization from improving the multichannel customer experience?" (Source: UX Matters, survey conducted by Econsultancy and Foviance.)

Many companies today are still organized in silos: different groups own different channels, they are not incentivized to share knowledge or work together, and they often are positioned to compete against one another for market share. When the front stage of the experience requires a collaborative effort to weave the end-to-end experience throughout touchpoints, these silos have problems connecting the backstage operations and flow, and ultimately cannot deliver the best experience to the customer. Even when groups do try to coordinate across channels, they have difficulty knowing when users cross from one device to the next, or even measuring how the touchpoints affect one another.

In a world where the user journey is becoming increasingly complex due to evolving technology and the proliferation of connected devices, a critical factor in designing an effective and successful experience is the extent to which organizations are committed to delivering it. This commitment demands strategic leadership aimed at establishing cooperation between teams and business units, and strongly promoting a central multi-device approach. Specifically, leaders can address the problem with such measures as building teams around ecosystem experiences rather than ones focused on specific devices. These teams can be then split into smaller groups with specific device expertise, while maintaining a close, continuous collaboration with one another, led by a high-level, end-to-end flow defined for the entire ecosystem.

It's important to note that this type of cross-team cooperation is not only a structural change, but also a cultural one. It's a big shift to move away from owning a silo to a operating a collaborative engagement model that focuses much more on group success. It carries wide implications in terms of responsibility, accountability, decision making, work processes, performance evaluation, and sense of ownership. Establishing such an organizational culture can take many forms, some of which will be determined as more companies jump on the ecosystem wagon.

THE WALLED GARDEN CHALLENGE

In the software world, a *walled garden* (or *closed platform*) is a system in which the service provider controls users' access to applications, services, data, and other content, allowing access to some of it and preventing access to other parts. Some examples include Comcast, Barnes & Noble (which restricts access to its Nook tablets), and Apple (which is probably the most well known of the walled gardens).

An *open platform* is the opposite case, where people get unrestricted access to the system content and services. It is based on open standards (often applied through APIs)[2] that allow third-party developers to integrate with the platform's services to power their own products. While an open platform is not necessarily open source, most open platforms are. The most prominent example is Android, which offers an open source–based platform for mobile carriers, OEMs (original equipment manufacturers), and developers. Other examples include Firefox, WordPress, and the *Guardian*.

As you may recall from Chapter 1, when defining a software ecosystem, I made the analogy to a natural ecosystem describing it as:

> [A] climate of multiple devices...smartphones, tablets, laptops, TVs, and other connected devices all interacting with one another and wirelessly sharing data. These interactions are shaped by the different ways in which individuals use the content and services that flow between devices.

In other words, multi-device experiences are defined by the underlying network of connections among devices, content, and people. These connections provide the energy that keeps the ecosystem alive and gives it meaning. Thus, the broader and larger this network of connections is, the more the ecosystem experience will flourish. This applies not only to connectivity and flow opportunities *within* a specific ecosystem, but also to potential integrations *between* multiple product ecosystems.[3]

The face of the mobile market today, however, is highly fragmented, forcing us to artificially split ecosystem experiences between multiple technological platforms (mainly the two dominant ones, iOS and Android) that are cut off from one another. Locking people into roped-off platforms this way not only defines and impacts communication flows and behaviors, but also establishes a mindset of platform-oriented ecosystems (rather than people-oriented ecosystems). This has several implications, both for consumers and for developers.

First, almost all multi-device experiences available today require consumers to use devices that all belong to the same platform. This requirement by itself binds people to platform-supported devices only (thus limiting their device selection) if they want to enjoy the benefits of the ecosystem offering. This limitation is more strongly felt in the case of a closed platform, such as iOS, that offers a narrower set of devices.

Second, even if people set up a platform-focused ecosystem, they might not be able to take full advantage of it. As we saw in previous chapters, many of the multi-device experiences integrate a social layer that is key to the experience—Party Play mode in collaborative games, active social communities in sports or activity ecosystems, and more. In such cases, it's not enough that the user has the apps up and running on multiple ecosystem devices—she needs her friends to be on the same platform as well.

From a developer's perspective, a common manifestation of this challenge is the "cold start" hurdle faced when first launching a product. Due to the cost, resources, and time to market involved in developing a product for multiple platforms, companies usually start with just one platform and add others later. The problem is that social systems require a critical mass of users in order to get moving and catch on—in terms of engagement, reach, and traction. Focusing on just a single platform by definition trims down the potential target audience. Furthermore, even when companies do launch their products multiple platforms, users might still remain separated from one another based on the platforms they use. With this split between platforms, users are unable to connect with one another and leverage ecosystem opportunities; thus, building and maintaining the critical user base becomes *much* harder, however great the experience might be.

Specific to walled gardens, developers are also limited in their ability to integrate their apps into the platform and use its services. They have much less flexibility in the way they can modify, access, or use native platform components, and thus might not be able to offer the same type of experience or features as in other platforms. This could lead to multiple mobile app variants that not only differ in platform-specific UI standards (like the position of the back button or the location of the tabs), but also present a deeper gap in the functionality and flow of the experience. Such fragmentation *within* product ecosystems can further hinder the interaction options and fluidity for people using different platforms.

RESOURCE AND TIME-TO-MARKET CHALLENGES

Building a multi-device experience is by definition more costly in terms of time, effort, and resources—especially as you go beyond developing consistent experiences that are replicated across devices and integrate complementary or continuous designs, which are context-driven and require adapting the experience to each device. As you'll recall, devices can play very different roles in such ecosystem experiences; thus, they could require different features, flows, and interactions that multiply the amount of work. Not only that, but all these devices need to work as a connected group, which adds the task of designing the integration points and experience transitions between them.

On the UX side, this means more work in each stage of the design process: additional research and design explorations are necessary in order to define the overarching ecosystem narrative across the board. This requires us to reexamine our current design approach in the following ways:

- Rethink use cases, contexts of use, and user flows in light of the new connected devices.

- Identify integration points and contextual triggers along the end-to-end experience.

- Define the multi-device experience patterns involved in the experience.

- Figure out what exactly should live on which device, when, and how.

Beyond that, there is the actual iterative work of building wireframes, mockups, and prototypes that translate these concepts into visuals. Finally, as multi-device experiences are still new and potentially outstretch existing mental models, we need to do more user testing and careful data analysis in order to continuously learn and improve the experience across the board.

On the engineering side, there's a lot of heavy lifting to do, including developing tailored experiences across devices, building contextual frameworks for data sharing and communication, storing all the data, developing separate interfaces for each device (potentially dynamic ones), and integrating mechanisms for machine learning and adaptive behavior. And I'm sure there's more.

At the very basic level, these new approaches limit the effectiveness of component reuse and the ability to use techniques like responsive design. But more importantly, a lot of the powerful contextual pieces of the experience require new engineering solutions to overcome existing challenges—whether related to response times, context detection (signals, analysis), or machine learning algorithms.

Such challenges come with the territory. It's important to see that these challenges are an integral part of this space: building a product across multiple devices requires more time and resources than building it on just one device. At the same time, given the increasing rate at which multiple devices are becoming assimilated into our lives, there's already a cost for *not* designing for multiple devices (one that will only rise as more and more devices join the space). Moreover, designing effective multi-device experiences that are better adapted to varying user contexts and task flows carries greater potential for impact, innovation, and success.

Ecosystems Don't Happen Overnight

I only hope we that we never lose sight of one thing—that it was all started by a mouse.

WALT DISNEY, 1957

We have reviewed some significant design and development challenges, no doubt. But they entail even greater opportunities.

Both types of challenges—organizational and developmental—require time and learning to overcome. We are taking only the first steps in building a connected world, and there's a lot to explore and iterate on. At this point in time, nobody can say how the future is going to look exactly, but we can start preparing for it by experimenting with new approaches for designing and building ecosystem products.

Building greatness doesn't need to happen in a day. You can (and should) think big, and plan for the broad multi-device narrative. Thinking through people's contextual journeys and identifying the sweet spots you can leverage *is* important. With that said, you don't necessarily need to launch the fully fleshed ecosystem in a single go. You can break down the vision into smaller steps and build your way from there. Start by focusing on the very essence—the two or three most important offerings in your product that set you apart from others and provide people with the strongest added value. This might be a more limited feature set involving only two devices, or a broader offering that is launched initially on just a single device but that prepares the ground for more devices joining progressively down the road, while building users' expectations.

In many cases, thinking about the smartphone experience first is a good exercise, since it is currently the prevalent device with the most constraints (small size, touch interface), and as such it forces you to focus on what matters most.

> **[NOTE]**
>
> Down the road this might not necessarily be the case, as smaller devices (like watches, glasses, and wristbands) diffuse in the market. These devices present further constraints and challenges beyond the ones we face with smartphones today.

Partnerships can be another means to deliver a rich multi-device experience to users. You don't necessarily need to build everything on your own: you can explore integrations with other products out there that complement yours, and create a bigger pie together.

The revolution is always on. Horses didn't just evolve into cars, or cars into airplanes (and who knows what's coming next). Each of these progressions involved a disruptive change in the transportation industry—a change that was first perceived as an unusual, impractical invention, and then became a luxury, and eventually turned into a commonplace mode of travel that people use every day.

We are going through a similar process with multi-device experiences. If we stick with the preceding analogy, looking at the ultimate IoT vision of ubiquitous computing and ambient intelligence we're probably somewhere between a horse and a car at this point. We still have many hurdles to jump, standards to establish, and a whole lot of learning and experimentation to do along the way, but the impact is going to be huge. By starting to address these challenges, we prepare for and inform bigger changes to come, bringing the future closer.

Discussion: Deconstructing the Internet of Things

SCOTT JENSON, GOOGLE

Scott Jenson has been doing user interface design and strategic planning for over 20 years. He worked at Apple on System 7, Newton, and the Apple Human Interface guidelines. He was the director of Symbian's DesignLab, VP of product design for Cognima, a manager of mobile UX for Google for five years, and a creative director at frog design in San Francisco. He has consulted to several early-stage startups, and is now back at Google, working on the Chrome web browser.

SMART TOASTER

When talking about the Internet of Things (or IoT), I frequently bring up the Smart Toaster™, as it is such a lightning rod. People just love to make fun of it. My favorite was the tweet, "I don't think my smart toaster needs apps," which (of course) was retweeted into the stratosphere.

When I read things like this, I just shake my head. You can't evaluate tomorrow's concepts by yesterday's tasks! Of course, a smart toaster doesn't need apps. A horse doesn't need wheels either. We just need to look at what *smart* means in a more nuanced way. The goal of this sidebar is to convince you that the Smart Toaster actually is a bold new vision of the future. If I can unpack what it means to be smart, so that even a lowly toaster starts to make sense, we'll be thinking about the IoT in a much broader context.

THE CLASSIC VISION

The classic vision of the Internet of Things is a fairly complex cascade of activity triggered by an event. For example, when I pull into my driveway, my garage door opens, the lights turn on, a status update is sent to my family ("Dad's home!"), the house has been preemptively warmed up, and the music in my car is seamlessly transferred to my home stereo. This is a great vision, but it also implies some very deep cooperation and standardization. We'll get there in time, but I'm still living in a world where my Bluetooth phone has trouble talking to my Bluetooth car stereo.

My point is that we shouldn't jump straight into the most complex vision of the future. It's confusing and excessively difficult, and it can lead to a backlash when we can't do it all at once. Small can be beautiful. Let's look a bit more closely at the smart toaster and figure out how to peel back this grand vision. Are there layers of functionality that are easier to obtain but still provide value? I'm going to talk about three: discovery, control, and coordination. Let's take a look at each and how it has value.

LAYER 1: DISCOVERY

This first layer is simple, very simple. At this level, a smart device just broadcasts a URL, wirelessly, to any nearby smart display. By *smart display*, I mean a phone, a tablet, a smart TV, or even Google Glass. This would allow me to walk into my kitchen, open my phone, and "see" that my toaster is offering up a URL. When I click on the device name, I go to that URL in the browser. It's that simple.

Now, to be honest, just broadcasting a top-level website is pretty boring—more marketing than real consumer value. But if that URL were to contain my model number, I could be directed to a very useful support site. Even further, if the URL contained my serial number, then things could get really interesting, as everything about my device and my interaction with it could be recorded. It could completely change customer support (and registration, and online instruction, and recycling, and...).

Companies would kill for this. They already put URLs and even QR codes all over their product packaging. To have this extend into the life of a product would be extremely useful. The problem is that they can't do this. Well, some companies do, but it's very expensive: it's called *writing a native app*. But this isn't just expensive, it also doesn't scale: no customer is going to have an app for every product in his house. If we could make the broadcast of a URL cheap to add to a product, and make it so any device could discover it, it would create a new "web race" where every device could take you to its website.

This would be the first, simplest form of the Internet of Things: things on the Internet. It would succeed because it is universal, like the Internet itself is. It also would start off as a bit unassuming—a bunch of Black & Decker products pointing to instructional videos. But once the ecosystem takes off, it will start to create a linkage between anything in the real world that wants to take you to something on the Web. Museums, airport kiosks, bus stops, kids' toys, and even dog collars could all sprout very useful websites that could in turn be a platform to more, higher-level services.

LAYER 2: CONTROL

Once you've taken that step, it's not that much harder to add a few dollars to your product cost to enable wireless control of the device. This is where people tend to misunderstand, as they expect the functionality of smart devices to be on par with iPhones.

If my smart toaster had only a single, trivial function—to change my "toast done" sound to a range of different sounds, from soothing Zen tones to goofy, kid-friendly slapstick—that would be huge! Yes, in the world of toasters, adding a few additional dollars to its production cost is indeed a big deal. There is no question that this is a risk, but I also know that there are many parents that would spend a lot more for a crazy, kid-pleasing toaster. The Nest home heating system (discussed in Chapter 6) has proven that high-end devices that break out of the norm can indeed justify higher price points.

If this extra "toast done" sound feature doubled the cost of the product, it would be a terribly bad idea. However, as the cost of system-on-a-chip devices falls, the cost of this addition will fall as well, becoming trivial over time. The trick is finding the right value/price point for these early, control-layer products. It will get much easier as the price falls. One daring company needs to take the first scary jump and validate the approach. But whoever succeeds will be immediately followed by the rest.

LAYER 3: COORDINATION

At this level, things start to get much harder. The previous two layers were pretty much solo endeavors. The only shared mechanism was a universal form of discovery. In fact, every smart device today, from Nest to Sonos to Withings smart scales, "goes solo" by writing its own apps. The value of discovery/control is already a well-known value for the trailblazing companies. The problem is that the only viable way forward is to write an app. If we could remove that barrier, many more products would be able to sprout interactivity.

However, once we enter the realm of cooperating devices, the level of complexity rises quickly. My toaster is now part of a broader home system that can:

- Log sensor information to a common data store.
- Store that information in a common format.
- Respond to a range of shared commands that all devices support.

These abilities are what most people associate with swarms of IoT devices: everything works together to share data and functionality. The difficulty with this level is not so much in making it happen technically but socially. In order for these scenarios to play out, companies need to cooperate and agree on certain APIs and communication protocols to get things to play nicely.

We have a terrible track record of device cooperation today. I can't even get my TV and Blu-Ray player to communicate over an HDMI video cable, and this is after a decade of standardization effort. Right now, the big companies are trying to create self-protecting ecosystems, attempting to crowd out competitors. But things are changing rapidly. A slew of new, scrappy Kickstarter/Indigogo projects are going to rally around a self-forming standard. The tiny mammals will outrace the powerful dinosaurs. Once something gains traction, it will build quickly.

This coordination effort will also likely to have deconstructed layers of its own, pushing data up and control down, but that's a separate topic. I very much want this third coordination layer to arrive, but I'm realistic that we have lots of experimentation and agreement to get through first. Fortunately, this is already happening with cooperating companies like Spark Devices, SmartThings, pinocc.io, and many more.

CONCLUSION

The Internet of Things is a big, complex beast, and we're in love with the most complex version of it—the coordination layer. While this layer is the most impressive of the three, we shouldn't ignore the fairly low-hanging fruit that comes from the first two: discovery and control. The discovery layer creates an entirely new way to link the real world to the Web, lowering the cost so any company can easily connect its device to the Internet without building an app. This is the first and easiest step. The control layer just takes it a bit further and allows you to connect and control the device. This is harder only because it is more expensive per device, but that cost will fall quickly. Both of these layers are still fairly easy because they're not beholden to anyone: you can control your device in any way you see fit, using any commands you want.

The only thing we have to build is the discovery system that needs to look for these URLs. This will open up an entire ecosystem of interactivity, one that—like the early Internet—starts off modestly but will grow into a platform to allow all sorts of products to flourish.

Ecosystem Adoption Challenges

Now we'll look at some consumer-focused challenges, which touch on different aspects of ecosystem adoption: setting up the ecosystem, getting it running, and dealing with app overload. These hurdles already impact users' engagement, even in these early days of multi-device experiences, where the focus is just on the core ecosystem devices. As the grand, ambitious IoT vision continues to be realized, it's going to get much hairier.

The earlier we can get users' adoption, and the more people we can get on board, the more we will be able to learn about what works, what doesn't, and how we can get better going forward.

THE CHALLENGE OF GETTING THE ECOSYSTEM UP AND RUNNING

To a consumer, one of the biggest hurdles to engaging with an ecosystem experience is just getting it up and running—and keeping it that way. Currently, to use one app on multiple devices, people need to install it separately on any device they want to use it on—a process that raises an already high barrier to entry. Just take a look at a common workflow for installing *one* app on *one* device (Figure 8-3).

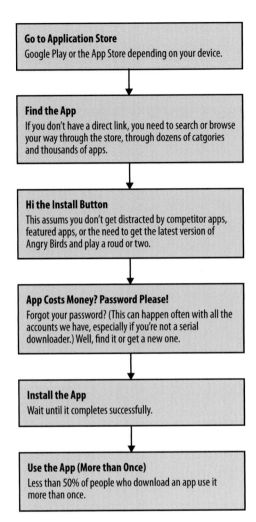

Go to Application Store
Google Play or the App Store depending on your device.

Find the App
If you don't have a direct link, you need to search or browse your way through the store, through dozens of catgories and thousands of apps.

Hi the Install Button
This assumes you don't get distracted by competitor apps, featured apps, or the need to get the latest version of Angry Birds and play a roud or two.

App Costs Money? Password Please!
Forgot your password? (This can happen often with all the accounts we have, especially if you're not a serial downloader.) Well, find it or get a new one.

Install the App
Wait until it completes successfully.

Use the App (More than Once)
Less than 50% of people who download an app use it more than once.

FIGURE 8-3
Common flow steps required for installing one app on one device.

Getting users' attention, time, and focus long enough to persist through an app installation for one device is nothing to take for granted, let alone when this process is required across several devices. If you also account for the registration or sign-in process that almost all apps require in order to use them, the hurdle is even higher.

Users might have some time to install your app on their smartphones on the train ride home while they're playing with it. However, by the time they get home (where their tablets wait expectantly), their minds are already somewhere else (like having dinner with the family, or putting the kids to bed), and they quickly forget or don't have the availability to address other devices.

Furthermore, with the very limited multi-device-experience education that products offer today, as discussed in Chapter 3, users are not typically informed along the product flow (contextually or at all) that there are more "parts" to the experience on other devices. Thus, it's easy to lose sight of the cross-device setup needed.

Apple tried to address this challenge by automatically syncing apps between devices. By default, any downloaded app is automatically transferred to other devices the next time the devices are synced (an automatic process that takes place when the user connects the device to the computer).[4] This setting helps streamline the ecosystem setup process, but it still embodies several challenges:

Device sync is detached from user flow
> The trigger for syncing apps across devices is the point in time when people choose to sync their devices. They might do that right before they actually need the app on a device, but they might not. This sync action is detached from the actual user flow, and thus there's no clear contextual tie (or guidance) between the task at hand and how the user can benefit from accomplishing it through the use of multiple devices.

Can't see the ecosystem for the apps
> When there are more than 100 or 200 apps on a device—a scenario that is not far-fetched—an auto-sync for all these apps across all devices pays no mind to context, and this convenience can actually obscure the bigger ecosystem picture.[5] With so many apps synced everywhere, most people probably won't even notice or remember how all the apps got there, and which ones actually provide a well-designed, multi-device experience.

Multi-device experiences often comprise different apps for different devices
> As it currently stands, many products that offer contextual multi-device experiences deliver them through separate apps (under separate names) for smartphones and tablets. For example, Allrecipes has an app (Dinner Spinner) for the smartphone, and an app (Your Kitchen Inspiration) for the tablet. A simple app sync between devices will not capture these connected multi-device experience ingredients.

Not only that, but if you think about the ecosystem setup process (as it works today) in the broader scope of the IoT world—with the watches, glasses, toasters, refrigerators, lamps, coffee machines, and whatnot—this challenge worsens. Can we really expect people to install, sync, and maintain apps for each and every device that takes part in the experience? Does it make sense to have people constantly engaging in app hopping for every connected thing they want to interact with in their homes or outside?

For all these reasons, we not only face a setup barrier in getting the basic multi-device experience up and running across devices, but we can also see that the current app paradigm cannot scale into the near future.

This latter point also brings up another challenge we already face: app overload.

Discussion: The Battery-Life Challenge

Battery life is a major usage barrier we've been facing for a while with all our portable devices—from laptops and media players, to smartphones and tablets, and now to watches, wristbands, headsets, and other wearables that are joining the charging party. It has come to the point that there's actually a wearable wrist charger, just for charging your portable devices through long days of traveling.[6] And yes—you guessed right—it needs to be charged as well.

As the owner of seven different portable consumer electronics I use on a daily basis, I find myself constantly in a charging race. It starts with the ongoing anxious lookout for battery level across all devices, making sure I don't run out of power on any of them. Some devices can go on without charging for five days, others for three days, and some need charging every day. However, battery longevity also depends on usage level (which is not always stable), so it's not necessarily predictable. To make things even more complicated, wearable devices that rely on a Bluetooth connection (like most do) eat up the battery life of the paired device (usually the smartphone) much faster than otherwise, aggravating the charging problem. But this is just half of the problem.

The other half is when you actually need to charge the device(s). Then, the race becomes one for a power socket. Most mobile devices today are shipped with a USB cable for charging, turning the computer into their main source of life. Being the owner of a MacBook Air—which comes with just two USB ports—I often run into the problem of having to decide on charging prioritization, due to too many "mouths to feed." Yes, I can buy a power adapter (or USB hub), but that's more work (and more things to carry around). Most of us just stick to the default configuration we get (a fact that applies to both software and hardware).

Planning the charging schedule ahead of time is also a bit of a stretch: with so many devices, it's quite hard to remember when you last charged each one. You mostly rely on the UI feedback on each device display, following closely that little battery icon and its diminishing color fill.

Until wireless charging is disseminated everywhere, or a different technological solution is found, the UI plays a key role in handling the battery battle. What should you consider in that respect?

BATTERY-LEVEL INDICATION

There are several options for providing ongoing feedback about battery status:

- Always showing feedback on-screen (as in mobile phones, tablets)

- Surfacing feedback on-screen contextually, only when the battery is getting low and your attention is needed or an action should be taken (as in the Pebble Watch)

- Not showing feedback on-screen at all, keeping the UI clean:

  - If the device has a screen, place the battery information in a designated area the user can navigate to in order to check the level.

  - If the device doesn't have a screen, alert the user when the battery is getting to a low charge state (more on that shortly).

Out of these three options, I personally prefer the first strategy—always showing battery information on the screen (the same way car dashboards show the fuel gauge).

Given the critical importance of battery life (and fuel level) information—both to people and to the actual product usage—providing a clear status indication helps establish confidence among users, without carrying a high visual cost:

- As long as battery level is good, people are reassured and experience a "feel-good moment," knowing they can continue using the product safely. This feeling is an important UX guideline: you shouldn't just give feedback to people when something goes wrong—make sure to also provide positive reinforcement when relevant. Making people feel good helps boost their confidence in using the product, and cultivates a positive perception of the product overall.

- When the battery level is going down, users can spot it right away and act upon it. Through color change, for example, their attention can be drawn to the battery information.

As much as I value a contextual UI treatment, where information is displayed only when it's needed (keeping the UI clean the rest of the time), it's not always the best solution. In some instances, using a persistent anchor that is always present enhances in terms of predictability, clarity, and user confidence.

INFORMATION SHOWN

The battery information can include:

- Visual indication only (a battery icon)
- Visual indication plus battery percentage
- Visual indication plus time left until battery runs out

As a general guideline, it's usually enough to display just a simple battery icon that provides a visual representation of the status. This is an already established standard that people are familiar with and know how to address. Furthermore, assuming we display this indicator at all times, making it compact and subtle helps maintain a clean, polished design that doesn't compete for a user's attention with too many prominent visual elements.

At the same time, providing a way to get additional info about the battery status can be useful, especially when it's about to run out and the user might need to take some action, like turning off services to save battery power for later. In this case, showing how much time is left before the battery runs out would be more useful and actionable (compared to just a percentage), as this is essentially the information the user needs in order to assess her next steps. If the design (and available real estate) allows, it would be helpful to provide some guidance about the ways the user can save battery power or the closest place where she can charge it.

This additional information can be displayed in a designated area (like Settings), or via focused "Battery Low" alerts, as discussed next.

"BATTERY LOW" ALERTS

When battery power reaches a certain low level—the level at which it requires attention, and possibly an action—you should alert the user about it.

This alert can take various forms:

- Changing the icon display
- Providing an auditory warning
- Displaying a pop-up alert on-screen, possibly with additional actionable data (like time left until battery runs out)
- Taking some automatic measures to help save battery power (dimming the brightness, for example)

An interesting design angle when it comes to multi-device experiences is the question of which devices should get this alert:

- Only the device it applies to
- The low-battery device plus other ecosystem devices

As mentioned in the discussion on notification strategy (Chapter 6), utilizing the holistic ecosystem constellation to support important message communication could be a powerful course of action—especially when it involves devices that have no screen or are not in immediate sight.

This means, for example, that if my wristband activity tracker is running out of battery, having an alert sent to my smartphone (in addition to getting some visual and/or auditory feedback on the wearable device itself) would be a good idea. The same goes for the Pebble Watch, where I might miss the notification on the device, and for smart monitors that are remote and other such devices.

To take this one step further, when it comes to communication devices—mainly the smartphone—I would consider notifying not only the device owner, but also other people trying to contact that person, when the device is about to (or already has) run out of battery. Given the always-on culture we live in today, and how heavily people rely on smartphones as a communication tool, you can easily get concerned when you're unable to reach others on their smartphones. Receiving an automatic out-of-battery notification when you're trying to contact the device owner, or during a communication thread in which the owner suddenly becomes unresponsive, could prevent potential stress and misunderstandings.

THE APP OVERLOAD CHALLENGE

Last I checked, I had 107 apps on my smartphone. Yet, on a regular day, I probably only use the same 14–16 apps, such as Messages, Phone, Google Maps, Facebook, Google Search, Gmail, Calendar, Alarm Clock, and News. A quick survey among my friends paints a similar picture: they have dozens of apps installed on their devices, but only use a handful regularly. A large study conducted by Nielsen in 2012 reveals app proliferation to be a nationwide phenomenon.[7] The average number of apps per smartphone in the US is constantly on the rise, jumping 28% (between 2011 and 2012)—yet people reported spending only 8% more time actually using those apps.[8] These figures go hand in hand with the booming supply in the app markets.

Everyday 641 new apps are posted to the App Store, adding up to more than 19,000 new apps every month.[9] In October 2013, Apple announced it had reached 60 billion downloads and 1 million apps in the store.[10] More than 4.5 billion apps are downloaded from the App Store and Google Play, combined, every month, filling up people's devices and creating more and more virtual desktops covered with colorful icons—all calling for users' attention (Figure 8-4).

FIGURE 8-4

A typical case of app overload on an iPhone, filling up multiple home screens.

With so many apps, the mobile experience becomes cluttered and difficult to maintain. Finding the good stuff gets harder and harder (both in the app market and on your personal device), and it's easy for a user to forget which apps he has, let alone locate one when he needs it.

The proliferation of apps is further intensified by companies releasing multiple apps for the same product on the same device: some apps differ in feature set, some are limited to a certain location or time frame, and with others the distinction is not always clear. This strategy is quite common among the bigger, more popular brands, which have the resources to build powerful multi-device experiences along with the ability to influence millions of their fans. A few examples include:

Nike+

> Offers Nike+ Running, Nike+ Training, Nike+ FuelBand, Nike+ Basketball, Nike+ Kinect Training, and more

Coca-Cola

Continuously releases new apps, like Coca-Cola Snow Globes, Coca-Cola Santa's Helper (for Christmas), Coca-Cola Freestyle, Coca-Cola My Beat Maker, and more

TripAdvisor

Offers Hotel Flights, SeatGuru: Maps+Flights+Tracker, and a separate city guide app for each city (e.g., London, New York, Rome, and dozens more)

With all these sibling apps, it becomes even more difficult for users to find their way through the app markets, let alone make a decision about the app that they need (and feel confident about it). If people take the safe route and install all the product apps on their devices, they further overload the home screen(s) with many apps that account for only a single product. Additionally, it becomes harder to differentiate between same-product apps because they usually share a very similar (if not identical) visual design.

With an already severe app overload problem when we're dealing with just four or five core devices, what will happen when IoT development gains speed (a process that has already started)? How will we be able to handle the overwhelming flow of apps without losing grip?

One Ecosystem Heart

One ecosystem heart refers to the idea of a single fluid entity running across all devices, one that adapts itself to the different contextual needs placed on the devices by users. Once the "heart" is up and beating on one device, it pumps the blood through all the relevant ecosystem vessels. The first device can be *any* device in the ecosystem, allowing for diversity in the ways different people engage with different devices.

As I look at the ecosystem adoption challenges we face, especially with regard to app overload, I can't help but wonder *what if*:

- Our ecosystem was based on a single "heart" (or app) that could distribute itself intelligently across devices?

- Instead of having to install multiple separate instances of the same product on multiple devices, people could interact with a single fluid app?

- One app could present itself (or relevant pieces of itself) contextually, on the relevant device, when people need it, and go away when its job is done (until next time)?

The distribution process across devices could be seamless, taking place in the background and triggered by context along the user journey. Triggers could include:

- Certain usage patterns on a certain device (e.g., registering for an event, bookmarking an item, playing a video, searching, zooming on an element, or clicking a certain link or button)

- A predefined location-, social-, or time-based context the user has entered (e.g., entering a venue, arriving at the office, getting on the train, watching TV with friends)

Alternatively, this ecosystem heart could be explicitly built into the product flow, so that while using the device, users are informed or guided to "expand" the experience to other devices. This could either be bound to the first-time experience (as part of the initial onboarding experience) or serve as an integral part of the flow on an ongoing basis—showing users the ways the experience could continue to and/ or complement other devices in the ecosystem.

The distribution itself can take place via a range of interactions, like voice input, promixity, gestures (like "tossing" the app between devices), taking a photo, or a physical connection between devices (such as a bump). These interactions could be fun and useful not only for expanding the user's own product ecosystem, but also in social contexts such as distributing the ecosystem to friends.

This experience modularity framework is software-based in essence. However, it can be accompanied by hardware customizations as well. Given the quick progression in the 3D printing world and the decreasing costs of hardware, devices can become dynamic not only in their interface design but also in their physical properties.

MY FIRST HEART AND ECOSYSTEM

As with most ideas, the idea of one ecosystem heart is not completely new. Before I joined Google in 2009, I worked at an innovative mobile startup called *modu*. Looking back, I can say that was probably the first moment that I got hooked on ecosystems.

modu invented, developed, and manufactured an innovative mobile ecosystem model focused on context (Figure 8-5). A tiny modular phone ("the modu") served as the heart, offering just the basic mobile functionality needed across all contexts (for instance, contacts, messages, and call log).[11] This little phone could then be placed into sleeves ("jackets"), which tailored the shape and functionality of the phone and adapted it to the context at hand. So, for example, a *Sport* jacket was designed as an armband (made of a special breathable fabric) for easy carrying during a sports activity. It was enhanced with additional sensors, offered built-in sports features, and had easily accessible buttons for controlling music, as well as a nice big display for the sports metrics during a user's run. The data could then be synced to the computer.

The modu phone was designed to also plug into other consumer electronics ("mates"), offering new experience opportunities by having those two devices connected to each other and able to share data.

FIGURE 8-5

The modu ecosystem of devices—the modu phone is in the middle, surrounded by selected set of "jackets" and "mates" it could plug into in order to provide tailored, modular solutions in different contexts.

Back then—and I'm referring to 2007, before the iPhone came out, before all these connected devices came into our lives—this concept of tailoring mobile experiences for different contexts was foreign to people. To explain when context shifts would benefit from a change in jacket, we often used the reference of *every time you change your shoes, you change your jacket.* Think about it: presumably we could all settle for a single pair of shoes for everywhere we go. For the most part, this would provide the functional and practical benefits we need, in the most cost-effective way. Still, we buy many (many) pairs and change them frequently, because we want to tailor the shoes to a context. We do this for more granular functional reasons (like boots for winter, sports shoes for running), fashion considerations (matching shoes with an outfit and/or accessories, keeping up with trends), and for specific events (such as a wedding).

What I found—and still find—most compelling about modu (besides the amazing group of people I was fortunate to know) was the visionary, context-driven thinking, both on the software and hardware sides. From the very get-go, I was fascinated by the idea of tailoring a mobile experience to people's needs in a modular way, simplifying it per touchpoint, and establishing a broader ecosystem narrative. The biggest multi-device design challenge we faced when building such an ecosystem was finding that delicate balance between consistency across the ecosystem and optimizing the experience to each device. This challenge translated to numerous detailed questions, on a daily basis, around flow designs, feature distribution, interaction models, and many other design details.

A lot of things have changed since 2007: we own multiple devices, we have a prosperous cloud technology, we can connect devices wirelessly, and the entire face of the mobile industry has shifted to touch-based, app-fed devices. Yet I believe that the essence of this contextual approach still applies today as we address multi-device experiences, both in terms of opportunities and challenges.

ONE ECOSYSTEM HEART FIRSTS

Two present-day products that already demonstrate the core idea of modular interfaces adapting themselves to contextual user needs are Everything.me and Aviate.

Search-driven adaptation: Everything.me

Everything.me offers a Dynamic Phone™ platform that constantly adapts itself by dynamically changing the home screen appearance and the apps surfaced on it, based on users' needs at that moment as expressed through their searches (Figure 8-6).

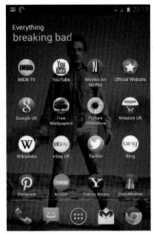

FIGURE 8-6

Everything.me (available only on Android), showing the way the phone UI adapts itself to each query entered. Tapping any app opens it with the query term inside.

For example, typing "sushi" in the Everything.me search bar will change the user's home screen background image to one of sushi, and surface to the top relevant apps the user has installed, like Yelp, OpenTable, and Google Places. The bottom portion of the screen offers apps from the cloud (using HTML5), which provide additional useful services that people would usually access through the browser; these are now easily accessible without the user's needing to download anything. Not only that, but when users go into any of these apps—say, the Wikipedia app, or the YouTube app—the results are already populated with the search term they entered, taking them directly where they need to go.

This combination of installed apps and cloud-based ones signifies an important step in blurring the lines between them, just like we had with desktops. This can potentially change the way people consume and interact with content and services on mobile devices as well. Thinking more broadly on the multi-device ecosystem—going into a world where everything (or at least core pieces) is operated from the cloud—turns that concept of one ecosystem heart that flows between devices into much more of a reality.

Automatic interface adaptation: Aviate

Aviate (Figure 8-7) is another example of an Android launcher that adopts the contextual approach, aiming to connect people to personalized information at the moment it's useful.

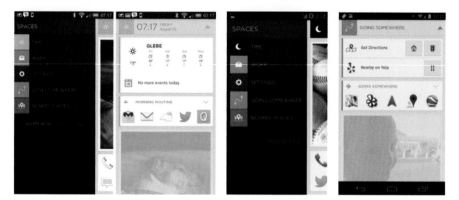

FIGURE 8-7

Aviate, an Android launcher, showing the changing home screen displays between "morning routine" and "nighttime," as well as between different spaces.

Similar to Everything.me, Aviate takes over the home screen and replaces it with an adaptive experience personalized to the user. However, it approaches it differently.

Aviate introduces several different "spaces" that represent different contexts: Time (the default space, which changes based on the time of day), Work, Nearby Places, Going Somewhere, and Settings. Users can access these spaces by swiping right and left, with each space offering a different display with a unique collection of apps and widgets.

While Everything.me relies on user input (i.e., the search term) as a trigger for its contextual behavior, Aviate changes its display automatically in a seamless manner, based on the user's location or movements. This means, for example, that when people wake up in the morning, the home screen shows their upcoming meetings and weather info, but when they're in the car driving to work, the display changes to traffic and directions. Also, the main Time space content changes through the day, from morning routine to a normal daytime to nighttime. Users can also manually move between spaces, but the real power lies in the automatic adaptive behavior throughout the day.

Intent-driven design

Everything.me and Aviate both highlight a few key principles related to the *one ecosystem heart* concept:

- We need to shift from app-driven approach to intent-focused design.

- The device usage is driven not by a grid of apps, but rather by user intent, which is served by the apps. Neither of these products broke completely from the apps paradigm (that would require a broader industry effort), but they adopted a different, more people-centered approach. In this approach, the leading factors are the users' journey and needs throughout the day, which drive the way they consume content and interact with the device.

- In many ways, both Everything.me and Aviate follow the intelligence path of Google Now (discussed in Chapter 2), putting the focus on automatically showing users what they need, when they need it, making the overall experience much more effective, simple, and delightful.

- These two products bring up the importance of an open platform in order to enable this kind of modular, contextual behavior. They are both offered only on Android, due to its open platform, which allows a lot more freedom in customizing the product design and behavior. The challenge of walled gardens was discussed previously, and it is already clear: as we move into a connected world, where ever more different things need to talk to one another and together create a meaningful experience, openness becomes a key success factor.

- Both products offer *contextual app surfacing*, simplifying device usage through surfacing only a selected group of relevant apps per context.

- Aviate adds another layer to that through its *dynamic app interface*. While Everything.me keeps a consistent UI template across all use cases (search terms), only changing the content within it, Aviate introduces a different screen display (layout, elements, design) for each space, based on the context at hand.

  Adding that layer opens up more opportunities for tailoring the experience to the context (and the individual). As we broaden the design scope to multi-device experiences, this capability becomes more important. The diversity of devices, their different properties and form factors, and the different needs and use cases they serve—all of these would benefit from a higher degree of customization and design freedom.

PERSONALIZATION CAN (AND WILL) GO FURTHER

This one ecosystem heart approach can go even further in terms of user and device personalization:

Personalized experiences on the same device

As more devices join the ecosystem—some shared by multiple people—being able to dynamically adapt the interface to each one would encourage adoption and increase engagement.[12] For example, when the five-year-old picks up the tablet, all she would see is her favorite set of games and educational apps, with no access to others' apps or data. When her dad uses the device, it would load *his* content, with all the latest books he's downloaded. When mom gets the device in her hands, she can immediately catch up on *her* emails, check out the latest guilty dog videos, and go to sleep.

This adaptive behavior should follow through to other devices as well, adhering to the 3Cs design framework. This means that the five-year-old, who started learning the basics of programming on the tablet at home (yes, there's an app for that!), can continue her education on mom's smartphone while they're waiting at the doctor's office. When mom gets to work, she can use her laptop to complete the email she started last night. Dad can continue the book he started reading during his morning run, utilizing the auditory version.

Personalized distribution across devices

The ecosystem experience could go beyond adapting the device interface to the individual user and also distribute the experience across devices selectively, based on the individual using the device. This could result in different people getting the piece of the chain that is relevant only to them. For example, two roommates could have the same app on their smartphones, but not necessarily have its counterpart on their tablets. To go back to the Allrecipes example, let's say one roommate is in charge of the grocery shopping in the apartment, and the other does the cooking. In that case, the continuous experiences could be split between the two, so that the first gets the automatic shopping list on the phone, but the other gets the cooking interface on the tablet, respective to each's role in this activity.

Adaptive content per context

What if, instead of offering multiple apps for the same product, we could update a single app entity with the relevant content per context? For example, instead of a dozen different TripAdvisor apps for each city, what about a single TripAdvisor entity that updates its content based on the user's location and/or upcoming trip itinerary? If he's starting the trip in Paris, the app would provide TripAdvisor's content on Paris, and once he gets to London the content would automatically update accordingly. Furthermore, when he's back home, we could build on dynamic app surfacing (as shown with Everything.me and Aviate) and potentially hide this app from the main home screen to clear out space for other apps that are more useful on a routine day.

These behaviors are more complex, but they are not impossible. As long as we focus on adapting to context, and moving away from an app-driven approach to a more modular experience design, we can progressively add in these capabilities. Starting from implementations like Everything.me and Aviate and broadening them to multi-device design (rather than just within-device design), we can make a first significant step into the new connected world.

Discussion: Multi-Device Experiences in the Service of Health

In Chapter 6, we saw a few examples, like BiKN and Square, where the smartphone is enhanced with new capabilities through hardware "jackets" (or accessories) that plug into the device. Through such physical connections, the smart device can get even smarter in a variety of ways, serving new, changing needs along different contexts and environments. The wireless connectivity complements the physical one, enabling ongoing conversation among the ecosystem devices. This conversation can take the form of data syncing across the different devices, all contributing to central ecosystem wisdom. It can also be a functional conversation, in which devices affect one another—for example, controlling one another using the technology embedded in those hardware jackets (like we saw with BiKN).

Let's expand our focus on multi-device experiences to include a look at products from the health and medical technology industry:

Medical technology is relevant

The medical industry is specifically suited for utilizing hardware accessories, due to its highly specialized requirements. It can leverage the computing powers of the smartphone (and other devices), but for many cases, an app is not enough. More advanced, sophisticated appliances are required to work in collaboration with the mobile device.

Medical technology is on fire

A prosperous entrepreneurial community is trying to develop a healthcare ecosystem through technology and innovation. As of this writing, there were 100 accelerator companies cultivating digital health and wellness startups, many of them solely focused on this industry (such as Rock Health, StartUp Health, and Welltech Funding).[13] This active startup community (operating side-by-side with established enterprises like Cisco, GE, Intel, and Verizon Wireless) further signals the worldwide potential and promise of health and medical technology innovations, and the impact they can have on saving and improving people's lives.

Medical technology is empowering users

One unique angle I find especially appealing in the present (and future) health-related ecosystems is the way they empower *us* as patients. If the Internet started altering the traditional doctor/patient relationship by offering greater access to medical information and turning people more into partners in their own care, this multi-device world takes matters one step further. Using the powerful set of connected devices we already own (especially mobile ones), people can get far more control over their health from the extensive information and tools available on these devices.

Let's look at a few examples.

OPTICAL SLEEVES—CELLSCOPE

CellScope is an early-stage, VC-funded startup that builds mobile hardware and software systems for disease diagnosis (Figure 8-8). Its optical sleeves turn smartphones into diagnostic-quality imaging systems for healthcare. These devices are patent-pending, and currently in the development and testing phases (not yet commercially available).

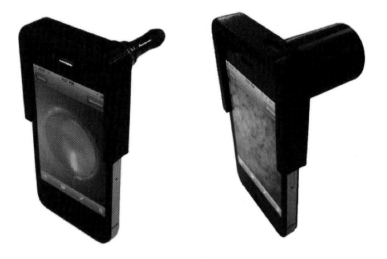

FIGURE 8-8

CellScope smartphone sleeves, turning the device into a diagnostic imaging system for healthcare. On the left, CellScope Oto, focused on ear infections; on the right, CellScope Derm, focused on skin care.

EAR INFECTION DIAGNOSIS—CELLSCOPE OTO

CellScope Oto (Figure 8-9) enables parents to diagnose and treat ear infections remotely, without having to visit the doctor's office. By simply picking up her smartphone and attaching the CellScope to it, a patient can instantly take a photo of the ear and share it with a medical professional so the doctor can prescribe treatment.

FIGURE 8-9

A parent using CellScope Oto on her child to diagnose an ear infection.

With ear infections being the most common reason parents take their children to a doctor, this product could save around 30 million doctors' appointments each year, according to CellScope.[14]

The convenience and immediacy with which parents can conduct the ear examinations at home relieves the high caseload of ear-related issues, as well as saving time, money, stress, and hassle for both parents and kids.

SKIN CARE—CELLSCOPE DERM

CellScope Derm (Figure 8-10) allows people to capture high-quality images of their skin in the privacy of their homes, which they can then send to their doctors for diagnosis.

Skin cancer is the most common of all cancers (nearly as prevalent as all of the others put together), afflicting more than two million Americans each year, and the numbers are rapidly rising. With a product like CellScope Derm, people can more easily and systematically address their skin care health. It allows users to:

- Practice skin self-examination privately at home, but also in a way more streamlined with doctor diagnosis (triggering higher accountability).

- Detect any kinds of changes in the skin more reliably by comparing to previous examination data collected over time.

- Enhance habit forming with monthly alerts set on the phone, online communication with the doctor, and the mere accessibility of the device at home.

FIGURE 8-10
CellScope Derm being used by a doctor.

MEDICAL TECHNOLOGY IN THE HOME

Bringing medicinal technology into people's homes through accessories that plug into our daily devices makes it immediately accessible, private, and convenient to use. As a result, it encourages early detection and action, which not only can save lives, but also can reduce the massive cost burden on the healthcare system. This could then allow allocation of resources to other diseases that are harder to cure or require more research.

From the UX design perspective, if we look at the CellScope product offering in light of the challenges just discussed, these physical sleeves serve as strong context signals that can be used to streamline the user flow. In other words, instead of users having to connect the hardware sleeve, look for the associated app, and then launch it, we could use the "click" moment upon connecting the sleeve to fire up the relevant app without requiring any user intervention. While digital context signals (place, time, etc.) can be quite blurry in terms of intent, buckling up the smartphone and the sleeve provides us with a clear statement. We can then use this declaration of intent in the design to create a continuous flow. For example, upon connecting the sleeve, the app can be triggered and offer a guided walkthrough on how to use it, breaking it down into the different steps.

ASTHMA MANAGEMENT—GECKOCAP

GeckoCap (Figure 8-11) is an asthma management product aimed at establishing medical inhaler compliance among kids by encouraging them to establish healthy habits and take control over their disease. In addition, it provides parents with tools to monitor their children's inhaler behavior and work together with them to increase their asthma awareness.

What is especially interesting in this example is that the hardware accessory is designed for the inhaler rather than the smartphone. This highlights again one of the most important principles discussed in this book: the design should not start from a specific device, but rather from the relationship between people and devices. In other words, it's not about "designing a jacket for the smartphone," but rather analyzing what users need and then choosing the device that will support them best in their task flow.

The GeckoCap ecosystem is built as follows: the GeckoCap itself is a colorful, Bluetooth-enabled rubber accessory that fits on top of the child's inhaler, and the cap contains an LED light that starts flashing when it's time to use the inhaler.

FIGURE 8-11

The GeckoCap ecosystem: an inhaler device equipped with a smartcap working in collaboration with the smartphone to create a kid-friendly experience.

When the child uses the inhaler (pressing down on the GeckoCap), it sends usage data to the GeckoCap website, which collects all of the inhaler data, including the precise times and the amount of medication left. Through the site, parents or doctors can track the child's inhaler behavior, from anywhere, making sure the child adheres to his prescription. They also get reminders/alerts for cases like the prescription running low or the rescue inhaler being used.

In addition, GeckoCap also empowers children to develop healthy habits by getting them involved in their own treatment in a fun, gamified way with a special dashboard designed just for kids. Kids can set goals with their parents and get rewarded with points and badges when they adhere to their inhaler prescriptions.

SUMMARY

Taking multi-device experiences beyond the boundaries of software modularity offers several important advantages:

- Incorporating hardware accessories or sleeves opens up new opportunities in terms of the functionalities our devices can provide, and thus the industries they can benefit. Medicine/healthcare is one prominent example. Education and environment are two additional routes.

- Instead of manufacturing more and more discrete devices, we can leverage the existing ones and enhance them with add-ons. This saves costs and resources for all sides, as well as electronic waste.

- Hardware customization also enriches design innovation opportunities and allows further personalization of the experience per context. If we go back to the gaming industry, for example, we saw that in many cases the smartphone is a great substitute for a game control in terms of function. However, one main thing it lacks is the form. The control's design, shape, style, grip, and other physical factors all contribute to the gaming experience (and the ergonomics). Plugging the smartphone into a "gaming jacket" could improve the experience even more, especially for "heavy" gamers.

- The industrial design of any device has important implications in terms of ease of use, ergonomics, convenience, and overall experience. Not only that, but aesthetics matter too—especially as we enter the world of wearables, where many devices (like watches, glasses, and wristbands) become part of our appearance, turning into fashion accessories.

  Offering a superior experience in that department can help create differentiation in the market. A good example is Misfit's Shine tracker (Figure 8-12), which stands out with its slick, compact, elegant design compared to others in the market.

FIGURE 8-12
Shine tracker device by Misfit.

A New, Disrupted (Human) World

So many of our dreams at first seem impossible, then they seem improbable, and then, when we summon the will, they soon become inevitable.

CHRISTOPHER REEVE

In his book *Creating Innovators: The Making of Young People Who Will Change the World* (Scribner), Tony Wagner cites research showing an important agreement among 77% of senior business executives in 12 countries:

> The greatest innovations of the 21st century will be those that help address human needs more than those that create the most profit.[15]

As a final note, I would like to take another peek at the limitless world of the Internet of Things, and pique your interest with some groundbreaking ideas on how this new economy of connections can promote global health and help humanity.

Beyond the horizon, we can easily imagine a fully networked world, equipped with trillions of sensors spread across the globe and beyond—billions of devices everywhere, and all of them connected to one another. This world is commonly envisioned as one of perfect ubiquitous computing: a utopian ambient intelligence where technology becomes invisibly embedded in our natural surroundings, weaving itself seamlessly into the fabric of our daily lives, attuned to all our senses, adaptive, and personalized.

An example of this might include a scenario where your front door automatically unlocks as you get home, the lights turn on as you enter, and a cup of fresh coffee is already waiting for you. It could include your car parking itself at night and waiting for you by the door when you need to head out for work in the morning, and delivering your groceries to you when needed so you never run out of milk. Basically, the embodiment of ultimate context awareness would be like having an invisible personal assistant who knows exactly what to do, at any given time, at any given place.

But it can go much further than that.

Such a world will also allow us to intimately hear the planet's heartbeat, sense the environment, understand climate changes, and manage our limited resources—in other words, help tackle the deep real-world challenges facing us now.

For example, a recent report by Carbon War Room and AT&T estimates that with the IoT, we could save 9.1 billion tons of carbon annually by 2020.[16] The beauty of this is that we could achieve it merely by using devices to do little things more intelligently, like automatically adapting air conditioners to the temperature (remember Nest?), optimizing the routes for truck drivers, loading container ships a bit more efficiently, or making sure crops get the exact right amount of water (Bitponics is a start).

Even more encouraging, the IoT can enable us to understand and predict climate changes, so that in addition to supplying the right amount of water, we could optimize the crops we choose to grow, take better care of them, and maximize the harvest quality. Along with better distribution systems, we could provide better distribution and delivery of food between places of abundance and places of scarcity, and relieve the hunger problem.

In an IoT world, we could also more quickly detect and fix many problems that reduce the clean water supply, such as industrial waste, unsustainable agriculture, and poor urban planning. This would increase the reach of drinkable water to areas in the world that still don't have clean water, and promote better health in those regions.

These are just a few examples. Given the extent of disruption the IoT is expected to bring, now is the time to start planning for such a world, where everything—people, information, and things—will be more connected than ever before.

What would *you* like a new, disrupted world to look like?

Summary

- Multi-device experiences carry huge opportunities, but as with any new technology, they also present certain challenges:

    ○ **Ecosystem design and development.** Organizational structure, walled gardens, resources, time to market

    ○ **Ecosystem adoption.** Getting the ecosystem up and running, app overload

- These challenges are solvable. Acknowledging them is the first step to working through them. The next step is to start taking action by researching, experimenting, launching, and iterating, as well as by engaging in more global collaborative discussions and initiatives.

- The concept of *one ecosystem heart* provides a way to address ecosystem adoption roadblocks. Everything.me and Aviate have demonstrated the first signs in the field for this line of thinking, adapting the UI per context.

- Ecosystems aren't built in a day, and while you should still plan for the broad multi-device narrative, remember that you can execute on it gradually.

NOTES

1. Tyler Tate, "The Rise of Cross-Channel UX Design," UX Matters, October 17, 2011, *http://bit.ly/1c79u39*.

2. API stands for *application programming interface*, a set of programming specifications and standards for how software components can interact with one another. Software companies release APIs to the public so that third-party developers can build products that are powered by their services. Some common uses for APIs include providing access to databases, hardware components (like sensors), and user interface elements.

3. The Amazon Kindle/Audible.com collaboration and Xbox/Nike+ partnership discussed in previous chapters are two examples of ecosystem integrations. Even though they are actually integrations between closed platforms, they still demonstrate the greater holistic value of such cross-ecosystem collaboration—both for product developers and for consumers.

4. Apple also offers the option to sync devices over WiFi. However, this option is not turned on by default, and requires that users (1) know that it exists, and (2) go to the settings, find it, and turn it on. In most products, more than 95% of users keep settings in the exact configuration that the device came with.

5. Data pulled between July and December of 2010 indicates that iPhone users have a median of 108 apps in total on their devices—20 that come preinstalled and 88 that users download (see Philip Elmer-DeWitt, "108 apps per iPhone," CNNMoney, January 28, 2011, *http://bit.ly/1cDjJZm*. This number is progressively on the rise.

6. The Universal Gadget Wrist Charger: *http://www.thinkgeek.com/product/ceca/*.

7. "State of the Appnation—A Year of Change and Growth in U.S. Smartphones," Nielsen, May 16, 2012, *http://bit.ly/1bf4IMp*.

8. The top five apps in terms of usage are: Facebook, YouTube, Google Play, Google Search, and Gmail.

9. Dan Rowinski, "Apple iOS App Store Adding 20,000 Apps A Month, Hits 40 Billion Downloads," January 7, 2013, *http://bit.ly/1i6ev04*.

10. Nathan Ingraham, "Apple announces 1 million apps in the App Store, more than 1 billion songs played on iTunes radio," The Verge, October 22, 2013, *http://bit.ly/1ad8Hzu*.

11. modu has been awarded the Guinness World Record for the world's lightest mobile phone.

12. This requires being able to reliably detect the person using the device, a point that takes us back to the importance of sign-in. Until we are able to offer easier (preferably implicit) ways for people to authenticate—such as habits, use patterns, other devices they have, and physical mechanisms (body temperature, skin texture, grip, fingerprint)—we need to get people to authenticate themselves through sign-in.

13. *http://bit.ly/1cKkV01*

14. Brian Dolan, "CellScope, Smartphone Diagnostic Startup, Raises $1M," MobiHealthNews, June 11, 2012, *http://bit.ly/1c4HM6Z*.

15. "GE Global Innovation Barometer 2011: An Overview on Messaging, Data, and Amplification," GE, January 2011, *http://invent.ge/1kYW2zh*.

16. Matt Cullinen, "Machine to Machine Technologies: Unlocking the Potential of a $1 Trillion Industry," Carbon War Room and AT&T, February 2013, *http://bit.ly/1fq17iR*.

[A]

Companies, Products, and Links

Multiple companies and products were mentioned and discussed throughout this book to illustrate the three design approaches, demonstrate their application in the field, and clarify additional associated UX design concepts and principles.

Following is the full list of these companies and products, along with the relevant links (ordered alphabetically).

PRODUCT	COMPANY	URL
Airbnb	Airbnb, Inc.	https://www.airbnb.com/
Allrecipes	Allrecipes.com	http://allrecipes.com/
Amazon Kindle	Amazon.com, Inc.	https://kindle.amazon.com/
Apple AirPlay	Apple, Inc.	http://www.apple.com/airplay/
Aviate	ThumbsUp Labs	http://getaviate.com/
BigOven	BigOven	http://bigoven.com/
Big Youth	Agence Big Youth	http://www.bigyouth.fr/
BiKN	Treehouse Labs, LLC	http://www.bikn.com/
Bites.TV	Bites Labs, Ltd.	http://bites.tv/
Bitponics	Bitponics	http://www.bitponics.com/
CellScope	CellScope, Inc.	https://www.cellscope.com/
Coca Cola	The Coca-Cola Company	http://us.coca-cola.com/
Eventbrite	Eventbrite	http://www.eventbrite.com/
Evernote	Evernote Corporation	http://evernote.com/
Everything.me	DoAT Media, Ltd.	http://everything.me/
Fab	Fab, Inc.	http://fab.com/
Facebook	Facebook	https://www.facebook.com/
Farmville	Zynga, Inc.	http://zynga.com/
Fitocracy	Fitocracy, Inc.	https://www.fitocracy.com/
Flex	Fitbit, Inc.	http://www.fitbit.com/

PRODUCT	COMPANY	URL
Foursquare	Foursquare	*https://foursquare.com/*
GeckoCap	Gecko Health Innovations, Inc.	*http://www.geckocap.com/*
Google Analytics	Google, Inc.	*http://www.google.com/analytics/*
Chromecast	Google, Inc.	*http://www.google.com/intl/en/ chrome/devices/chromecast/*
Google Drive	Google, Inc.	*https://drive.google.com/*
Google Maps	Google, Inc.	*http://maps.google.com/*
Google Search	Google, Inc.	*https://www.google.com/*
Hulu Plus	Hulu	*http://www.hulu.com/plus*
IKEA Catalog	Inter IKEA Systems B.V.	*http://www.ikea.com/ms/en_GB/vir- tual_catalogue/online_catalogues. html*
IntoNow	Yahoo, Inc.	*http://www.intonow.com/*
KL Dartboard	Key Lime 314, LLC	*http://www.keylime314.com/page16/ index.html*
Lumoback	LUMO Body Tech, Inc.	*http://www.lumoback.com/*
Marvel's *The Avengers*	Marvel	*http://marvel.com/avengers_movie*
Mashable	Mashable, Inc.	*http://mashable.com/*
Mint	Intuit, Inc.	*https://www.mint.com/*
modu	modu	*http://www.modumobile.com/*
Nest	Nest Labs	*https://nest.com/*
Netflix	Netfix, Inc.	*http://www.netflix.com/*
Neura	Neura, Inc.	*http://www.theneura.com/*
Nike+	Nike, Inc.	*http://nikeplus.nike.com/plus/*
Nike+ FuelBand	Nike, Inc.	*http://www.nike.com/us/en_us/c/ nikeplus-fuelband*
Nike+ Kinect	Nike, Inc.	*http://www.nike.com/us/en_us/c/ training/nike-plus-kinect-training*
Nike+ Running	Nike, Inc.	*http://nikeplus.nike.com/plus/ products/gps_app/*
Pad Racer	SMHK Ltd.	*http://padracer.com/*
Path	Path	*https://path.com/*
Pebble Watch	Pebble	*https://getpebble.com/*

PRODUCT	COMPANY	URL
Philip House Design	Philip House	*http://www.philiphousenyc.com/*
Philips Hue	Philips	*http://www.meethue.com/*
PhoneGap	Adobe Systems, Inc.	*http://phonegap.com/*
Pocket	Read It Later, Inc.	*http://getpocket.com/*
Polar	Input Factory Inc.	*http://polarb.com/*
POP	Woomoo, Inc.	*https://popapp.in/*
Real Racing 2	Electronic Arts, Inc.	*http://www.ea.com/real-racing-2-ios*
Roku	Roku, Inc.	*http://www.roku.com/*
RunKeeper	RunKeeper	*http://runkeeper.com/*
Scrabble for iPad	Electronic Arts, Inc.	*http://www.ea.com/scrabble-paid-ipad*
Shine	Misfit Wearables	*http://www.misfitwearables.com/*
Slingbox	Sling Media, Inc.	*http://www.slingbox.com/*
SmartThings	Physical Graph Corporation	*http://www.smartthings.com/*
Spotify	Spotify AB	*https://www.spotify.com/*
Square	Square, Inc.	*https://squareup.com/*
Sugru	FormFormForm	*http://sugru.com/*
TripAdvisor	TripAdvisor, LLC	*http://www.tripadvisor.com/*
TripIt	Concur Technologies, Inc.	*https://www.tripit.com/*
Trulia	Trulia, Inc.	*http://www.trulia.com/*
Tumblr	Tumblr, Inc.	*https://www.tumblr.com/*
Twitter	Twitter, Inc.	*https://twitter.com/*
Untappd	Untappd, LLC	*https://untappd.com/*
Up	Jawbone	*https://jawbone.com/*
Withings Smart Baby Monitor	Withings	*http://www.withings.com/en/babymonitor*
Xbox SmartGlass	Microsoft Corporation	*http://www.xbox.com/en-US/smartglass*

[*Index*]

Symbols

3Cs framework
  complementary design, 95
  consistent design, 21
  consistent experience vs. single
    activity flow, 62
  continuous design, 53
  expanding, 170–171
  expanding 3Cs framework, 167
  integrating approaches, 131
  Nike+ ecosystem flow diagram
    and, 189
  overview, 4–7
  using as building blocks, 132–134

A

A/B testing (Netflix), 238–241
accelerometer, 100
action phase (Hook model), 157
actions providing feedback from users, 220
activity duration (continuous design),
  54
activity trackers/sensors, 183
adaptive content per context, 279
adaptive design (Learning thermostat), 171–173
ad designs/campaigns, 244–245
adoption challenges (ecosystems),
  262–265
advanced vs. beginner users, 106–108
agenda-centered (conferences), 75–76
alerts/notifications (Quantified-Self
  apps), 183–185
Allrecipes
  integrating consistent/continuous
    design, 143–147
  sequenced activities flow, 68–73
alternative input methods (Google
  Search), 35–36

Amazon Kindle
  collaboration with Audible.com,
    288
  single activity flow, 59–61
American Music Awards (AMAS),
  116–117
analytics, multi-device. *See* multi-
  device analytics
Android platform
  advent of, 9
  Android/iOS platform designs,
    42–46
  Android Market, 11
  app development errors, 45–46
  Aviate app, 276
  Everything.me app, 275
  Pebble epaper watch for, 193
  Slingbox ecosystem on, 122
APIs (application programming
  interfaces), 288
Apple AirPlay (single activity flow),
  55–57
apps
  app markets, 82–83
  app overload challenges, 269–271
  in-app notifications, 83–84
  introduction/development of App
    Store, 11–13
  syncing across devices, 264
Ashton, Kevin, 168
asthma management (GeckoCap),
  283–284
asynchronous ecosystem relationships, 123
Audible.com, 59
augmented reality (AR), 201–204
automatic interface adaptation, 276
Avengers second-screen app, 119–121
Aviate app, 276–278

D

Darwin, Charles, 250
data. *See also* multi-device analytics
collecting user (gaming), 103
extracting actionable knowledge from, 173
tools for gathering, 224
deep hierarchy navigation model, 22
dependent vs. independent goals (ecosystems), 234
Derm, CellScope, 282–283
Designing for Behavioral Change (O'Reilly), 217
Designing for Emotion (A Book Apart), 208
desktop computers
activity notifications in, 183–184
controlling Xbox with, 124
Google Drive design, 61
Slingbox integrated design, 140
Trulia design optimization for, 41
device-agnostic vs. device-specific goals (multi-device analytics), 234
device-focused complementary analysis, 237
diagrams, flow (mapping ecosystems), 189–191
Dick Clark Productions (DCP), 116
Dinner Spinner app, 68, 143
discovery layer (IoT), 259–260
dynamic contexts (Google Now), 37–38
Dynamic Phone platform (Everything.me), 274–275

E

ear infection diagnosis (CellScope Oto), 281–282
Econsultancy surveys, 251–252
ecosystems of multi-devices
adoption challenges, 262–265
applying A/B testing to, 239–241
concept and structure of, 2–3
current usage of, 1–3
design and development challenges. *See* challenges
experiences developed from single device, 110–112
goal conversions for, 232–233
gradual evolution of, 257–258

guidelines for selection of features/devices, 150–153
vs. Internet of Things, 171
mapping with flow diagrams, 189–191
measuring ROI of, 243–247
new TV ecosystem standard, 154
non-TV ecosystem of controlled devices, 173–174
one ecosystem heart. *See* one ecosystem heart
"Please Don't Ruin the Ecosystem", 111
principles relating to, 18–19
promoting value of, 148–149
educating for continuity
app markets, 82–83
first-time experiences, 81–83
in-app notifications, 83–84
overview, 80–81
promotional messages, 82
engagement, designing for, 155–161
epaper technology, 192
EPG (electronic program guide), 125–126
Evans, Dale, 217
Eventbrite (continuous design)
examining user workflow, 73–75
expanding continuous flow, 75–80
overview, 72–73
Evernote website, 81
Everything.me Dynamic Phone platform, 274–275, 277–278
Eyal, Nir, 155

F

Fab app, 142
Farmville game (virtual goods), 245–246
first-time experiences, 81–83
fitness trackers, 179–180
flat hierarchy navigation model, 22
flexible images (RWD), 30
fluid grids (RWD), 30
form factor, optimizing for (consistent design), 27
forms, sign-in, 65–67
foursquare sign-up form, 64
FuelBand, Nike+, 183

G

gaming
Apple AirPlay, 55–57
augmenting games with smart
devices, 101
collecting user data, 103
extending experience of, 99–100
Farmville, 245–246
game controllers, 100–102
KL Dartboard, 108–109
lowering barriers for entry, 105
multi-player game experiences,
128
multi-tasking game setup, 101
optimizing smartphones for, 101
Pad Racer, 105–106
personalizing games, 101
Real Racing 2, 98–102
Scrabble for iPad, 102–106
Tumblr for Android, 107
virtual goods model, 245–246
GeckoCap ecosystem, 283–284
gestures, standardized, 27
Get Directions button, 27
goal conversions (ecosystems),
232–233
goal flows (Google Analytics),
234–237
Google Analytics
building design model, 226–227
challenges to overcome, 227
defining visits (sessions), 231–232
determining what to measure,
225–226
goal flows and conversion paths,
234–237
overview, 224–225
Google Chromecast, 5
Google Drive (single activity flow),
60–61
Google Maps iPhone app, 149
Google Now, 37–38
Google Search design, 32–35
gradual engagement (sign-up process), 66–67

H

habits, user, 155–156
hamburger icon, 22–23

hardware accessories, augmenting devices with (BiKN),
176–177
health and fitness. *See* medical
multi-device experiences;
Quantified-Self movement
heart, one ecosystem. *See* one ecosystem heart
Heineken Star Player app, 109–112
Hewlett-Packard portable computer
ad, 7
history of portable computers
ads from 1980s, 7–8
App Stores, 11–13
single-device design, 8–9
smartphones development, 9–13
tablets, 16–18
Hook four-phase model, 156–160
hover states, 27
HTML5 apps, 13
Hulu Plus (consistent design), 45–47
Hulu Plus Wii U (integrated design),
153–154
hybrid apps, 14–16

I

IA (information architecture)
adjustments, 22
consistency across devices, 29
IBM 1984 portable computer ad, 8
Ikea 2013 catalogue (augmented reality), 201–204
independent vs. dependent goals
(multi-device analytics), 234
integrated design approach
3Cs as building blocks, 132–134
acceleration of user expectations,
136–137
achieving user goals in different
ways, 144
adjusting features sets based on
user needs, 135–136
Allrecipes, 143–147
Bitponics, 161–162
design approaches completing
one another, 140–141
Dos and Don'ts of, 137–139
ecosystem guidelines, 146–149
Hook four-phase model, 156–160
Hulu Plus Wii U example,
153–154

About the Author

Michal Levin, Senior User Experience Designer at Google, has extensive practice in UX design for web, mobile, and TV. She joined Google in 2009, becoming the first UX designer in Google Israel, and later moved to headquarters in Mountain View, California. During her time at Google, Michal led the UX design in a variety of product areas including data analytics, data visualization, search, business applications, and security.

She has presented at leading international UX conferences on the concepts of ecosystem design and designing for different screen sizes. In addition, she has been the UX mentor at UpWest Labs—a startup accelerator—since 2012. Prior to Google, Michal worked as UX specialist at Modu, a startup that developed an innovative mobile ecosystem, and as Senior UX expert at TZUR, a leading UX design consultancy in Israel.

When she is not designing, Michal loves to attend live concerts, dance, and run. She recently finished her first Tough Mudder challenge.

Michal holds two bachelor degrees from Tel Aviv University: one in psychology and business management, and a second in communication.

Colophon

The animal on the cover of *Designing Multi-Device Experiences* is a carpet chameleon (*Furcifer lateralis*). This species, also known as the white-lined chameleon, is endemic to the entirety of Madagascar, except the northern part. The carpet chameleon can be found between 390 and 6,316 feet (120 and 1,925 meters) above sea level.

Adult male carpet chameleons mature at three months of age. Females can lay up to three clutches a year, which consist of between 8 and 23 eggs at a time. The eggs must be kept at a steady 75 degrees F (24 degrees C).

Have it your way.

Get even more for your money.

Join the O'Reilly Community, and register the O'Reilly books you own. It's free, and you'll get:

- $4.99 ebook upgrade offer
- 40% upgrade offer on O'Reilly print books
- Membership discounts on books and events
- Free lifetime updates to ebooks and videos
- Multiple ebook formats, DRM FREE
- Participation in the O'Reilly community
- Newsletters
- Account management
- 100% Satisfaction Guarantee

Signing up is easy:

1. **Go to: oreilly.com/go/register**
2. **Create an O'Reilly login.**
3. **Provide your address.**
4. **Register your books.**

Note: English-language books only

To order books online:
oreilly.com/store

For questions about products or an order:
orders@oreilly.com

To sign up to get topic-specific email announcements and/or news about upcoming books, conferences, special offers, and new technologies:
elists@oreilly.com

For technical questions about book content:
booktech@oreilly.com

To submit new book proposals to our editors:
proposals@oreilly.com

O'Reilly books are available in multiple DRM-free ebook formats. For more information:
oreilly.com/ebooks

O'REILLY®

Spreading the knowledge of innovators   oreilly.com